Janice E. Sullivan

As a 5 year-old child, Janice could have never known what mayhem and destruction her life would lead her to. Riddled by tragedy and death, she would find herself back in the arms of the man who had taken her virginity at the age of five. A mans life that had been filled with drugs, murder, and deceit. In her heart, Janice always believed the nightly visits paid to her by her cousin- were out of love and not the horrible sickness she would later come to discover. This book is a collection of thoughts and memories trapped in the author's mind. While spirituality and survival are the overarching theme, the underlining story is about societal failure, and its effect on the youth.

CUCUMBERS
Have Thorns And
Snakes Love
STRAWBERRIES

Janice E. Sullivan

Books are available at bulk purchases, for details.
Contact: T and L Global Marketing @ 404-697-6022
www.cucumbershavethorns.com

Copyrights

Dedication

———•••◆•••———

Dedicated To:
Jeanette Milton and Charles Edward Sullivan—
my parents, whom I loved very much.

Janice E. Sullivan

Table of Contents

Janice E. Sullivan

Foreward

Upon first hearing the subject of Janice's book, I thought I really don't want to read a book that is filled with depressing accounts of a child molestation....but I had promised Leroy Decosta, a business associate of mine and the husband of the author, that I would read it and give him my thoughts. The draft arrived a few days later and I sat down to read ''just a few lines.''

Well five chapters and sometime later I was interrupted by the ringing of my office telephone. It was then that I realized that Janice had virtually swept me away from my daily grind and taken me to another time and place that on the surface seemed ordinary.....but in fact, was shrouded in family secrets and sexual abuse...abuse that would emotionally cripple an innocent young child for most of her life.

Janice masterfully weaves her story in a way that the reader is transplanted into her often troubled life as a young child, abandoned teen and emotionally and physically abused young woman. She takes the reader on a very personal and true journey through one of life's hell-holes as she exposes one of the best kept and most dreadful of family secrets-child molestation. One element that makes Janice's story so intriguing is the fact that most of us can relate to many of the characters in her book. We all seem to have a relatives or friends with personalities similar to the ones she writes about....but thankfully, most do not have the sick, moral flaws and they don't engage in the abusive behavior that some of her family members inflicted upon her. Their abuses would cause emotional scarring that she would carry for most of her life. But the scars would also remind her that, that was not how she wanted to live. The scars would give her the courage to believe that through faith, spiritual guidance

and determination...even the most down-trodden can lift themselves up...step beyond a life of abuse and social ineptness...to a
life of fulfillment, happiness and true love.

    With the proper exposure...this book will become a best
seller!

-JP Beaty Senior Producer
Kelsher Communications, Inc.

Acknowledgments

I would like to extend my thanks to every person who has supported and helped me in the past. I now know that without experiencing what I have experienced, I would not be the person I am today. For that, I am grateful.

To my husband, Leroy Decosta, my biggest supporter, thank you for making me feel as though I can do anything.

I give honor and respect to my favorite uncle, Pastor Oliver Thomas, who has proven through his own endurance that God is a good God.

With as much love as my heart can bear, I give a special **thank you** to my brothers, Charles Milton and Willie McDougle, and to my sister Deborah McDougle, for constantly giving it their best.

Know this: If you have done your best then you have never failed....

To Cynthia Jo Goodman M.D. of Decatur, Georgia, I extend my gratitude and appreciation for your honesty. You helped me when I didn't know I needed help.

To Betty Reedy Gunn of Atlanta, Georgia, without whom I could not have written this book. You answered when the Lord called. And fought to see this through when I wanted to give up. You have been an inspiration. Your talent, your spirit, and ability to just *be*, frees those who are around you. Thank you for allowing me to share in that space.

Janice E. Sullivan

Preface

——◆——

Cucumbers Have Thorns and Snakes Love Strawberries is a true story about the most unspeakable secrets—revealed and released.

As a survivor of physical, emotional and sexual abuse, I have looked in the mirror many times and asked:

"Who should I be mad at?

Who should I blame for stealing—like a thief in the night—my innocence, and my childhood?"

Each time I tried to point a finger at an individual or the system that was supposed to protect children like me, I always returned to the same answer: No one!

Why? Because my story isn't about blame or confronting the perpetrators. It's about digging deep, and recovering and reviving the love, acceptance, and forgiveness buried deep inside me. It's about being empowered. It's about becoming whole again.

Self-empowerment is what has given me the strength to write this book of horrors, detailing how a lost soul, holding on to only a child's prayer, *overcame!*

Cucumbers Have Thorns and Snakes Love Strawberries is a compilation of painful memories once trapped in the deepest, darkest recesses of my mind. The book's purpose is to provide insight, and call to the forefront, those of us who have ignored the cries of the wounded and often forgotten children—children who have suffered unimaginable horrors through the hands of the very people assigned to protect them. It is not intended to lash out, but to yell out, to all who will hear.

I have chosen to change the names of family, friends and abusers. I hope in time, each may face their truths and deal with whatever demons have followed them from the past to the present.

It is important for the reader to visualize in graphic detail what I experienced as a child, who was trying to make sense of the senseless. I have not embellished, nor have I lied to make myself look good or to make circumstances or people appear better or worse than they were.

Many times, my heart felt so heavy it hurt to take a simple breath. While a part of me yearned for someone to rush into my tangled life and give me a huge hug and make everything better, another part of me turned callous, hard, and unfeeling—often behaving as if I didn't need anyone, whipping out sarcasms and hurtful words at every turn. Yet, even then, it was the comfort of a kind soul that I needed most.

I always desired love and companionship far more than I was willing to admit. I believe it may have been that same desperate longing for love, acceptance, and companionship that eventually caused me to leave my husband for my molester.

This book is a gift of liberation to anyone who carries the shame and burden of a childhood gone wrong.

Prologue

As I sit at my desk, I take a deep breath, close my eyes, and slowly place myself in the past. My mood changes and I begin to type mechanically as each thought tries to find its way to the pages.

My first memory is of a dimly lit room. A television is playing, but I hear no sound. I see myself standing in the distance. I am five years old.

As I stare out into the living room, I see my father in a wheelchair. My mother must be somewhere near because I can smell the aroma of her fried chicken, even now. This is a precious moment because I feel love all around me.

Other images of my past materialize in front of me. It's hard to describe what I feel. Each scene plays for just a few seconds and is gone. Suddenly, I am someplace else.

No matter how hard I try to remember, I am faced with blanks from my past. I am not sure if I should be glad that my mind chooses to keep these scenes hidden, or if I should be worried that the blanks indicate a more serious and deeper problem that I am not yet ready to address.

Reluctantly, I move past this image; my mind flashes forward and I find myself with my father again. We're in Fort Frederica, my hometown. Fort Frederica is a small place tucked away on the south side of St. Simon's Island, part of the Golden Isles on the Georgia coast. It's the kind of place where everyone is either family or friend.

I see my father riding me on the back of his wheelchair. I am holding on ever so tightly. I clinch my hands tighter, hoping not to fall as the wheelchair labors down the long, rocky, dirt road.

The day is warm and glistening, limbs of moss-laden trees sway back and forth as if serenading to the melody of a lazy summer breeze. I am happy. My father is my hero.

I often try to imagine what my father was like before the accident. I've heard many stories of how handsome he was in his newly pressed military uniform. My aunts told me he was one of the island's most sought-after bachelors. They said my father was so cool he ironed his money before putting it in his wallet. He was said to be a real ladies' man; however it was my mom who captured his eye, and, according to him, his eyes had never seen a more beautiful woman. My mom was five-foot-five with a pecan-brown complexion and a perfect smile. My mom said it was my father's strong, slim physique that attracted her to him.

She often told my brother and me the story of how they met. She bragged casually about how neatly-shaven and well-manicured he was, and how his hair always had to be cut just right. He was a proud man.

My fingers begin to slow down, and the typing stops abruptly as I feel my mood begin to change. I close my eyes and try hard to hold on to these happier times, but they vanish. I continue to sit with my eyes closed in an attempt to recall something more, but there is only an ominous darkness.

Suddenly, and appearing out of nowhere, I see an image of my brother, Junior, run past me. At first glance, it looks as if he is playing, but he is not. I see a frantic and terrified look on his face. Something is terribly wrong. I turn around and gasp in horror. It's my father. He's been drinking again. He is chasing my brother; the wheels on his wheelchair are spinning as fast as they can go. The alcohol has clouded my father's ability to reason. He is frantically trying to catch my brother. My father is convinced that if Junior will just stand still, he can shoot a wooden match right out of his tiny hand.

As my father whirs past me, I see the determined look on his face. He has a small gun in his lap and his hair is no longer neatly cut, but wooly and uneven. He has put on weight and is sweating profusely as he tries to help the wheels of his chair go even faster.

My brother is exhausted from running and stops to catch his breath. Thinking he is out of my father's reach, he bends over gasping with his hands on his knees.

As if he has forgotten he is chasing his son, my father takes aim, pulls the gun's trigger and strikes my brother in the forehead.

Junior falls to the ground.

I rush to my only sibling and best friend, unsure of his fate. As I kneel down beside his motionless body, my heart begins to race, but is put at ease as my brother, with blood streaming down his face, tearfully gazes up at me.

Thank God it was only a pellet gun, or my brother might not be here today.

Although my brother's wound eventually healed, I don't think he ever really got over what happen that day. That day, like so many days, would never be mentioned again by my brother, or me.

Although Junior was my best friend, we were different in so many ways. He was a momma's boy, always helping with the cooking and cleaning, sticking close by my mother's side. I, on the other hand, was a loner. I always wanted to eat, but was never one to help with the cooking. I would do practically anything to get out of doing my chores. My brother always tried to tell me what to do, but I had a mind of my own. I was five-going-on-fifty, and he, only two years older than me, was no match. I knew how to get my way. I exhale and ease slowly back in my chair. I can almost hear the words of my mother and aunt as they discuss the horrible accident that caused my father to morph into someone I no longer knew.

It all started one night during a horrific storm, when my father was on leave from service. The storm was so bad, it knocked the lights out of our house and the surrounding neighborhood. The gusting, howling, winds and torrential rains were so fierce they forced the branches of the giant moss trees to bend and kiss the ground. With every flash of lightning, black skies turned to day, while raindrops, as sharp as pebbles powered down on our neighborhood.

The storm, however, wasn't enough to deter my father from going out and getting the lights back. My father, trained as an electrician in the military, climbed to the top of the utility pole located near the side of our house, hoping to repair the loose wire that would bring the lights back on.

As he neared the top of the pole, my father tried to steady himself by grabbing onto a nearby branch. He almost had it when another piercing, crackling sound ripped through the air.

My father reeled around as a bolt of lightning struck him. It hit him so hard he was knocked to the ground. He lay paralyzed from the waist down, pants on fire, and unable to move. My mother, hearing him scream rushed to his side. She did all she could to put out the flames, but it was too late. The damage had been done.

His legs were burned so badly they had to be removed. Weeks later, at the age of twenty-six, my father left the hospital a cripple—a condition far too much for him to bear.

As time passed my father became a different man. He slowly drifted to a place no one could penetrate. He started drinking heavily. The bottle became his best friend and constant companion.

As I sit reminiscing, another image appears. My mother is pulling my brother and me off the school bus, just a few blocks from our home on St. Simon's. She had had enough. The drunken bouts and obnoxious behavior by my father was just too much for her to bear.

The drastic impact that day would have on my life and the life of my family would not unfold until years later. Fourteen years would pass before I'd see my father again.

My mother left so abruptly that day, she hadn't thought out a real plan for our future. So we moved around a lot, going from town to town, and to relative after relative.

Eventually we ended up in a Belle Glade, Florida, which is the where my story begins....

Janice E. Sullivan

Chapter One
Getting It All Out

———— ·•·━●━·•·————

Where do you begin when there is so much inside that wants out?

I wish I was a big strong wind, and that just by blowing, I could clear the air of all the sadness and hurt I have held inside for so long. Never again would I experience the pain of remembering the darkest, deepest secrets of my life. Just as quickly as this whole mess started it would end, and everyone would understand what I had been through, and all the hurt I felt. Nevertheless, since I am not that wind, I will take a long, slow sigh and begin to tell my story....

Belle Glade, Florida was a dangerous place to live, but as a child I found it fun and exciting. It was there I learned from my Uncle Dutch how to file down pennies to look like dimes, to trick the coke machine into giving my brother and me free sodas. When filing pennies became too much work, I would go down to the corner store hoping to earn spare change by helping the neighborhood drunks gather empty bottles. But whatever pastime I engaged in, you could be sure it involved broken glass, which was everywhere. It littered the walkways, the street, the parking lot. Any place you found a flat surface, you found broken glass. Sometimes I'd just sit and marvel at it, the sun's rays making it appear as jewelry shining on the concrete surface. But not even glassed jewelry, kissed by the sun, could beautify this dilapidated neighborhood. The puke-green, four-story rooming house with its chipped stairwells, graffiti-covered walls, and pungent urine smell was where we called home. Each floor had twenty small rooms and a foul-smelling community bathroom located at one end of the building. I would often sit on the cement walkway, outside our room and dangle my feet under the metal railings as I watched the tenants pass below. Sometimes, out of boredom, I would run my hand back and forth along the aluminum rail that stretched from our room to my Aunt Katie's room, only a few doors away. Aunt Katie is the reason my mother moved to Belle Glade in the first place.

Belle Glade was very different from the island. I had to travel at least five blocks from home to find a safe place to play. Everyday, I would rush off to my favorite place to play and climb for coconuts. It was so beautiful and different there. The ground was covered with white, smooth sand and dates that had fallen because they had become too ripe. Everyday I would pass the same two little old ladies sitting on their porch, and everyday they would ask me the same question:

"So how's our girl doing today?"

And everyday, I would reply, "Oh, pretty good."

I said it so much that after a while 'Pretty Good' became my nickname. Even strangers would yell to me from their porch, "Hey, Pretty Good!" while waving their hands and smiling. I'd smile and wave back as I ran by.

I think, because I had always been a happy and cheerful child, the idea never crossed anyone's mind that each night in our community shower, I was being molested.

Let's call him Mike.

Mike was fourteen when we had our first encounter, and I was five. He was the son of my great Aunt Katie whom I spoke of earlier...therefore, he was my second cousin. Ever since I can remember Mike had spent most of his time in and out of jail for either fighting, stealing, or selling drugs.

Mike resembled Link from the seventies hit series, "Mod Squad." He was dark with clear, smooth, chocolate skin. He wore an African dashiki with a band around his head most of the time. And for the most part came across as hip. He stood about five-feet, six inches, but acted as if he was six-foot-six. He wasn't afraid of anyone.

Everyone knew I was Mike's favorite cousin. It wasn't unusual to see me tagging along behind him when he visited his friends. He always took good care of me.

Yep! Nothing was too good for his little cousin, "Pretty Good," not even an occasional finger in her vagina every now and then.

Being five years old, I trusted Mike completely. So when he said he needed me, I believed him and would do whatever he asked whenever he asked.

One day he took me in the community shower of our building. In broad daylight, with people coming and going all around us, he laid me on the wet concrete floor, leaving the door partially ajar. He began sliding his finger in private part and kissing me as if I were a grown-up. He climbed on top of me and prepared to place his manhood inside me when we heard a noise. Mike became frustrated by the sound in the hallway, and sucked his teeth in disappointment.

"Someone is coming," Mike whispered in my ear as he jumped up and ran towards the urinal while pointing for me to get behind the shower curtain.

As soon I ran into the shower and closed the curtain, my brother, Junior walked in. He looked around the shower stall as if sensing something was wrong. Slowly he walked towards my direction. Just before he could uncloak me, I pulled the curtain back, jumped out of the shower and yelled, "Gotcha!"

I'd pretended to scare both he and Mike, which proved even more that I was a willing participant. My brother, never acting the wiser, looked at me with a frown that usually meant I had gotten on his nerves.

"Quit playing," he said grabbing me by my hand, as he escorted me back to the room where we lived.

I often wonder whether or not my brother knew what was really going on between Mike and me.

I guess I should have told my mom or some adult when all

this was going on, but Mike had convinced me that we were doing nothing wrong, and to say something to someone would be to betray him, Oddly enough, the first real memory I have of my mom comes with the first memory of my stepfather.

Marvin Baker met my mother one day as she worked in the sugar cane fields of Belle Glade. Marvin was straight 'off the muck', as they say (this meant he could not read or write). He was the kind of man that didn't mind being with a woman with two children, especially a woman like my mom, who was strong, smart, and pretty.

Marvin was a man with big dreams and high hopes. My mom took to him right away. He would come by our room, say his hello's to us as we were being escorted out to play. We'd sit outside the door listening to them laughing, and then things would get quiet. Marvin would emerge later, and be on his way. My great aunt, Katie, called Marvin one of the ugliest men she'd seen in a long time. Marvin had a really big nose, which covered the better part of his face. He stood about 5'9" and would often smell of his work. My mother however thought he was perfect in his own way. After several months of courtship, Marvin convinced my mother to move up north with him. My brother and I were not sure where we were going or what we would do once we got there, but Marvin quickly calmed us with the promise of a better life, and my mother was more than happy to believe him.

We ended up in Newark, New Jersey. It had only been a few weeks since we arrived and Marvin had already bought himself some fancy clothes, and began living his dream. As my mom, who was now pregnant, lay back to have Child Number Three.

Marvin wasn't around much during my mother's pregnancy and I could tell it bothered her. But she settled in just the same and made Newark our new home.

Marvin hung out with a lot of women, especially white women. Although he wasn't that attractive, he was fun. He knew how to make you smile even in your worst moments. And women back in those days seemed to need to smile.

Marvin told my mom he was using the other women to get ahead. He had big ideas for all of us and he said a white woman was our ticket. This was a side of him we had never seen before. He was confident and sure of himself as he spoke about the white women that, until now, he would have never dreamed of having a conversation with, let alone any type of relationship. He told my mom not to worry, so she didn't, and like always, Marvin came through. On the rare occasions when my mom would dare question Marvin for returning home in the early morning, the next day he would come home with just enough gifts to make everyone forget his infidelity.

Nevertheless, things were great! We had a beautiful double-wide trailer with all the trimmings, new friends included. We grew closer to Marvin as he became someone we could rely on. Having more confidence in himself, Marvin decided to deal with his illiteracy. He openly asked for help, and began studying everyday with us from our school lessons.

My mother also knew how to make things fun and comfortable for Marvin. She pretended to be our teacher, popping Marvin's hand as she did ours, when there was a missed word or lack of attention to the lesson at hand. This would cause us kids to roll all over the floor laughing as Marvin took his punishment.

I remember the fist time Marvin signed his name without using an X. That night mom made his favorite cake, and we got to lick the bowl for being so helpful.

Marvin had done well in a short period both on and off the job. He was very proud of himself. He was promoted to night supervisor where he worked as a janitor. He couldn't wait to show us the big building he was in charge of at night. He started taking Junior and me to work with him, promising us we could earn extra money. Well, turns out that on our second night of being employed, Junior, who loved to snoop, was caught on tape taking money from one of the executive's desk.

This cost Marvin his job.

It didn't take long for things to go downhill. It became really tough for us and the strain of not having Marvin's income began to take its toll on my mom. She was more irritable, constantly talking about how lazy Marvin had become. I heard her screaming at Marvin one night because we were going to lose the trailer. A few days later Marvin came running through the door yelling for us to pack our bags.

"We're leaving town tonight," he said, never bothering to explain why, and rushing us along barely giving us time to grab our belongings. I didn't know it then, but I know now that Marvin almost got himself killed that day over a tall, skinny, white woman named Carol. The same white woman I would learn to call Auntie on our trip back to Florida, as she too threw her bags in the car.

Most people tend to overlook children, not realizing that they understand far more than they receive credit for. Marvin was no different. I had witnessed on several occasions the secret touches he and "Aunt" Carol had exchanged as my mom lay drained from taking care of the baby and keeping the house clean.

I never said anything because I, better than anyone, knew the game of secret touches.

Mike had taught me that sometimes a person needs more than certain people can give.

"Not for anything bad," he would say as he pulled his pants up over his knees. "But just because they do."

I am not sure why my mother allowed this woman to come with us, but she did.

Jumping on the road so abruptly still left open the business of where we were going. I think it may have been at a rest stop that my mother called Belle Glade and found out from a friend that my great aunt, Katie, Mike's mother, had moved to Daytona Beach.

So, to Daytona we headed—back to the sun and Mike, my favorite cousin.

I had not seen Mike in over two years and I couldn't wait to see him again. When I look back, even then, I never had a bad thought or feeling towards Mike. He was actually the one who took care of me the most, taking me with him everywhere he went and making sure no harm ever came to me. I felt special because he always wanted me near him. Not once did it occur to me to fear him. After all, I was his special girl. Even when we lived in the same house and he eventually had his own little girl, Mike would still creep into my room.

"Just a little," Mike would say trying to calm me as he started pushing his manhood inside of me. "I don't want to hurt you," he would add, giving me a smile as he told me that one day I would be able to take it all like a big girl.

Although I was only seven, I remember feeling how couldn't wait to be his big girl.

Janice E. Sullivan

Chapter Two

Cucumbers Have Thorns and Snakes Love Strawberries

––•·•◆•·•––

Once we arrived in Daytona Beach we moved into our own place. My mom was on Child Number Four, and Marvin, who was always off somewhere working on his next plan to make us rich, had become bitter and no longer related to us in the manner he once did.

Maybe it was because Aunt Carol left. I'm not sure, but whatever it was, it was clear that things had changed. My mom told us Aunt Carol had made her way back up north, working as a lady of the night, which, in layman terms I knew, meant whore or prostitute. So, when Carol pulled back up in our yard one afternoon, I couldn't understand the fanfare or the open-armed welcome she received from my mom. I sat quietly listening as Carol explained to Marvin how quick and easy the money was.

"This is our way out," she exclaimed. She let Marvin know that the only reason she came back was to take her sweet brown daddy back with her. She said she needed his protection as she hustled her way to freedom. Marvin smiled at the idea as her hands roamed all over his body. Neither of them paid any attention to my mother and me standing only a few feet away. I would like to think that my mom had no idea what was going on as she packed our bags, yet again, for another move north.

On the way to Syracuse, New York, we made one stop to pick up Marvin's daughter, Pam, who until now, had not been mentioned before. As she walked out to the car I remember looking at her and being afraid. Although she was only a year or so older than I was, her small frame, and even smaller steps towards the car, indicated how timid she was. As she came closer, I could see that her neck and one arm was covered with white

31

patches. I wondered how a person could be white and black at the same time. I imagine we must have seemed absolutely horrible as we squeezed up close to each other so that we wouldn't touch the marks on her arm.

We would find out later that Pam had received her skin discoloration from a pot of boiling water thrown on her by her very own mother. We would spend months after the trip trying to touch and sometimes even kiss her spots. We wanted her know she wasn't different and that we, her new family, were no longer afraid.

As we continued to travel on the highway, I stared out at the tall buildings and thought there must be a lot of important people inside. I pressed my face against the glass of the car window to get a better view. I longed to be like the people on television, whom I felt must live in such huge buildings. Even as a child I would pray as hard as I could, asking God for help. Although I didn't know what I needed help for, praying seemed to relieve me of the heaviness I felt inside. It was as if I could hear him say, "Don't worry, you are My child and I will take care of you."

When we finally arrived in Syracuse, things didn't go according to Marvin's plans. Even amongst pimps there seemed to be some sort of a code when entering new territory. And Marvin, like every other pimp, had to establish himself. In the meantime, while Marvin was "establishing himself," we worked.

My mother didn't approve of us doing field work, but Marvin was not going to carry the load by himself.

He told my mom, "There's one thing I know for sure and that's field work ain't never hurt anybody. It took care of me all my life, so why shouldn't it take care of us now?"

Marvin convinced my mom that we would have to contribute to his plan. Before we knew it, we were traveling back and forth, going from field to field picking apples in apple season, potatoes in potato season, and cherries in cherry season. We would drive hours away from Syracuse, just to catch strawberry and cucumber season in the other surrounding states. I loved cherries and wished we could pick them forever. We became part of a traveling network of field hands and we would often see the same people from season to season. Marvin had become so good at slave labor he would gather up a bunch of drunks off the street corner each morning to go with us to work in the hot sun—not to decrease our load, mind you, but to increase his. Their pay was as much Wild Irish Rose as they could hold and still be able to make it to work the next morning.

One day, I ran off from Miss Mattie, the woman who often helped keep and eye on us when my mother couldn't come to work. I ran off to sit with some of the men who worked in the field. As they talked amongst themselves, I leaned against Big Joe's inner thigh and chest, while playing with the long whiskers that hung from his chin. When Miss Mattie noticed I had slipped off, you could see the dust that rose from beneath her feet as she angrily stomped through the rows of strawberries headed in my direction. When she finally reached us she stopped dead-smack in the middle of their little circle. The shadow that cast over us let the men know she was not to be messed with. Reaching down in one swift motion, she grabbed me by my arm and snatched me to my feet. She then dragged me off, taking just a moment to look back over her shoulders and gave the men a nasty look. While dragging me along behind her, she suddenly stopped and placed her hands on both my shoulders. She looked down at me, and said, with a stern, but worried look, "Baby as long as you live, always remember: *Cucumbers have thorns and Snakes love strawberries* ." Although at the time I didn't understand it, I would never forget her words.

She took a long, deep breath, sighed and slowly removed her hands from my shoulder. I could tell she was troubled by the whole thing. She grabbed my hand in hers once again, but this time with a little less aggression, and began speaking about the dangers of young girls and old men.

"Yes ma'am," I said after each warning, hoping she wouldn't tell my mom.

That night when we returned home I discovered the reason my mom didn't come with us to the fields was because she was planning yet another party at our house. Marvin was back on track, and had now earned enough money to get a fancy car, and the loud colorful clothes that pimps often wore.

It had been two years since we left Daytona and my mom and Marvin were becoming a part of the in-crowd, one party at a time. On many occasions the adults coaxed us into dancing for them until the party really picked up. I was an excellent dancer and solid for a nine-year-old. All of us children would be in the middle of the floor dancing and thriving for their attention. Needing to be the main attraction, I would always give it just a little bit more by mimicking a few moves I had learned from the adults.

My mother's younger brother Dutch had moved to Syracuse shortly after we had, and when it came to dancing, he was my biggest fan. He and his friends would cheer me on until finally the other kids would stop dancing because all eyes were on me.

This was the first time I had spent time with my Uncle Dutch since we'd left Belle Glade. It was he who had taught my brother and me how to file down the pennies to get free cokes. Although he was my uncle, we never really referred to him as such. I think it was because we all played together as kids. He looked the same as when we left. He still had his baby soft hair that naturally waved up when he wet it. He was very slim with fair skin. He was always bopping around singing Otis Redding's songs, with a toothpick hanging out his mouth and a small cloth that hung neatly from his back pocket. In his mind he was The Man. He had even acquired the nickname "Bell Glade" because of his unique, country style that he had made cool. He and most of his friends were about ten years older than I was and used to call me their little girlfriend. I'd go around bouncing from lap to lap, giving out tight hugs and kisses.

I guess I shouldn't have been surprised when the molestation started again, but I was.

I once wanted to blame the molestation exclusively on me, but looking back, I now know it was a sickness, which haunted my family. A sickness that had been passed down from one generation to the next. I hadn't fallen into the sexual grip of a family friend or a stranger. No, once again, it was a relative. My very own uncle had now taken on the role of my molester.

Many nights he would slip into the room where I slept with my step-sister, Pam, and my baby sister, Dedra. Pam and I had two twin beds so my little sister would fall asleep in either bed. When I'd hear him enter the room I would shut my eyes as tight as I could and pretend to be fast asleep. As he crawled on the bed, I would squeeze my eyes even tighter and prayed that he would just finish and leave. On those nights, I would lie still, hollow inside, as he would penetrate the small hole that made up my vagina. My uncle would place his hands over my mouth, partially covering my nose, as he lay on top of me pulling my panties aside. Forcing as much of himself as he could inside me. Other nights he would place his penis between my legs and rub it back and forth against my vagina and backside as I lay curled in a fetal position facing the wall, numb to all that was happening. I didn't understand that this was rape or molestation. Back then we called it "doing the nasty." And everybody did the nasty but no one ever told.

One night while my sisters and I lay in bed asleep he came into my room. Putting his hand between my thighs he pulled my legs apart. My sister began to toss and turn, as if she were about to awaken. This ran him off. However, I knew he would be back. I got up and moved to the floor so he would have all the room he needed, fearing I would get in trouble if my sisters woke up and caught us doing the nasty.

When he returned he was surprised to see I had moved and was now lying on the floor. He began his advance by pulling my underwear completely off this time. I didn't move, I pretended to be fast asleep. I don't know why I got on the floor that night, I don't even know why I pretended to be fast asleep, but I did.

After that night, my uncle's midnight callings turned into walks to the store, which were really clandestine trips to a nearby park. There he would lay me down on the cold grass behind the bushes as he pleasured himself, placing his manhood inside of me. This time I thought it was my fault. I felt I was the bad person, not him. After all, I must be asking for it because it wasn't happening to anyone else.

The molestation was often and went on for what seemed like years. Eventually, however, he would move on and the nightly attacks stopped—never to occur again. My Uncle Dutch would still come around, teasing and playing with all of us kids as if nothing had ever happened between us.

I never had the courage to say anything about the molestation to anyone. I know my mom was around during those times, I can see her in my mind's eye, laughing and busy planning one of the many parties she and Marvin gave. Not once did my mom check on us during all of her good times. Maybe she thought we were safely tucked away in our bed.

Chapter Three
Untitled

——— •··•●•··• ———

Well, like with any good pimp, when things are good, they're really good. Marvin had become crystal-quick (smooth and smart). Girls flocked to him, begging to be part of his entourage. They knew he was a much kinder and giving pimp than they had worked for in the past. He treated them like family. Marvin's doors were open to any woman or girl who wanted to be in the business. But the more girls Marvin took in, the more it cost him. Every night his girls were being hauled off to jail by the truckload and every morning Marvin would send someone down to get them out. That was one thing about Marvin, he had a big heart and you could always count on him. He didn't care who you were—fat, skinny, big, tall, ugly—it just didn't matter to him. If you were in his stable, he was going to take care of you.

But Marvin had a lot to learn. Until now, he had only experienced the upside of pimping. Now, he was faced with not only the police, but pimp rivalry. The streets were no longer safe for him or his girls. He needed to do something—and he needed to do it soon.

Early one morning Marvin woke my step-sister, Pam, my brother, Junior, and me. He said he had something for us to do. Sleepy and not knowing what was going on, we got dressed and Marvin drove us and one of his buddies over to the old Darling Ice Cream Parlor on Castle Street. It had closed down a month prior but had not been emptied out. We listened as Marvin explained how he wanted us to climb through the window and open the back door. Although what we were doing felt wrong, we did as we were told.

That night we loaded up all the restaurant equipment our

truck could carry. We took everything from the freezers to the sinks. Marvin even had me grab the register. He left nothing behind but the memories of a once thriving business.

A week or two later Marvin opened a record shop/restaurant where you could get anything from my mom's down-home cooking, to costume jewelry that would flatter even the funkiest outfit. He even added a candy and ice-cream section in the back for the neighborhood kids, which, of course, included us.

Marvin had found a way to come through for everybody. He rented the upstairs of the building and divided it into small rooms.

His plan was brilliant.

Marvin was on top again. He was now setup for business in the middle of South Avenue, the number-one street for prostitution. It was where the coolest-of-the-cools hung out. Prostitutes flowed in and out with their patrons; pimps ate bar-b-que chicken, sweet potato pie, and collard greens, while grooving to some of the smoothest tunes of the day. Money was coming in by the fistful. It seemed too good to be true—and it was.

Both Marvin and my mom were good targets for any wannabe, gold-digging man or woman.

It's no wonder things got out of hand.

It seems that Barbara, my mom's best friend, was having an affair with Marvin, but so were my mom and Barbara's husband. Each would tip around thinking no one knew, but I knew. So when things hit the fan and shirts and bras were being torn off, it didn't surprise me at all.

As a result, mom and Marvin called it quits. The only remaining question was: Who did we kids want to go with? One by one, each of us gave our answer. So far, there were two for Marvin, which were my step-sister, Pam, and brother, James, and one for Mom, which was my brother, Junior. My sister Dedra was only three years old, so she didn't have a say. I was next. Although I really didn't want to choose, I knew I had to, so I thought for a moment. Now, aside from my real dad, Marvin was the only father-type I had ever known, and, of course, there was all that candy and ice cream to consider. On the other hand, Mom would be so hurt if no one wanted to come with her.

"I'll go with mom," I said missing the ice cream as soon as the words came out of my mouth.

We didn't know then, that this would be the beginning of their many breakups. A few months would pass before they would rekindle their so-called 'new found love.' This time Marvin promised there would be no more lies, pimpin', or runnin' women.

"I'm going be a legitimate business man and we're going to be the family we were meant to be," he declared as he gave all of us a big hug.

Marvin kept his promises to be a better mate and stepfather, we did all sorts of things together. We spent the weekends at the movies, or my personal favorite, the amusement park.

"No more fields for us," I thought as the days went by.

Somehow, Marvin pulled it off. He had us all convinced that this was a new day. But he never really went legit. That promise, like so many others, didn't last very long. One day he just woke up, grabbed two or three whores along with his daughter, and headed back to Florida. My mom was devastated. She was left with no money and no means of supporting herself or us. Within a few weeks she also headed south, but this time, without us. She said she needed a fresh start and promised to send for us kids later.

We were left with my grandmother, a cheating, drunken step-grandfather, and my Uncle Dutch who, at one time, couldn't keep his hands off me. My grandmother and her husband had moved to Syracuse after they had heard how well my mom was doing.

Living with my grandmother was different from living with my mom. My grandmother lived in the upper level of a two-story house. It was considerably small and had just one bedroom. They didn't have the money or fancy items to which we had become accustomed. I recall the fans that constantly blew to keep the house cool during the summer. It must have been during that time that we found out I had asthma. I recall being deathly ill as the doctor explained that asthma is a condition I will have for the rest of my life. I knew it couldn't have been easy for my grandmother back then. She was stuck taking care of four kids, one of which was now always at the hospital. My Uncle Dutch and his two kids had also taken their place on the floor with us. I can only imagine how trapped she must have felt as my sister, brother, and I sat patiently waiting for my mom to return.

The year we spent with my grandmother felt like a lifetime. But just like she promised, my mom popped up out of nowhere to pick us up. With a new husband in tow, she enters the house with a certain air and what appears to be a new lease on life. Although my mom and her new man are married, we were told to call him "Mr. J. D.," so we did. It didn't matter to us; after all, we didn't know him and he wasn't our father. He was nothing like Marvin, who I still call Daddy to this day. No, he didn't reach out to us at all; in fact, he barely spoke.

After formal introductions, my mom pulled us aside to explain how Mr. J. D. would take care of us from now on. She smiled as she talked about how different things were going to be. The next day we packed our bags and rode off into the sunset as one big happy family.

Mama was right about how beautiful West Palm Beach was. There were mangoes and coconuts hanging from every tree, just waiting for little hungry hands to pluck them.

I liked this new life and made friends quickly. Although I was only eleven, I was able to find a little helper's job at a plant nursery pulling weeds. It wasn't very glamorous, but it would give me extra money to buy the things I would need when I started the sixth grade.

In this new town no one knew anything about my past, and I liked that. I worked hard at doing everything I could to be the best child possible. I joined the safety patrol (an honor back then), took ballet, played the violin in our school orchestra, and won the county competition for the in-school essay contest. My essay was entitled, "If I Could Be a Hero, I'd Be…." For me it was Harriet Tubman. She was strong and fearless, always doing what she believed in. My essay was so good it was published in the *Daily News*, one of West Palm Beach's local newspapers.

As hard as I would try, it seemed I would always find a way to be underfoot. I would be practicing either too early, or too late. And safety patrol, Mr. J. D. complained, was said to be keeping me out too long, leaving little time for chores and homework. By the time the school year was ending, I had managed to get myself restricted from practicing my violin in the house and told to quit safety patrol. This should have been the first sign that Mr. J. D. wasn't as happy with us living with him and my mom as I thought. I reminded myself that even though things were changing a bit, they were still better than what we had left—'*way* better.

After months of practice and hard work, it was time for city-wide orchestra concert. I thought about how proud my mother would be after she heard me play the violin. She and Mr. J. D. had laughed when I told them I may be one of a few students selected. They both mocked me and wanted to know who my competition was. I didn't care that they thought it was funny. I knew I had worked hard to learn my piece, and although I may not have been the best, I gave it my best and it paid off because I was one of a few from the string section selected.

The next morning, I got up before the sun came up. As always, I raced to the balcony to greet the huge orange ball that covered the whole sky. It was a special time for me. I felt safe in the glow of God's arms.

This particular morning, however, was like no other. This would be the day all my practice and hard work would be seen by hundreds of people. To me, this was one of the biggest days of my life. I pranced around the house pretending to play an invisible violin. I anxiously waited outside my mom's bedroom for her to open the door and head to the kitchen to have her morning coffee so I could remind her about the concert.

Janice E. Sullivan

As I stood waiting, I wondered what all the whispering was about. Hoping a surprise celebration was being planned for me after the concert, I leaned in just a bit closer so I could hear more clearly. The pain of what I heard that day is still fresh in my mind. As I stood at the door listening to Mr. J. D. and my mom, this is what I heard:

"What you should do is teach her a lesson for not folding those clothes like you asked," Mr. J. D. said, concerning an incident from last week.

What happened was that, while my mom and I were at the Laundromat, I was told to dry and fold the clothes, while she ran to the grocery store. Instead, I went off to play with my friend who lived nearby. My mother returned to find the clothes still in the washers, and I was nowhere to be found. The time had gotten away from me. By the time I returned my mother was sitting on the bench folding the clothes that had just finished drying.

My mother didn't respond to Mr. J. D. as she opened the door of their bedroom and walked out. To me, the fact that she did not respond to him meant she felt he was just as crazy as I did. She knew how hard I had prepared for the concert. Although little was said that morning, I ran off to school happy about the day's upcoming events.

When I returned home from school, I couldn't wait until it was time to get dressed for the concert. I had had my outfit picked out days earlier and I hurried as I put it on. My mom was sure to walk in the door around 5:30 p.m. since we needed to be at the school before 6:30 p.m., and there was no way I was going to be late.

As I anxiously looked out the window, I continued to glance back at the clock. The hand seemed to move faster than it ever moved before, first five-o'clock, and then five-thirty, then six, and six-thirty—still no car and no mom. Around 6:45 p.m. I hear my mom and Mr. J. D. coming up the walkway. I ran to the door screaming, "Mom hurry! We're going to be late!" I yelled, looking out the door as she calmly walked up the stairs leading to the front door.

"Late for what?" she said glancing at me with a detached look on her face.

Still excited I redirected my attention to the devious look Mr. J. D. had on his face as he brushes past me, also heading up the stairs.

While still watching him I looked at my mother and said, "Ma, you know my recital is tonight."

"Oh, that. Well, you're not going." She says matter-of-factly, but with a chill in her voice.

My heart dropped. I thought to myself, "Do anything but this!" "Mom, I'm sorry for whatever I did, but please, don't take this away from me." She didn't say another word, as she walked up the stairs not giving me a second look.

I cried all through dinner, until finally Mr. J. D. couldn't take it anymore.

"What is she crying for?" he asked my mom as if he didn't already know.

"She wanted to go to that recital tonight."

"Well she can't cry blood," he said looking at me as the tears streamed down my face.

He then turned to my mother and said, "Let's go to bed, she's just looking for attention."

To me that was the first time my mom had sold me out for a man. Compared to this, the other stuff didn't even matter.

By the middle of summer, my mother had shipped my younger sister, Dedra, and my oldest brother, Junior, back to my grandmother. I knew James and I wouldn't be far behind. I thank God that before that day came I would have the chance to witness my first miracle and learn first hand the power of prayer.

I had taken a baby-sitting job for a white couple across the street. They had a little boy who was mentally disabled. Although he was only two, it had been confirmed by doctors he would never be normal (whatever that means). I had done a good job the first few times I kept him, so the Smiths used me whenever they needed a sitter. I was glad because I wanted to be away from everything and everyone at home. I did my best to stay out of Mr. J. D.'s way.

One night while I was sitting for the Smiths, I laid the little boy on the couch for a moment while I went to the kitchen for a soda. I knew he was not to be left alone because he often threw himself violently, but I promised myself I'd be quick. It was in that second that I heard a crash.

The little boy had thrown himself on the floor, hitting his head on the corner of the coffee table, causing a cut just above his eye. As I saw blood run down his face, I became hysterical and began to cry. It seemed I just couldn't do anything right.

Everything was going haywire. I had a step dad who hated children, and a mother who was so wrapped up in him, she was shipping us off one by one. And now, as if things couldn't get any worst, I was going to be barred from the one place I had to run. I was sure the Smiths wouldn't entrust me with their only child again. Before I knew it, I was on my knees, praying as I had never prayed before. I asked God to help me. In my heart, I questioned what I could have done for so many things to be wrong in my life. I prayed until I fell asleep with the little boy in my arms.

When I awoke, Mrs. Smith was taking the child from me so she could put him in bed. My heart sank as she brushed his hair back to give him a kiss. When she didn't say anything about the bruise, I sat straight up, startled, as she turned to take Junior to his room. I jumped up thinking she must have overlooked the cut. I knew I had to tell Mrs. Smith what happened, so I called to her to come back in the room.

"The baby hit his head," I said nervously as I brushed back his hair so she could see the hole in her son's head. It was gone. There wasn't a trace of blood or a bruise anywhere—not one sign of an injury.

"He seems okay now," she replied, looking at her child, who was fast asleep. That night I walked home, thanking the Lord.

Chapter Four
I Got Your Back

———◆———

It was late summer and just as I predicted, my little brother James and I were being placed on a Greyhound bus, and shipped back to my grandmother in Syracuse. I can still hear my mother telling the driver to keep a close watch on us.

Then she bent down, looked me in the eyes and whispered, "I've wrapped some money in this handkerchief. Don't take it out in front of anybody. If you need money to eat, go in the ladies room and get what you need and then put it back. You understand?" "Yes Mama," I replied as tears rolled down my face. James, who was six at the time and didn't know what was going on, stood looking up at me with a smile on his face.

We got on the bus and like any eleven-year-old, by the time we reached our third stop I had spent all the money my mother had given me. We pulled up in the Washington D.C. terminal, scared, broke, and hungry. We had a three-hour wait, and our bus wasn't scheduled to arrive in Syracuse until the next afternoon.

As tears again rolled down my face, I asked God what we should do. In the middle of my prayer, a tall, pregnant, brown-skinned woman walked over to me. "Scared, huh?" she said. "I bet you're hungry too, right?" She didn't wait for a response. "Well, come on, lets see what they have here to eat."

The lady made small talk while we ate. She told me she would sit with us until her bus arrived. As I watched my brother bite into a fried chicken leg, I asked her where she was going.

"Syracuse, New York," was her reply.

I was ecstatic. Her words were music to my ears.

Overjoyed, I replied, "So are we."

I knew we'd be safe the rest of the way.

As the cab pulled up to my grandmother's house I saw my brother Junior, and sister Dedra sitting on the porch waiting for us.

Where is my Granny? I wondered, as Junior paid the cab and helped us with our stuff.

Granny had just moved into a new house. There was little furniture, and clothes were thrown everywhere. As I walked into the kitchen my granny was sitting at the table with a beer in her hand. She appeared drunk. Junior said she started drinking heavily after our step-grandfather was sentenced to 25 years to life for the murder of his girlfriend's husband.

My grandmother did not give us much of a greeting, and started laying into me right away. I figured it must have been because of the look on my face, which showed my shock at our new living conditions. While reaching for another beer, she stared at me as if I had invaded her privacy.

"Ya mama already told me you think ya uppity. So don't come in here with that look on your face like you smell somethin' or you got somewhere better to go, because you don't. Go put that stuff away," she said looking me up and down.

She was no longer the grandmother I remembered. She had aged so much in just a short time.

This house had three bedrooms. Two of the rooms had a bed and other furnishings, but the third had a worn mattress on the floor and nothing else. James and Junior would share a bedroom, and Dedra would sleep with Granny in the other. I quickly discovered that the room with the mattress on the floor would be mine. I didn't care just as long as it wasn't forever. Besides, Mom told me Granny just needed someone to look after her for a while, and promised to come get us soon.

We had been with our grandmother a few months when we got the news that our grandfather had had a stroke while in prison, leaving him partially paralyzed on one side. He would soon be paroled and returning home. This was great news because Granny would no longer be alone. My mother would surely be on her way to get us. So we waited.

When my grandfather returned home, his first official act as boss was to inform the family that we would be moving from 'this big drafty house' (as he called it) to the projects where he was sure the bills would be cheaper. The projects to which my grandfather was referring were three blocks away from where we now lived, but it was a whole different world. It was a tough neighborhood, and many of the people who lived there were either out of work, on welfare, on drugs, or all three.

I thought to myself, "Could things get any worse?"

If my grandmother wasn't drinking, my grandfather was bossing us around. We were afraid of him he was 6'9" and his left shoulder, due to the stroke, slumped in slightly. He also shook a lot and his left arm jumped up and down uncontrollably as he tried to hold it close to his side. The stroke left him in pretty bad shape, but somehow he still managed to terrorize us anyway.

I was excited the day we went to see our new home in Albert Terrace, also known as 'Brick City.' A courtyard separated the two long rows of buildings that faced each other. Each building was divided into sections, and each section had two doors and a small front porch shared by two families. We walked on the porch where we would soon live. As the door opened, I could see a small living room area with two sets of steps. One set led down to a tiny basement, and the other led upstairs to a mini-kitchen. A door on the second level led to a fenced-in backyard that separated one tenement from the other. A young girl my age was sitting on her back porch. I went over and introduced myself. She told me her name was Colette. She couldn't have been more than a year younger than me, but she was pretty well-endowed for her age. Her hips and butt were huge compared to the small waistline that sat on top of them. Aside from all the hips and butt, we sort of looked alike. We were the same height, had the same pecan-brown complexion, and both of us wore our hair in pigtails. We talked for a moment and I liked her right away.

Colette said she hoped we would move in, and so did I. I

left Colette and returned to the rest of my family. I followed my grandmother from the kitchen as she went up another short flight of steps leading to the first bedroom. I was surprised to see so much space, because the place didn't look very tall from the outside. We continued up another flight leading to a small bathroom and the bedroom that would be occupied by Junior and James. I looked up at what appeared to be the last set of stairs and rushed to see what was at the top. There it was—the room that would be mine and sometimes Dedra's. I ran to the window and looked out over the neighborhood. I could see just about everything in the complex. I liked the room because I would be away from everyone. I went back downstairs to hear what everyone else thought. My grandfather, of course, was being his normal miserable self, but my grandmother thought it would do just fine, and so did my brothers, sister, and I.

I wanted to tell my grandmother how much easier living here would make it on Junior and me as there were many nights when we had to carry my grandfather all the way home from the liquor store, which now would only be a few short blocks away.

Well, my grandfather must have figured that much out for himself, because within the next week we were packed and ready to make the move.

I liked that the new place allowed me to spend time alone. I often sat in my room thinking of West Palm Beach. Although a lot of time had passed since my grandfather got out of prison, I still held onto the dream of my mother coming to get us. It seemed as though my grandmother hated me for refusing to let go of what I knew life could be. I constantly fought against my surroundings, which didn't help matters. My grandmother even refused to buy me or my younger brother, James, clothes for school after everything we had brought from Florida was stolen as they hung out to dry. She only bought clothes for Junior and Dedra, who she said were appreciative. I never let it bother me because I had learned to be resourceful and often borrowed clothes from my friends. But for James, it was a different story. His clothes were ragged and soon kids started to pick on him. They called him cruel names like Mr. Dirt, and that bothered me a lot.

Every meal my grandmother prepared was basically the same: beans and rice for breakfast, lunch, and dinner. She would cook up a pot of food and sit it on the floor for James, me, and sometimes, my three cousins to share. We would look at each other intensely with our spoons positioned like shovels. I didn't realize the derogation of it all. We fought to get enough. Sometimes we would use our utensils as swords, knocking the food off each other's spoon in a war of survival, while only a few feet away, my grandmother and Dedra sat at the table enjoying their unrushed and unshared dinner.

Junior had wised up and was gone as much, and as long, as possible. I, on the other hand, had to be creative. Colette, my new best friend was always willing to share a plate of whatever she had with me. But my little brother, once again, wasn't as lucky and had to endure the mistreatment all by himself.

One day, I sat James, now eight, down and explained to him that he would have to find a way to help out. He needed to earn a dollar or two so we could make it. James really did want to help out, so every Tuesday he would take the trash out for the owner of a nearby restaurant in exchange for two chicken dinners. He also earned another two dollars by cleaning the lot of another business.

As for me, I couldn't leave the front porch or eyesight of my grandmother, whichever was closest. I believe she resented the fact that I hadn't succumbed to her attempt to belittle me. Whatever she did was okay with me because all my friends would gather around our porch and play with me until I had to go in.

It had been quite a while since we moved in with our grandmother, and we had received a care package from my mom only a few times. Each package had a different address and no mention of her return. My grandmother was drinking more and more each night. We had to lift her from the chair and walk her up the stairs as she leaned her dead weight on us. Since my grandmother was always drunk, and my grandfather was preoccupied with his new girlfriend, I was left free to venture out into the neighborhood with my friends.

Fortunately for me, my friends all had at least one positive relative in their family and I made the best of it. Unlike most kids who emulated the traits of their parents, I admired and tried to emulate the positive qualities of the people I came in contact with. Taking on different mannerisms, I slowly began to mold myself into the person I someday hoped to be: I took grace and poise from one, a light laugh from another, respect, good taste, and determination, from others.

Being free gave me the opportunity to admire the girls dressed in the latest fashions, their hair always done-up in such pretty styles. I too wanted to dress and be pretty. So when I learned how the others always seemed to have the latest stuff, I wasn't reluctant to try their technique.

I was thrust into a crash course of shoplifting 101. I'd skip school and go to department stores with my friends who were experts in the art of stealing. It wasn't long before I had all the latest stuff, too. James was no longer wearing sandals in the winter and we had food to eat. Oh, yeah, we had food. I learned to conceal an empty bag under my blouse, carry it into the store, and then fill it up as I walked from aisle to aisle making my selections. I would then take the now-stuffed bag to the front counter, explaining to the cashier that I forgot to leave it up front when I came in.

I had become good at shoplifting food—no, let me correct that— I was great! But clothing stores were a bit different, and I found myself being brought home by the police on more than one occasion. That didn't make my grandmother happy, but even that changed once she saw that a case of beer was just as easy to steal as a candy bar. Our trade-off was I would keep the fridge filled with Schlitz Malt Liquor and she would leave me alone.

It was somewhere during this time my grandfather lost his girlfriend and started hanging around the house more, but I wasn't about to let him ruin my truce with my grandmother. I supplied the beer and she left me alone. That was the deal and he wasn't going to mess that up.

A new look, a new attitude, and street smarts had been added to my portfolio. I wasn't going back to feeling helpless, and spending all my time trying to figure out, "Why me?" or "Why not me?"

My grandfather constantly complained about my being gone. He said he wanted me around the house more, in case he needed me.

Turns out he had his own reasons for wanting to keep me underfoot. I remember him staring at me one day in the kitchen, it was as if his eyes were trying to penetrate through my clothes. I watched him out of the corner of my eye as I walked past him headed towards the stairs that led to my room. I felt like he was a predator, and I, his prey. He would lean back in the kitchen chair and spread his long legs wide open.

"Come give Granddaddy a kiss," he would say, his speech slurred. He would reach for me trying to pull me up close to him with his good arm, which seemed to have taken on a new found strength. I could smell the stench of alcohol escaping from his skin as if it too needed to get away from this horrid man.

As my grandfather pulled me close, I became trance-like and just stared at the beautiful woman he had tattooed on his arm. She was so perfect, just lying there naked on her side. Her head was propped on her hand as her long hair draped slightly over her breast. The tattoo was that of my grandmother when they first met years ago.

It was hard to imagine the woman who now sat only two chairs away, drunk and over three hundred pounds, could have ever been as strong and as vibrant as the image I saw before me as I struggled to get free from her husband.

I wasn't afraid anymore, and I wasn't about to take another round of molestation. I pulled away snatching so hard I almost fell back over his foot. As I ran upstairs to my room, each breath became harder and harder as the anger of what had just happened mounted. That night, I lay on the mattress sobbing into my pillow, wondering how the little kisses I used to receive from my grandfather could turn into a forceful attempt to stick his tongue down my throat.

There were other times when his advances were more suttle. He would pretend to accidentally brush against my breasts as he waved his so-called, stroke-afflicted left arm uncontrollably. But I knew, I could feel the disease flowing though my body.

"How could this be?" I thought.

I didn't know how long I could keep my grandfather off me. I tried to tell my grandmother what was happening. Although on one occasion he tried to grab me with my grandmother sitting just a few feet away. She sat watching me twist and turn trying to get free from his clutch, but said nothing.

"Grandma," I yelled. "Tell him to quit trying to put his tongue in my mouth!"

My grandmother looked at me as if I had done something wrong.

"Go to bed right now!" she yelled.

"But Granny," I exclaimed.

Before I could say anything else, she cut me off with her stern throaty voice, "Go to bed now!"

Tears rolled down my face but I quickly wiped them away. My grandmother had taken his side and there wasn't anything I could do about it. Feeling he now had carte blanche, my grandfather began coming into my room late at night, lying down beside me and feeling all over my body.

His touch sickened me.

The first night I jumped straight out of bed and ran into my grandmother's room, screaming and crying. Again I tried to tell her what was happening, but when I reached the doorway, she was lying on the bed in the nude, passed out. I tried to pull her arm to wake her. After a few aggressive tugs, she sat up just in time to see my grandfather coming down the stairs. He stood in the doorway with his bad arm half raised, shaking violently. He dragged his left leg in behind him. He was dressed in black socks that went halfway up his calf, and a pair of boxer shorts that had the fly wide open, exposing his penis. He stood there like the towering giant I would remember in my nightmares from that night forward. Pausing only for a second, he walked past me and climbed into bed, where they both fell fast asleep. Nothing was ever said.

I got my mother's address off one of our care packages, I wrote her so I could tell her what was going on. But my letter went unanswered. Once again, I was left again to fend for myself. I had begun carrying a pocketknife in my bra. I was fed up and would do whatever I had to if he (the man I called Grandfather) ever came in my room again.

In my mind's eye, it feels as though I had cried out for help so many times; in hindsight, maybe I wasn't crying loud enough. I believe no one heard me, because no one wanted to hear. No one paid attention to my movement, my silence, my behavior—no one asked why I had changed, no one wanted to know.

I remember once when I went to the dentist to have a cavity filled, I waited until I was almost under the gas and pretended to be drowsier than I actually was. I started moving my head from side to side as if I was talking unconsciously, murmuring about what was going on at home. I even pulled out my pocket knife to show what I was going to do if he tried it again.

"Who?" asked one of the assistants, speaking softly.

"My grandfather," I said, pretending to be semi-conscious, letting my body relax, knowing now, I would finally get some help.

When I awoke, I expected to see police officers waiting to take me to some great foster home, where I would be safe, which is what eventually happened to Marvin's daughter, Pam.

Marvin had left Pam with "Aunt" Carol so he could run errands. Before Marvin could return to the house, the cops had raided it. They took Pam into custody and she was placed into a foster care program. The bust had something to do with prostitution and drugs, I think. It could have been that a black man living with nine women—and only one of them black—was bound to spell trouble sooner or later.

I saw Pam once or twice after that. We'd give each other a hug and just stand there in an awkward silence, never really having much to say. As she walked away she promised to keep in touch, but I knew she wouldn't, because she never gave me her telephone number or asked for mine. I guess she wanted to put the past behind her.

To my disappointment, there wasn't a single officer anywhere. I was greeted by only the sad face of the dentist. That day, he watched me walk out of the door and back into the world that he could afford to pretend did not exist. Realizing no one really cared, I took a deep breath and headed up the sidewalk. With one broad stroke I wiped away the tears and any hope of rescue.

Some of the most valuable lessons I would ever learn were the ones I wasn't looking for. They would prepare me for something greater than I realize. Take, for instance, something as simple, but important, as feminine hygiene. This lesson would come to me not a moment too soon.

One day, while hanging out with my friend, Joyce, at her sister's house, I asked if I could use the bathroom. When I went in and closed the door, I noticed a red, hot water bottle hanging from the shower. I remembered my mom had the same bag and she said she used it to stay fresh. Later that evening, when my friend's sister announced she was going to the store, I dashed for the bathroom and filled the bottle with water. I then inserted the nozzle in my private. I had noticed a strange odor coming from my feminine area lately and wasn't sure just what to do. When my girlfriend's sister returned home and went into the bathroom, she was livid. I tried to lie but she knew. When she saw the water well up in my eyes, she stopped yelling and began to ask me questions about myself, and what I did or did not know about being a woman. She took the time to fill in all the blanks.

A few weeks later, at the age of 12 ½, I had my first period.

Janice E. Sullivan

Chapter Five
My Mother Is Coming!

The school year ended as quickly as it began and I was glad; it was summer and time to have some fun. I had made several friends who were as close to me as my own sister and brothers. Although I spent a lot of time crying that year, it was because of these friends that I spent just as much time laughing.

I dreaded being home, especially when my grandfather was there. No matter what I did, it didn't stop his attempts to molest me. Although I had made a vow to cut him, I never got up the courage. However, I was able to get off a few good knees to the groin while pretending to toss wildly as I slept.

My grandfather wasn't like the others in that he never tried to have full penetration. Instead he wanted to defile and degrade me with his touch. He would rub all over my body with his rough, callous hands while breathing heavily in my ear; each of his touches becoming more sickening than the last.

I hated him. The smell of his skin along with the rough feel of his unshaven face haunted me nightly. I would get sick to my stomach just thinking about it. I had had enough and it would not have taken much to push me over the edge.

I thought if I could just keep my grandfather from drinking, maybe he would leave me alone. I began dumping out the bottles of Smirnoff vodka and replacing them with water. When he found out, he was furious and went into an alcoholic rage—cursing and yelling throughout the house. I had no idea about alcoholism or its affect on someone when they couldn't have it. All I knew was that I wanted the abuse to stop.

There was a silent war going on between me and my grandfather and he was determined to win. He began telling my grandmother vicious lies about me. My grandmother would believe them and restrict me to my room. When he was sober he would come into my bedroom, sit boldly next to me on the bed and start doling out grandfatherly advice. He was a big, tall man and I was intimidated by his presence, but at the same time amazed that he could now treat me as if he himself had done nothing wrong.

One day, he found the knife I had hidden under my pillow and showed it to my grandmother. He told her I was fighting in the streets and causing trouble all over the neighborhood. I tried to convince my grandmother that none of this was true, but she refused to believe anything I had to say. She didn't want to hear that the knife I had wasn't to fight off the people in the streets, but to fight off the man she called her husband. She stomped into the bedroom to call my mom. Looking back at me with disgust, she closed the door in my face. I sat on the hall steps listening to them as they talked.

"She's completely out of hand," my grandmother complained.

"Oh, you're in trouble now, mister," I thought to myself. "You may have my grandmother all sowed up, but my mom is a different story."

I sat quiet as a mouse, listening for some sound of refute. But instead, I heard my grandmother say, "You're right. We'll just do what we can with her."

My heart fell and I was shattered. Why hadn't my mom come to my defense or at least asked to speak to me? Surely, she wouldn't just automatically believe everything she'd heard.

Didn't she want to hear my side of the story?

All hope of being rescued by my mom ended on that day, and I did the only thing I could think of that would keep me out of my grandfather's clutches. I hung out at anyone's house that would have me; I joined Colette's church and choir, and when it wasn't open, I took to the streets. I stayed clear of my grandfather any way I could until it was bedtime. Then I would sit up all night, making little noises so he would know I was still awake.

It didn't take long before I realized my grandfather was a coward. He would only attack when he was drunk and thought I was asleep; startling me seemed to give him additional pleasure. There were nights I would sit up until early morning trying to avoid my grandfather's advances. It worked, but not for long. Each night, I prayed for God's protection as I lay in bed listening to the radio and escaping into the words of a familiar song. I followed the lyrics imagining each love song was about me. No matter what happened, I felt safe in the arms of God and the rhythm of the music.

One evening, after weeks of trying (often unsuccessfully) to stay awake through the night, I just couldn't take it anymore and decided to confide in my friend Shelia, who lived a few doors down from me. Her father and my grandfather drank and ran women together. I felt if anyone could understand what I was going through it would be her. When I got to her door, she was smiling. She was always happy to see me.

As we walked through the kitchen, only the light over the sink was on but the aroma of an earlier meal still lingered in the air. We went upstairs to her bedroom. We spent a few minutes looking out the window. Then I sat down on her bed. Unlike mine, Shelia's room was warm and cozy. There was a lamp and table in one corner and a tall dresser with four drawers against the wall. She had pictures torn from popular magazines taped over her bed. She didn't have a mattress on the floor, she had a real bed. I felt small and poor surrounded by all her things.

Although I had heard the rumors about her father, I wasn't sure how to start the conversation. I felt that, she, like me, just wanted to forget it. But now it was time to talk. I needed to know how she made it stop.

I found we had more in common than I thought. She too had gone through several forms of molestation, including from an aunt. We both sat shocked as we listen intently to the other's story. She talked openly about the late night attacks she had endured. My jaw dropped as she told how she was forced to give oral sex to her aunt. I couldn't believe it. I didn't even know what that was. "Wow!! I'm sorry," I said, giving her a hug.

When it was my turn to tell all, I held back. I didn't mention Mike or my uncle. I was afraid. I thought she might be making up the stories of being molested, so that I would tell her everything. She would then tell everyone else about my horrible secret. Besides, how could all of this have happened to her with all the stuff she had?

That night I only spoke of my grandfather and the things he did to me. I didn't care if she told people about him; I wanted everyone to hate him. She said she had been where I now was. When I asked what she did to make it stop, she said "nothing". "One day it just did". We thought hard on what I should do, but no answers came. I was surprised at myself. I didn't cry or feel the hopelessness that had eaten away at me earlier. Instead we sat there talking freely about the worst violation a young girl could experience as if we were telling a secret about a boyfriend we weren't supposed to have. We had become bonded by a secret and we had no one else we could trust.

We made a pact that each night, after I was sent to bed, I would climb out of my brother's bedroom window, which was one flight up from the kitchen, drop down to the yard, jump the fence, run to her house, climb up to her window, and spend the night. Then I would return home just before it was time for school. It seemed like such and easy plan when we thought it up, but in actuality, it took some real work and determination to pull it off. And pull it off we did! My grandfather would look at me each morning as I sashayed by him, smiling as I closed the door on my way out. I knew he would try to spoil my new strategy, but for now, I was winning.

Each morning I would head off to school feeling victorious…
…but *never underestimate the enemy.*

Caught up in my new win, I hadn't noticed that no one had made a fuss about my late night outings. They just let me continue without saying a word. Then one morning out of the blue my mom popped up. She, my grandparents, along with Mr. J. D., were just sitting there looking at each other as I came down the stairs after one of my late night escapes.

I missed you this morning when we got in, my mom said. I thought I'd stop by before you went to school, to let you know we were here."

I couldn't say anything. I wanted to go into a hundred explanations, but nothing came out. There weren't any of the hugs or I-missed-you's from my mom that I had dreamed about. There were only conspiratorial looks between them, while glancing at me. They sat around the table and each began their evaluation of poor, out-of-control Janice as if I wasn't there. Well, I decided to do as they did and act as if I weren't there, either. I looked at them blankly, and then went on about my morning, got dressed and headed off to school.

That day I swear I could hear each second tick off the clock, as I sat at my desk in a fog from my mom's unexpected visit and the trouble it appeared I was in.

Let 'em go ahead and tell my mom all those lies, I thought. She'll find out for herself. The best part was that mom was back to pick us up and I was going home. Once we were together again, I could tell my side of the story. She would then know the truth and be furious.

I was ready to go. I mentally made a note of the things I wanted to be sure and take. After school, I ran from the bus excited, not wanting to hold up our departure. As I entered the house, I looked in the kitchen. It felt as though time had stood still. They were all still sitting there just as I had left them. Had it not been for their clothing I would have sworn they had never moved.

My mom was a lot more talkative this time, and even gave me an outfit that matched hers to put on after she braided my hair. Once I was all cleaned up, my mother said Mr. J. D. was tired so she was taking him back to the hotel. I ran to the car and jumped in the back seat. I wasn't going to let my mother leave me again—no way!

After we dropped Mr. J. D. off, we stopped by the store to get us both a snack. My mother didn't say much at all during the outing. And I didn't say anything about what I had been going through either. Instead, I just asked my mom to please take me with her.

I fought back the tears as she responded, "We will see," giving me her best motherly look.

Once we were back in the projects where I lived, I took my mother around from door to door, showing off our twin outfits. After I had exhausted my list of friends we went back to my grandmother's where I was then asked by my mother to excuse myself. I went upstairs making sure to sit on the top step so I could still hear what they were saying. I heard my mother and grandmother talking about my mother's plans to leave the next day. This was all I needed to hear. I jumped up off the step, ran in my room, and began to pack for my trip back home. I ran around that evening collecting all the things I wanted to take with me. I then made a goodbye trip to each of my friend's house, telling them my mother had come for me and I would be leaving in the morning. We all hugged and gave each other a kiss as we promised to write.

Happy and excited, I ran all the way home. By the time I had gotten back to my grandmother's house my mother wasn't there, but I just knew she would return for me. I tried to encourage my baby sister and brother to get their things ready as well.

"Mama didn't say we were going," said my brother.

"Grandma, said you ain't going nowhere," my little sister chimed in.

I gave them the, 'Okay, but I'm gonna miss ya look' as I turned towards my room running happily up the stairs.

The next morning I sat with my bags lined up at the door. No one said anything as I sat in the chair next to them waiting for my mom to walk in.

My mom finally showed a few hours later. She came in, sat

down and talked with my grandmother a few minutes, then, she stood up and made her announcement.

"Well, Mama, I guess we're gonna run."

I jumped up asking loudly, "Mama, you want me to put these bags in the car?"

"No, baby we'll put them in the car when I get back," she said as lovingly as possible.

"Oh, you're coming back?" I questioned.

"Yes, I'll be back," she said while bending over to give me a reassuring kiss.

I sat in that chair all day waiting for her to return. I stared out of the window until it was late into the night. Eventually, reality sat in. I began to cry as I bent over to pick up my bags and headed back to my room.

She wasn't coming!

Janice E. Sullivan

Chapter Six
How Did I Get Here?

My mom had lied about coming back, and my grandmother wasn't interested in anything negative I had to say about my grandfather. At this point, I was way beyond caring what anyone thought about my behavior, and it wasn't long before I started slipping out of the house for reasons other than to get away. I began stealing on a regular basis, and I was brought home by the police just as often. Knowing I couldn't go to jail until I was fifteen, I had been offered a free ticket to trouble—and I took it. Most of the time, after I was caught stealing, a police officer would come pick me up, take me to the police station, then call home for someone to come get me. My grandmother would explain that she didn't have a car so she couldn't pick me up. I was put in the backseat of the police vehicle and returned home with a warning to my grandmother and me. I think somewhere in the back of my adolescent mind, I thought if I got into enough trouble my mother would come for me.

Although my grandfather had found another girlfriend and wasn't around much, I felt my life was a disaster, and I hated it and everyone who participated in making it that way.

I would find myself praying for something to happen to my grandfather, and it did. One day a nurse from the hospital called my grandmother with the news that he had another stroke.

It doesn't bother me to say it wasn't bad news. I did feel sorry for my grandmother, however, because she seemed to take it very hard. After all that man had done to her, when she heard the news, she still cried a river of tears over him.

For the first time, I saw a deep sadness in her and could almost hear her heart crying out for help. The wrinkles on her face mirrored the pain she was suffering in her soul. We both sat in silence, until my anger turned to pity. I think she felt better that I was there, but the bond we shared momentarily was interrupted when she began gathering up items and placing them neatly in her purse.

I asked her matter-of-factly, "So, where you going?" not caring that her husband was in the hospital.

"I'm going to the hospital to see your grandfather," she replied, sounding irritated.

"How are you going to get there?" I asked, not really caring about her response. Before she could answer, the doorbell rang. I dashed downstairs, thinking it may be one of my friends. Instead, it was a woman I had seen before—my grandfather's girlfriend. I couldn't believe she was actually standing in the doorway of my grandmother's house asking her if she had packed everything my grandfather wanted. My grandmother told her she had, as the sad defeated look in her eyes returned. I watched my grandmother walk down the sidewalk with the woman who had taken her husband, and now was taking her pride. I cursed and hated my grandfather on her behalf. I thought about how, yet again, my grandmother was being abused by another man.

She had had five husbands and eight children. Three of the girls had been molested by their fathers, one of which became pregnant. They didn't keep the child and behaved as if the situation had never occurred.

After that day, I worked hard at being more understanding rather than angry towards my grandmother. I realized it wasn't me my grandmother had given up on, but herself. As far as I was concerned, I could not understand how she could waste her time pining away for a man who, I don't believe, had ever done one good thing for her. Although I felt really sorry for my grandmother, that day I lost something for her and I never saw her quite the same. But I couldn't dwell on the day's events.

It was close to my birthday, and my friend, Marsha, who lived in the building behind me, and I had made plans to go to a huge block party that weekend. I grabbed the phone and called Marsha. We agreed to meet in front of her house so we could head to the mall to "get" something to wear. We walked to the bus stop excited about the new outfits we would soon have. Some older girls, known to be big-time boosters pulled up and asked where we were headed. We told them we were going to the mall. Knowing we were two of the more skilled shoplifters in the neighborhood, they asked if we wanted to ride with them. We were thrilled by the invitation, so we quickly said yes, and piled into the car.

When we got to the mall, things went smoothly. The other girls had already stolen everything from leather coats to a television. Marsha and I, however, focused only on what we needed to wear for the block party. We would never steal just to steal. It was always out of necessity.

Everyone was ready to go except Quanessa, who we called "Q." She wouldn't leave without a pair of shoes she had seen in the window of one of the stores. Since shoes were one of the easiest items to lift, we agreed to one last store before heading home. Q got her shoes and we were back in the car within minutes.

These girls were considered to be heavy-hitters in the neighborhood, and it was an honor that they had invited us at all. So when Q, while laughing and talking about our success, pulled out a joint, lit it, hit it, and passed it to us, I didn't know what to say or do. I couldn't let them know I didn't smoke. So like a pro, I took a long drag and passed it to Marsha.

It wasn't long before the station wagon was filled with smoke, and without warning, the air passage in my throat narrowed, my muscles tightened around my chest, and I began frantically gasping for air. The music appeared to get louder and louder, breathing became more and more difficult, and I knew I was having an asthma attack.

I yelled, "Please turn down the music. I, I can't—"

Before I could finish my sentence, I heard sirens, and suddenly the blaring music was replaced by a man's voice yelling through a megaphone.

"Pull over. We have you surrounded."

When we got out of the car I quickly took a puff of my inhaler, which brought back my ability to breathe and the reality of what was happening became clear. Marsha and I had both been caught before, but this time, the police had guns drawn and we were being thrown to the ground like common criminals while they yelled at us. Crying like babies Marsha and I were loaded in the back seat of the police car and hauled off to jail.

When we reached the police station, Marsha and I found out that the car we were in had been stolen. To make matters worse, we were not only in a car with what the police called "repeat offenders" who all had records as long as their arm, but they were in possession of marijuana as well.

Q and her friends were older than Marsha and me and they all had children of their own. Q, who hadn't been out of jail for more than a week, had just blown, once again, any opportunity to get her kids out of foster care.

Thank God, we had our bus passes, which identified us as being under age. The sheriff looked at our district then called the inner city police to pick us up. Boy was I glad to see them. Once we were out of earshot of the other officers, I tried to make light of the situation. I joked with Officer Dan, who had taken us home many times before. He was one of the coolest white officers we knew. This time his attitude was different. He didn't smile or give us the father/daughter talk he had given many times before.

Instead, Officer Dan said, in an ice cold voice, "You've crossed the line girls. It's not a game anymore."

He was so angry at having to come so far to pick us up, he wasn't the least bit pleasant. In fact that day he ended our conversation with one of the most callous statement he had every made to us.

"It's okay," he said, "I know the next ride I take you on will be your last."

That left things deafly quiet for the rest of the ride home.

Marsha's mom showed up at the station to pick her up. As for me, this time the officers offered no assistance at all. As far as they were concerned, I had stepped way out of bound. I was no longer a kid out doing mischief. I had made the decision to hang out with the "big boys," or as in this case, "big girls," and would be treated as such.

When they called my grandmother, they didn't offer to take me home as they had in the past. They told my grandmother, unless someone picked me up, they would have to call the juvenile detention center.

That day, my grandmother, who was overweight and could barely walk a short distance, walked four miles to the precinct to collect me.

"See you next time, Janice," I heard Officer Dan yell out as I disappeared out the door.

While my grandmother and I walked home, Officer Dan's comments continued to play in my head. I looked around at the buildings and people that made up the projects where we lived. I realized that I didn't hate where I lived, I hated the life I was living. I had become caught up in the pain and constant battle of what it meant to live in the ghetto. I was on my way to becoming just another statistic.

As we approached the steps that led to our porch, I paused to take a good look at my grandmother. Her breathing was labored; the long walk had been too much for her. I felt guilty for adding to her already troubled life. When we entered the house I grabbed my granny by the arm and helped her up the flight of stairs leading to the kitchen and carefully placed her feet in a chair. She seemed too tired to fuss.

That day, remembering what Officer Dan had said, *"See you next time, Janice"*, I took a long look at myself and felt ashamed. As I removed my grandmother's shoes from her swollen feet, I said in a low and determined voice,

"No you won't."

And I never stole again….

Janice E. Sullivan

Chapter Seven
Putting It All Together

———·•◆•·———

Although my grandfather had not come home after his release from the hospital, my granny was still happy to see him stumble through the front door a week later. As soon as he walked in the house I could tell he had been drinking - the stench of the alcohol came up the stairs long before he did. He strolled over to my grandmother, who was standing over the stove cooking, as if he had been home all along. He slapped her on the butt, then reached into his back pocket to pull out a bottle of lemon-flavored gin. My grandmother lit up as this man, whom she hadn't seen in a week, gave her mere scraps of the affection she deserved.

I watched him pour glass after glass as my grandmother drank and laughed like a schoolgirl with a crush. I could see she was past her limit, but still she drank as if she was welcoming back a long lost boyfriend. He poured, and she drank, until every drop was gone.

My brother, Junior, who came home as infrequently as my grandfather, decided to drop in as well. He stopped at the top of the stairs appearing surprised to hear so much laughing and joking. He stood watching in silence, quickly realizing as I had that my grandmother had had far too much to drink. As he stood watching them, his reflection cascaded off the window in front of my grandmother. My grandmother, now drunk, did not realize it was a reflection, and began talking to the glass pane in front of her. At first, I snickered and tried to conceal my amusement. Then my grandmother started to cry as she spoke to the reflection in the window. She told Junior of a pain she had never mentioned before.She called out to him in a smooth coaxing voice. It was eerie. "Come here son," she said beckoning to the reflection.

"Grandma's sorry."

Tears began to well in my eyes as I too, felt her pain and loneliness. My brother, standing not three feet away rushed to her side. He placed his hand on her shoulder. "Shh," he said attempting to quiet her. "I'm right here, Grandma, I'm right here."

He then helped her up the stairs to her room, and laid her down for the night.

I'm not sure what my grandmother was referring to, but whatever it was upset my brother so much he left without saying what it was for which he had actually come home. I watched the front door slam behind him as he left.

My grandfather was now downstairs in the living room and I was left sitting alone at the table. With everything that had just happened, I wanted to disappear too. I eased up from the table and headed towards the back door. At that very moment, my grandfather called me. I stood frozen, debating whether or not to pretend I didn't hear. He wanted me to turn on the television for him. I was only two feet away from the back door and could have easily made a run for it. If he had waited just a second longer I would have been gone.

Slowly, I turned and walked towards the dimly lit room where he was. I paused, as I stood at the top of the five steps that separated me from him. I looked around the room but his tall, ominous frame was muted by the dark, heavy drapes that hung from the window. The thin streams of light from the street lamp granted access to an insidious stare that sent chills up my spine.

Suddenly, I panicked like an animal that realizes it has been tricked into the hunter's snare. I began feeling sick in the bottom of my stomach. I quickly I tried to calm myself by repeating in my mind, "He wouldn't dare try anything."

I hurried to turned on the television set and attempted to make my escape.

Obviously drunk, and barely able to sit up straight, he leaned back on the sofa. Just when I thought I was out of danger, he asked me to get his cigarettes that had fallen under the couch where he sat. Reluctantly, I knelt down to pick them up, but I couldn't find them. I felt around a little longer before giving up.

As I rose to stand up, he grabbed my wrist.

"Oh, here they are," he said, with a tone that wasn't grandfatherly at all. It sounded almost sexual as he motioned me towards his lap. I followed the tilt of his head with my eyes, I was too afraid of what was going on to actually move. There they were, in his lap next to his penis that was hanging out in plain view. I felt my heart race as I tried to figure out how to get out of this situation. I was pinned between the table and the couch where he sat. He held my wrist even tighter as he pulled my hand towards his erection.

I was terrified.

How could the man I called Grandfather be doing this? Didn't he understand that what he was putting me through would traumatize me for life? But those were my thoughts, not his, as he placed my hand around his penis, forcing me to stroke it. I turned my head while tears ran down my cheek so I wouldn't have to look at the pleasure on his face. In an effort to reposition me, he then pulled me around beside him and sat me on the couch. As if there was nothing wrong with what he was doing, he started to moan.

Each breath I took was accompanied by severe pain in my throat and chest.

"Oh God, help me," I thought. "Help me please."

I wanted my mother more than ever before. I wanted her to come in and kill the S. O. B. that would dare do this to her little girl. Suddenly the door swung open and Junior walked in. He looked at my grandfather and then at me.

"What's wrong with you?" he asked.

Looking at him, but too afraid to speak, I didn't say a word. Although the room was dark, I hoped Junior would see the plea for help in my eyes as he picked up whatever it was that brought him home again.

My grandfather, who had placed a throw pillow over his

lap, answers on my behalf.

"It's all right," he said, putting my head on his shoulder. "She's just missing your mother," he added as my brother headed back out the door.

"I'm fine now, thanks," I said stiffly, lifting my head from my grandfather's shoulder. I wanted to spit in his face as his eyes meet mine, but all I could deliver was a cold stare.

I heard the front door close, and I realized my brother was gone. I jumped to my feet and ran up the stairs and out the back door.

That night I didn't run to catch up with my brother, nor did I run so I could tell anyone about what had just happened. I just ran.

Everything around me was a wreck. Even though we were siblings, Junior and I had been shipped around, and separated so much that we had no emotional connection between us. My brother lived in his own world, suffering from his own hurt and I lived in mine. I continued to walk around for hours, eventually running into some friends who were on their way to a party in the next town. I decided to go with them. I didn't care what time it was or if I would ever return home.

We arrived around midnight and the party was still going strong. It was a house party, which meant there were more people than room. So we sat with some guys outside on the hood of their car to watch the action.

One of the guys pulled out a case of beer, and passed it around. I didn't take one at first but decided later, with a little encouragement, to go ahead and have one. I drank the beer a lot faster than I thought I would. Before I knew it, I was on my third beer, talking and laughing as if the nightmare I had experienced a few short hours before had never happened.

Five-thirty a.m. rolled around and the guy driving the car was too drunk to drive. Not willing to take the risk of being stopped, he pulled over next to a pond just a mile or two from the party. The driver, who was only a year or so older than me, said he just needed to sleep it off for a few hours and then he would take me home as promised.

On the drive back, I thought about how I would get in the house without being caught. With any luck, my grandmother would be hung over from all the alcohol she had consumed the night before, and would still be asleep. As we pulled into the projects I noticed how quiet it was when no one was stirring about. I saw, for what seemed like the first time, the trash that was everywhere as I walked up the walkway. I paused for a few moments just to really take in the place I called home. I noticed the fencing that separated the projects from the outside world. The fence was constructed so that anyone who needed to get outside or in the projects would have to walk all the way around. Not me though, I squeezed through the fence and the pole that was attached to it and entered my grandmother's backyard. The small opening was a great short cut for a child or those who were thin enough to make it through. Looking back over the fence, as I let out the air I had been holding, the thought "Why won't someone clean this place up?" Raced though my mind.

I rounded the corner of the building leading to our house. Finally, I was at the back door. My plan was to do the following: climb up onto the part of the roof just over the back door; go through my brother James's bedroom window and slip quietly up to my room, just a few feet away. My plan sounded foolproof to me, only, when I reached the roof and tried to open the window, it was locked. I tapped on the pane attempting to get my brother James's attention. He was already awake but he just lay there staring at me as if afraid to move.

In a further scan of his room, I noticed my grandfather standing in the doorway of his closet with a cigarette in his hand.

He started yelling, "Get the hell off that roof!"

I climbed down the same way I went up, which was a lot more difficult, but I made it. When I walked in the house my granny was standing next to a green garbage bag with my clothes hanging out of it. I looked down at the bag, and said nothing.

"I want you out of this house, right now! You've come up to be nothing but trash and you're too hard-headed," she said, as she held her head, still feeling the effect of the alcohol from the night before.

My brother, James, and sister, Dedra, sat on the steps listening, and looked up at me to see what I would do. I was determined not to cry as I tried to reason with my grandmother. My voice cracked as I tried to get the words out, I knew if I continued to talk, eventually a tear would fall. And I would never give my grandfather the pleasure of seeing that. So I stood there silently abandoning any idea of trying to make my grandmother see it was her husband who had driven me out.

My grandfather walked over to the door and with one shove, pushed my clothes completely out the back door.

"And don't you come back!" he yelled as he jerked open the door even wider so I could get out.

As I turned to leave, I stopped to look at my grandmother, hoping she would intervene. I was now unable to stop the tears from flowing as my grandmother turned her back on me.

I vowed that day that they would need me long before I would ever need them. Bending over, I gathered my clothes, which had spilled all over the ground and left. A few weeks later, just before he turned sixteen, Junior packed up and left my grandmother's house for good. Even now, almost twenty-seven years later, I still ask myself why didn't I tell him or anybody what was happening to me. Although I may never really know, I feel it may have been the fear of being an outcast.

Chapter Eight
Lost and Found

———————•◆•———————

For the next few weeks I spent the night with as many friends as possible. This worked out well until word got out that I was homeless, which snatched the welcome mat from under my feet. No one wanted their child hanging out with a homeless, streetwise, troublemaker.

How quickly their opinion had changed of me. It was only yesterday that they considered me to be polite and well-mannered. This put my friends, who were still trying to remain loyal, in a tough position. They would have to choose me over their parents. I knew most of them would still let me in their homes to take a bath while their parents (or, in most cases, parent) weren't home. But I didn't want to see them in a position like my own, so I was content just to get the few meals they were able to sneak to me.

During the day I would visit anyone I could, showing up sometimes too early for even my closest friends. But they still would let me in so I could fall asleep, as I pretended to be watching television. Luckily for me, it was summer and there was always a late-night block party where I could hang out until daylight.

One night, close to the end of the summer, I was over at Marsha's house. Everyone had gone off to bed except Marsha. I knew she was tired and would have really preferred to be asleep, but she sat with me knowing I had nowhere to go.

It must have been around 1-o'clock a.m. when Marsha's mother got up to use the restroom, and heard us talking. She asked me to leave, and then yelled at Marsha for having company so late. I looked over at Marsha as I stood up to leave. She looked at me, both of us realizing it was too late for me to go anywhere else for the night.

Marsha stood up without saying a word to me as she yelled upstairs to her mom.

"Sorry ma, we didn't know it was so late. She's leaving now."

Marsha pointed towards the pantry while at the same time opening her back door.

"See you later," she said, yelling loud enough for her mother to hear her. Pretending I had left she slammed the back door, put her finger over her lips and tiptoed me towards the pantry where I would sleep, covered with one of Marsha's coats. She waved good-bye before heading off to bed. I could hear her mother talking and tears fell from my eyes as she complained about me to the one friend I had that night.

The next day Marsha said I couldn't hang out at her house anymore. She did think, however, that if we explained my situation to her older sister she would let me stay with her for a while. She was right. That night I moved in with Tara. I remember feeling so happy to have a place to go. I never knew how important having a place to call home was, even if it wasn't a happy one.

Tara and I got along great. Not wanting to become a burden I babysat for her while she worked. Plus, I did all the housekeeping to help pay for my stay. I didn't have a room of my own, but it was okay with me. I just wanted a place where I could feel safe and call home.

It was two months into my stay when Tara came in with the news that her baby's daddy planned on moving in with her. I knew him, but we never really got along. As far as I was concerned, Tara could do better. He was mean and only came around when he needed something. I knew once he moved in, my time there would be up. When Tara's boyfriend finally did move in, he immediately began to complain about everything I did. Unfortunately, it was just as Old Man Winter rolled around that things hit the fan between Donald and me. Tara asked me to leave and I fully understood the position she was in. She, like most women when faced with choosing what their heart knows is right and what their man wants, will chose the latter. She did offer what help she could by asking her other sister Denise if I could crash with her for a few days. I was especially thankful for that gesture because the nights had started getting very cold.

Since the problem wasn't between Tara and me, Denise agreed to give me one week to get myself together. I don't have to tell you how quickly time flies when you need it to stand still. So a week later, there I was, once again, with nowhere to go. I didn't cry this time as I gathered my clothes yet again. I just thanked Denise for her kindness, told her I had found another spot and left.

I had lied.

As I walked down the sidewalk of Pioneer homes on that cold winter day, my heart ached. It had been months since I had seen anyone in my family. I desperately longed to see my brothers and sister. I went back to the neighborhood, and paced back and forth on the corner by the park where they often played. I waited patiently for them to arrive, and, like clockwork, they both came shooting around the corner, racing to be first on the swing.

As I walked over to them, my heart sank deep inside my chest, and I felt a pain I hadn't experienced before. I wanted so much to say to them everything was going to be all right as I took their hands in mine. I wished I could take them away from the life they were now living. Instead I had to settle for a few bad jokes and as many hugs as I could squeeze in as I played with them.

I didn't ask about my grandmother nor did they mention her. Somewhere deep inside I wanted them to say that my grandmother wanted me to come home, but they didn't. The snow would be falling soon and I would need some kind of a plan. I tried calling my mother at her old job in West Palm Beach. My heart and mind were racing with all the things I would say if she answered.

A voice came on line. "Hello."

"Hello, can I speak with Julissa?

"Julissa-Who, baby?"

"I'm not sure. Maxwell I think," I said sounding puzzled, realizing that I didn't know my own mother's last name.

"She no longer works here, but if I see her who should I say was calling?"

"No one, thanks," I said, sadly placing the phone back on the receiver.

It was getting colder and colder as each night passed, but I was determined not to tell anyone I had no place to go. When asked, I would just say I was staying with a friend. I didn't feel that their inquiries were genuine. Nor were they to offer me a place to sleep, but a mere inquisition to see what was going on with the kid who had been thrown out.

How could I tell them I was sleeping in the hallways of various apartment buildings? And how I was being run off nightly, by the superintendents who would lock the door to keep, not just me, but several like me out of their halls? How could I tell them that I was on the street because my grandmother's husband, who had been sexually molesting me was the cause of my being thrown out?

I never once gave a care to the homeless people I had seen in the halls of the very buildings I now took refuge in. And now, here we were, fighting together for a warm place to sleep. Until then, I never knew people lived their whole lives, moving from one building to the next, one hallway to the next. At fifteen, it was hard to figure out what went wrong. Why had all this happened to me? My desire to do what was right seemed to fade away each day as my future began to look dimmer and dimmer.

I learned a lot of things while hanging out in those halls. But the most important was this: If I could get through this day (meaning the day I was in) then I'd have a chance to succeed in the next.

The guys offered me a drink, as we bunked down for one of the coldest nights we'd faced. I reflected on how good the three beers I drank at the house party that night had made me feel, and eagerly took a huge swallow. They were right about one thing, after a few drinks the world didn't matter so much. Drinking with them wasn't as bad as I thought it would be, and the liquor made me feel warm inside. I guzzled it down each night until I would either laugh until I made myself sick, or cry at my self-thrown pity party until I fell asleep. In most cases, I spent half the night doing one, and the other half doing the other.

By the time winter set in, the alcohol had started making me sick. Before I could even take a drink, the smell would cause me to throw up. My stomach would continue to heave but there was nothing left to come up. I hadn't had real food in weeks and I was living off a few snacks here and there. Eventually, without having the alcohol to fall back on, the weather became unbearable and I became very ill. I was an asthmatic and I knew I was in deep trouble. I could hardly walk without my lungs feeling as if they would collapse any minute. I didn't know what to do. I didn't want my friends to see me so sick because I had always been one of the tough ones, able to handle anything. Now here I was— lonely, hungry, and destitute.

Not knowing what to do, I sat against the wall shivering, thinking of all the times my grandmother had nursed me back to health after all the long nights we spent at the emergency room. I was scared. I felt this time I wouldn't make it through another night. I knew the only choice I had was to accept defeat and return to my grandmother. I struggled to keep my balance as I headed towards the projects. The walk seemed to take forever, but in reality, where I lived now was just a few short blocks from where I once lived. On my walk back to my grandmother's house, I reprimanded myself for being so cocky. Why did I challenge my grandfather? Why hadn't I just taken it?

"Because it's wrong!" I said out loud, answering my own

thought. Shaking, and barely able to form a fist, I stepped up onto the little porch that led to the back door of my grandmother's house.

There I was knocking, in the middle of the night, holding on as best I could as the door slowly opened. I didn't say anything, feeling so sick I could hardly talk as the water filled my eyes. My granny opened the door wider, looking at me, but never saying a word. As the door widened I thought it was a gesture for me to come in, but I was wrong. Instead, it was my grandfather, who stood like the gatekeeper of hell, hovering over me, watching me sweat and cough. My grandmother looked up at him.

"She's sick, Elbert," she said in a half-pleading voice.

To my horror, her comments didn't budge him and he didn't flinch as he pushed the door closed. Being too sick to move, I slept on the stoop outside my grandmother's doorstep, listening to my brother and sister cry. Their faces pressed against the glass as they looked out at me freezing in the dead of a New York winter.

The next morning before the neighborhood could wake up, I woke up, sat up and prayed. I had made it through another night.

I asked the Lord again, "Why me?" I listened for some sign or answer, but heard only silence, until the sound of a roaring ambulance passed by. I would have never thought that that was the sign I had prayed for. A sound that meant tragedy or death to others, was now the sound of life to me.

"That's it!" I thought, knowing with an asthmatic condition as serious as mine, the doctors would at least keep me overnight.

I stood up and walked towards the bus stop to catch a bus that would take me to the hospital. I didn't have any money so I would have to use an old trick I had used many times. I would have to pretend to have lost my transfer slip and needed to get home. This was a trick my friends and I used many times to get to the mall. The bus drivers were suckers for kids, not wanting to have the weight of something happening to a poor child on their hands. As I started out for the main street, I thought about how sick I was. I also thought how now, for some reason, I felt better and maybe even stronger just at the thought of a bed and some food, even if it was hospital food. That was the last thought I had before I collapsed in the middle of the street.

The next thing I knew, I was in a hospital bed with tubes in my arm and people talking all around me. I hadn't made it to the bus stop. Instead, I had passed out in the street. No one knows, to this day, who called the ambulance. Could it be that the sound I heard earlier was on its way for me? I hadn't made it a block away from my grandmothers when I collapsed.

Walking pneumonia, compounded with asthma, almost took my life. The doctors waited until I could talk without gasping for air before they began probing me. They wanted to know who I was, and where I lived. I pretended it was still too much for me to bear, but I knew eventually I would have to give them the information they need so they could contact my family.

At first, I gave them my mother's information the best I could. I knew if anyone could find her, it would be the police. But they also wanted information on the person I was living with now. I gave them my grandmother's phone number, not because I wanted to go back, but so that the news of my near-death experience and how they had contributed to it, would hurt them.

Two days went by, and then three, but not a soul showed up to even see if I was still alive. The nurses had started telling me what the police would do if they didn't locate someone to which I could be discharged.

"Time for me to go," I whispered aloud to myself, as I prayed again before drifting off to sleep. I remember being half-asleep when I heard the one thing that has been more important to me than anything else in my life. That night, I swear I heard the Lord call to me. His voice was calming as He said, "Don't worry. I'll be right here for the rest of your life."

Each word gave me a feeling of peace. That night, for the first time, I drifted off without crying. The next morning something about me was different. I want to say I grew up. I knew I would be all right, as I walked out of the hospital realizing I really was - totally on my own.

Once again God would show his grace allowing Collette's mom to take me in, even though she had three children she was raising alone. She was one of those moms everyone looked up to, and the guys looked at. She was young, hip and in good shape. She was undoubtedly her own woman. She didn't care that my grandmother lived just over the rail. Nope, didn't bother her at all. She opened her doors freely and without question after hearing what had happened to me.

Later that winter I was also blessed to get a job at Church's Chicken as a runner, taking food out to awaiting cars. Of course, I had to lie about my age. But it is my belief that the manager, who had given my brother James a job emptying trash last year, knew I wasn't sixteen. He had often seen us eagerly gobbling up the chicken my brother received as his pay. He didn't even question me. He just told me to be there tomorrow, on time, and gave me a pat on my hand as he stood up. It took me a few months but I saved enough money to get my own place.

Since I was only 15, Marsha's sister, Tara, came to my rescue again. She convinced a guy she knew and worked for to let me rent his studio apartment. His building stood directly across the street from the projects where my family lived. I could see the backyard and porch of my grandmother's house whenever I walked outside. I lived in a two-story, light-grey building. A grocery store occupied the first floor and blasted, soulful music from speakers mounted just above the door. On the side of the building someone had painted a huge red, black, and green flag.

Across the street sat Martin Luther King Junior Elementary School, which faced a big, red, wooden house that had long since been condemned. I sat on the steps looking out over at my old neighborhood that now appeared totally different.

The neighborhood was alive with emotion and so was I. I had a smile on the inside that no one could take away. Things were coming together, thanks again to Colette and her mom. My new home was quite cozy. Colette's mom had given me some old furniture she had stored in her basement. The tattered orange and white sofa had a hole in the middle, but I didn't care. We just placed a pillow in the hole and covered it with a towel. She gave me her old end tables too, and a few other odds and ends that would help make my little place a home. Adding my own finishing touch, I placed a few pictures that I had torn from a magazine on the walls. I remembered how warm and cozy my friend, Sheila's room felt that night as we shared our deep, dark, family secrets.

I admit it wasn't much, but I had saved up for it, and I was proud of my accomplishment. Having a front view of the projects where my sister and brother still lived made it extremely hard not to miss them even more. However, I did as my grandmother wished, and stayed away. I found out my brother, Junior, had moved about fifty minutes away to Auburn, N. Y. We had spoken briefly on many occasions, but we never discussed why I was now out on my own. As far as he knew I was too hard-headed and my grandmother had no choice but to put me out.

Working a job and coming home to my very own place was more than I had hoped for. Yet, on nights when everything was still, I sat in a corner chair with my legs tucked under me, staring at the walls, reminding myself how blessed I was, while feeling an almost unbearable loneliness. I was alone and lonely, a condition that could turn into your worst enemy.

A lesson I would soon learn in the worst way.

One night, while sitting alone on the stoop in front of my building, a guy walked up and asked if he could sit with me. Of course I said yes; I was just happy to have someone to talk to. He said his name was Richard. We had such a good time talking and laughing that one night turned into another, and then another. Soon his visits became a ritual. He would show up nightly and just sit with me and talk for hours. We never talked about him or where he lived or anything personal. I had learned during my time on the streets that those things didn't really matter. Besides, most of the time people, including me, only told you what they thought you wanted to hear.

We were two weeks into our friendship when Richard showed up with a bottle of gin. As we sat drinking and talking my mind drifted back to the guys I had shared many a bottle with just to keep warm. I had forgotten all the promises I had made to myself on those shameless nights in the hall, swearing through wind-chapped lips, that if I ever got on my feet I would go back for them. Now here I was in front of my own place drinking and laughing, and those bad times were now just bad memories. I tried to enjoy that night in spite of the haunting thoughts of the people I had left behind. I told myself I wasn't on my feet yet, that I was barely making it. If anybody knew what barely making it was, I did. And it was nowhere near what I had now. I was ashamed that I hadn't kept my word. I hadn't even tried to take food back to where I knew they would be.

I sat with Richard for a few more minutes then excused myself so I could get out of the night air. I was feeling tired now and not having as much fun. My guilt had gotten the best of me.

The next morning I woke up, wheezing and dizzy.

"I don't feel so well," I said aloud while holding my head.

I had developed a cough a few days before, but I ignored it. Obviously, the cool air of last night had made it worse and I was having tough time breathing. I didn't have a phone so there was no way to let my job know I wouldn't be in.

I lay on the couch not able to move. I would sweat for a while, and then I would have chills. As I lay there lonely and afraid, I wondered if anyone would care if I died. I also wondered what everyone would say as they stared into my coffin. Who would take the blame for what had become of me? I hoped everyone would blame my grandfather as I pulled the covers tighter around my shoulders, trying to fight off the chills as I drifted off to sleep.

Later that night there was a knock at my door. I didn't open the door right away. Instead, I asked in a tough voice, muffled by my hands, "Who is it?"

A voice said almost apologetically, "I'm sorry, I thought my friend lived here."

"Richard?" I asked, half-heartedly and surprised.

How could I have forgotten my friend who showed up to sit with me each night? Surely, he would care if I died. I let him in and fell back on the couch drained.

I was sick the better part of three days but Richard stayed the whole time. He fed me and gave me everything I needed to help me regain my strength. He sat in the chair all day, watching me fall asleep and wake up, only to fall asleep again. He sat in that chair until I felt better and was able to care for myself.

It had been two days since I was feeling better and back on my feet, but Richard continued to stay. I wondered when he planned to leave, but since he had sat with me twenty-four hours a day, every day, while I was sick, I didn't have the heart to ask him to go.

I was sure I had been fired from my job, but I was too embarrassed and afraid to approach the manager who had given me a chance and ask for it back. Richard told me the manager would think I was lying. He said he would help me with the rent and anything else I needed. I accepted his help.

Whenever I had to go near the restaurant I would cross over to the other side of the street, sometimes pulling my jacket over my head so as to not be identified by someone at Church's. Just like that, I had lost my job and gained a live-in boyfriend in less than a week. Richard wanted to spend every moment with me. He would always try to kiss or hold me, but I would say I wasn't that kind of girl. I didn't mind the two of us lying on the couch watching television, but I didn't want to be touched. Later, I found out from Richard's sister why he could spend so much time with me.

He didn't work!

He hung out in bars every night and before he moved in with me, would sleep where ever he could. One day, he said he wanted me to get to know his family. I could tell from their reaction as I met them, that Richard hadn't had many girlfriends. His sisters were nice enough and we got along well. Both of them loved to have fun and I hung out with them everyday, which was just as Richard had planned. They were what I called party girls. Everything was always about getting ready for the club. What are you going to wear? How are you going to do your hair? It was always about the club.

So, like them, I eventually found myself in the clubs seven nights a week, dancing and getting guys to buy us drinks. Since I was only fifteen at the time I hadn't had any experience in clubs, but I, of course, took to it quickly.

My favorite club was this little Spanish hole-in-the-wall on the west side of town. I loved the Latin music and spent my nights learning how to Salsa. Soon I could Salsa better than any Spanish girl. Most of the guys would wait for me to show up and hope I would be their dance contest partner. There was something about the music that brought me to life. It gave me a feeling of freedom that I only felt on the dance floor.

"You dance with such grace that it could have only been given by God himself," said Juan, one of my dance partners, after winning yet another contest.

I felt good. I met a lot of people at the club, each calling themselves my friend, but yet I knew nothing about them. Many times I'd wanted to trust and believe that someone wanted to be around me for me—just me—but I was always let down. I don't know why, but I thought this time would be different.

Since Richard had paid the rent and bought food last month, I was left alone with very little to do with my time. After gaining all my popularity, it wasn't very long before I started going over to the west side of town not just at night, but during the day as well. The west side was where all the Puerto Ricans and Cubans lived. There had always been some sort of unspoken territorial rule between the blacks and Puerto Ricans that no one crossed— a silent agreement that faded as day turned to night. But I believed

I was different, and in no way did this rule apply to me. I saw no harm in hanging out on their side of town, day or night. After all, it wasn't like black people didn't live on that side of town. So I crossed the line to visit my Hispanic friends.

I was fascinated by the Puerto Rican culture and their way of life. I loved their big families with lots of children and the way everyone helped for the good of the whole. What they had I wanted and needed.

I hadn't seen Richard in two weeks. He left the house one night and just never came back, and I surely wasn't going to go looking for him. I knew I never wanted a relationship with him in the first place, but his absence caused another problem. Without him, I could not pay my rent and needed to earn some money. I had fallen in love with the Hispanic community so when two Cuban guys named Raphael and Manuel asked me to teach them English so they could understand a basic conversation, I agreed. My prayers had been answered. I could not only put the threat of being homeless behind me, I could also spend time with my new-found friends. Although I didn't see the harm in going to the Hispanic neighborhood to teach my friends English, Juan, my Puerto Rican dance partner and now boyfriend, along with several others, warned me to stay far away from them. I probably would have if I had not been given three weeks to pay my rent.

Wanting the lessons to be kept on the hush-hush, I had the first session at my apartment. My brother's girlfriend was also there. She also hung out at the club and the guys were familiar with her as well. She wasn't there because I felt threatened in anyway, but because there were two men coming to my apartment.

Things went fine until the guys left. Sharon and I had decided to walk with them a little ways out of the neighborhood. We had only walked a few blocks when a couple of black guys who lived in the projects across the street started calling Manuel and Raphael names for being on the black side of town. They, not understanding what was being said, kept walking and looking back every so often as the two guys approached them.

I didn't know these guys and it didn't matter that I was black too. If I took Manuel and Raphael's side I would get beat up as well, so I stayed out of it.

The two guys beat them up pretty bad and there wasn't anything I could do but watch in horror. When Manuel and Raphael were finally able to escape, they fled in shirts covered with blood.

I ran back upstairs and entered my apartment shaking. I could only imagine what was going to take place when the guys returned to their community bloodied and bruised. I knew everyone would blame me because I should have known better. I knew the rules although they didn't and they trusted me.

I didn't want to see Manuel or Raphael again.

I didn't know what to say or how to act if and when I was confronted by either side. No matter how many times I practiced, I couldn't come up with a convincing enough role for the scene that would have to play out. I decided not to go back to the club until Friday which was four days away. I hoped it would give things a chance to cool down. I knew I would have to go down to the club early, it would be empty then. Entering a full club would place the burden on me to either approach them as if nothing had happened, or to walk in, have a seat, and wait for someone to approach me about what had happened. Either way, the pressure would be on me, but if I was already sitting at the bar when they came in, the burden to approach or speak would be on them.

As I walked up to the club that Friday night, I began to question my plan and my hands shook as I twisted the doorknob.

"Take One, Scene One," is what I thought as I entered the bar.

I walked in, grabbed a seat, and ordered myself a Slow Gin

Fizz. That was the one drink that didn't make me sick, plus it tast good. As I sat sipping on my drink, I took a long look around the club. Somehow, it didn't have that warm and fuzzy feeling that I had felt in the past when I walked through the door with tons of people waiting to greet me. This time, I entered a place that had walls that were peeling and dingy. It smelled of old cigarettes and spilled liquor. I began to wonder how I ended up coming here in the first place. That's when I remembered Richard. He's the one who brought me to the club and then just disappeared. He hadn't been around in weeks and I had no intention to go by his family's house to look for him. Thank God for that. There was something about him that I could not put my finger on and really didn't want to.

The door opening broke my train of thought.

"Take Two, Scene Two," flashed across my mind as the night shift waitress came in.

"Hey girl," she said, "You here kinda early."

"Yeah," I said trying to appear as if nothing was wrong.

She put her purse down and went immediately to the point.

"Chile', why you let them boys come over to the south side? You was wrong!"

I looked at her and tried to explain that I never thought that things would end up like they did.

I'd been around all types of people, but I'd never known hate or racism. Most of the people in the club didn't know I was only fifteen and that most of my life I had been so preoccupied with my own family drama that I didn't have time to experience open hate between two groups of people.

But there I sat, all made-up and holding a drink. Who would believe I was fifteen? Most people thought I was around twenty because of the way I talked and carried myself. I had been through a lot and knew a lot for a kid my age.

It really was like a movie for me, my life I mean, because I felt like I had all these characters inside of me waiting to enter Stage Left. They consisted of the many people I had known who possessed a quality that I found to be intriguing or different in some way. And as each scene of my life opened up, I would call on a particular character to make each moment a flawless take. But upon whom do I call now? I had been totally naive to the danger my decision would cause.

Soon, an almost empty club was transformed into a tightly packed house with couples dancing rhythmically. But I sat on the bar seat, sweating, still scared, yet determined for the drama to play out as I had rehearsed so many times in my head.

The door to the club opened again and again but neither Manuel nor Raphael walked in. I got up to fix my clothes and leave, when I realized three of the men who lived with Manuel were standing right next to me. One was a very slender, tall guy with an afro so big it made his face appear very tiny. The other was short with piercing eyes that scared me. He had always been very quiet because he spoke no English. Looking at the two of them, you would have thought they were black.

The tall, thin one was leaning back with his elbows on the bar and facing the crowd. He blew a huge puff of smoke into the air and said, "Let's dance." I could feel he wasn't being friendly, it was almost a demanding gesture as if to intimidate me.

I paused and sat my purse down, pretending the music was too loud for me to hear. He gently tugged at my arm, motioning at the dance floor. I had never gone out on the floor with him or any of the other guys who seemed to like other men, but I didn't want to be insulting.

As we made our way to the floor, I wasn't sure what was happening or how to act. Here was this person in front of me dancing—no, mimicking—me. It was as if he had rehearsed my every dance move. It was eerie, like looking at myself on the dance floor. He was a little more theatrical, but I recognized myself in his moves. After our dance, I walked back to my seat and sat alone. None of my many dance partners came around to ask me to dance or talked to me.

The bartender on the nightshift was usually the interpreter for most of the people who weren't bilingual. So when he began to give me the message that Manuel had sent, it didn't appear strange because he had given me messages before. The message was that Manuel still wanted his lessons but he didn't want anyone to see his bruises. He had asked him to ask me to come to their house the next day. I agreed, thinking it was the right thing to do. The next day, around 5:30 p.m. my friend, Sharon, who was with me the day they came to my apartment, walked with me to Manuel's place. That way, after the lesson, we could all walk to the club together, and put things back to normal. When we arrived, the house was filled with Manuel's friends from the night before. There were several people I had never seen. They all looked black, giving away their identity only when they spoke.

Although we sat speaking in both Spanish and then English, something was different. No one seemed to be interested in learning and there was just too much commotion as people were constantly running from room to room.

Manuel suggested we sit in what appeared to be the television room. I hadn't seen a television anywhere else, so that must have been where they all gathered. Within five minutes, you could hear a pin fall. I looked around and everyone except Sharon, Manuel, Raphael and me, had left. This made Sharon and me uneasy so we suggested that we meet them later. We used the excuse that we needed to make another stop before heading to the club. We slowly stood up and headed towards the front room. If it had been possible to see my heart racing through my blouse, Manuel would have probably jumped back to the wall. My heart felt as if it was leaping out of my chest and across the room with every breath I took. I walked towards the room where we had left our jackets, but they were nowhere to be found. Raphael saw the despair in my eyes and pointed to a room down the hall. Sharon and I both walked towards the room. We were a little angry now and made sure they knew it. Our hope was to transfer our anger into the guys so that whatever plans they had, they would change their minds.

I reached the room first, grabbed the coats off the bed and turned to pass Sharon her coat when a scuffle broke out. By the time I looked up, Raphael had a butcher knife as long as my arm around Sharon's throat and his hands placed over her mouth. Manuel, not giving me a chance to react, quickly reached behind his back and pulled out another knife. He placed it against my spine with one hand and pulled my hair with the other, snatching my head back so hard I thought my neck would snap. Frightened and mad, my face filled with anger. I was ready to fight back. Instead, I calmed myself and listen to the inner voice warning me that this wasn't the time.

I looked back at Manuel from the corner of my eye as I transformed into yet another character I'd seen on television who had found herself in a similar situation.

I said as calmly as possible, "Why are you doing this?"

I did as she had done and tried to reason with Manuel. I thought of what I would say next as I glanced over at Sharon who had started crying and begging for her life. She had not realized she was talking a mile a minute to someone who didn't even understand a word she was saying. Without crying and with the most confused look I could muster, I looked at Manuel and made motions with my hands while speaking slowly.

"Why, Manuel? What's wrong with you? I thought we were friends. Why are you doing this? What did I do?", I said speaking far faster than I knew he could interpret.

After a moment, I could feel the tension on my hair lighten just a little bit. Sharon was more frantic than ever, slumping over as Raphael punched her in the face. He threw her on one of the beds with the knife pointed at her jugular. I saw her give up in spirit and in action, but I couldn't. I didn't fight, but I wasn't giving up yet either. I looked Manuel directly in his eyes and sat on the bed. He was then staring in my eyes and I could see that he cared. That, to me, was my way in. I let small tears roll from my eyes as I looked at him and pointed towards the door that lead to the other room. Motioning to him that I didn't want anyone to see us, Manuel raised me off the bed and pulled me towards the door that lead to another room.

Once we were in the other room I spoke in the broken English we had used to communicate.

"Why are you doing this? I thought we were going to take our time," I said, playing the girlfriend role. "Are you mad at me? Who told you to do this to me? Please don't, Manuel," I said, while all the time looking at him with as much love and bewilderment as possible.

I could tell he was beginning to think about what he was doing because his facial features were softening. Just as I felt he was calm enough to be rational, we were startled by a horrible scream coming from the room Sharon was in. Without thinking, I dashed towards the back, opening the door to the room we had just left. I was sickened by the sight of Sharon lying with no clothes on, legs spread wide, and Raphael between them. His hands were caked with the blood from the deep slash he had made on Sharon's arm. It was at that moment that the acting ended and I began to cry. I must have been crying so hard, I lost it, because out of nowhere came a hard blow to my face that literally threw me back. Manuel and Raphael were talking in their native tongue, bringing back all the fury I had seen earlier in Manual's eyes. He pushed me into the wall and began shoving me back towards the front of the house.

This time he pushed me onto the couch and unzipped his pants while yelling, "You suck! You suck!"

At the same time he slashed me across the arm. Although it drew blood, somehow I knew by the way he moved that his actions were to scare me, not to hurt me.

…I paused, and continued to tell my story to the judge.

Sharon and I had been called to testify against Raphael and Manual, forcing us to relive that night.

"There was something in his eyes that just made me know things had gone too far, and for him there was no turning back.

95

He was still holding the knife but he wasn't threatening me with it. "

I heard myself saying to the judge as I sat in the witness box recalling the events that would decide the fate of the two men that held us hostage that night.

"How did you get out? The judge asked.

"Someone passing by heard Sharon scream and they called the police, sir."

"Then what happened?"

"Well, Your Honor, I heard an officer on a bull horn asking everyone to come out with their hands up. At that point, Sharon, who was half-dressed, ran up front to the living room. I then slowly turned to Manuel, and looked him in the face. He was afraid. I put my hand over his and took the knife, then Sharon and I ran out."

"The guys were arrested and then Sharon and I were taken to the hospital for tests. I told the officers over and over again that nothing had happened to me but they still made me go to the hospital to fill out a report."

The judge turned his chair towards me.

"Young lady, it almost sounds as if you're a witness trying to help the defendant. Has anyone threatened you?" he asked.

I looked at him and said, "No sir. I'm just trying to tell the truth about what happened because I really don't think he would have hurt me."

The judge, then turned his chair back to the front of his stand, looking bewildered as he said, "Very well, you can step down."

Sharon's testimony was different. She cried and yelled as she told her story. When she finished the judge took a brief break before coming back and announcing his decision.

Raphael received seven years in prison and upon his release, he would be sent back to Cuba. Next Manuel's name was called. As he stood up my heart sank, because I knew what I felt that night was true and he deserved another chance. I felt helpless as the judge spoke. He used a much lower tone as he sentenced

Manuel to one year in jail and two years of probation for assault with a deadly weapon. He explained to him that it was my testimony that saved him from the charge of rape and kidnapping. Advising him he should thank me because his true feelings were to do the same with him as with his co-defendant. He then dismissed the court.

Sharon's family looked at me with disgust as they left the courtroom holding their daughter in their arms. There wasn't anyone there waiting to hold me or ask if I was okay. I watched Sharon's tear stained face and partially limp body disappear around the corner. And then I got up and walked down that long corridor alone. Sadden by it all I thought back on what made me do what I did. It was Sharon. That night at the house she took several hundred dollars off Raphel. It puzzled me that in all the confusion she could think to grab his wallet. I'm not saying what she went through wasn't traumatic, no, not at all. Just not as traumatic as she now made it seem. That along with what we found out after the incident just made me want to be fair in what I actually felt. A few days later we found out what everyone else already knew. I could not believe it. Manuel and the Cubans he lived with were a part of a government program. The United States made a deal with Fidel Castro, in the seventies that allowed him to release some of his most violent criminals on our doorsteps. These criminals were deliberately dropped off in this country and no one knew who they were or what they were capable of doing. That alone made me shudder. I couldn't bring my self to imagine what could have happen.

As I filled out the jail logbook to leave money in Manuel's account so he could get the cigarettes and things he would need, I decided never to return to the club.

Because Sharon and I were both under age our names were left out of the story that hit the papers the next day, but everyone knew it was us.

Janice E. Sullivan

Chapter Nine
Is There Some Kind of a Mix Up?

———••◆••———

As I sat in my favorite chair listening to the joyful music coming from the church around the corner, I thought to myself how quiet and drama-free my life had been lately. The choir was in the middle of singing a song about 'holding on' when tears suddenly began streaming down my face and I was overcome with feelings of hopelessness and despair. With all that had happened in my life over the past few years, I knew I should be thankful for the blessings I had received lately. After all, I had a roof over my head for at least another month, thanks to Sharon, who had given me some of the money the night we were attacked.

I decided to go to the church and give thanks because, although my life was in no way perfect, things were working out and I knew an angel was watching over me. So, with that thought, I got dressed and headed out the door. As I approached the church the music grew louder and louder. I felt I was being lifted up by the song and couldn't turn back even if I wanted to.

When I reached the church, I went inside, took a seat, and started crying again. I thought about how blessed I was to be there, and remembered the promise the Lord had made to always be with me. I left the church feeling reassured. Although things hadn't always happened the way I wanted them to, I knew I had to hold on to His word, and I did.

I became a regular on the night the church held bible study. One of the ladies, who saw me each week without a bible, gave me one—carrying case and all. I took it everywhere. I read it whenever I got the chance. It made me feel safe knowing the word was with me no matter where I went.

Then one night, while sitting on the front stoop of my

apartment building reading my Bible, Richard walked up. His presence startled me. It didn't take much to see he was drunk. His eyes were all a-glazed and wide, like a wild man. As he took a seat next to me and I scooted over further than necessary. We talked, but I was not as friendly as I had been in the past. In fact, I was scared, knowing all that I knew about him. After Richard disappeared, the people at the club told me how violent and dangerous he was and that he was known to be a heavy drug user. Since he had stopped coming around, I never gave much thought to him popping up again.

Richard insisted on telling me about an incident that happened a few weeks earlier, so I sat back and listened, not wanting to upset him. He said he had spent the past few weeks in jail for something he did not do. He had been accused of snatching a woman's purse and assaulting the woman and her date on the campus of Syracuse University. He told me that because he had been seen running down the hill from the campus, the police pinned the charge on him. He admitted he had been drinking but he knew what he had and had not done.

I listened to Richard slur his words and watched the horrible white foam around his mouth. I could barely look him in his face without feeling sick. When I couldn't take it anymore, I stood up, stretched my arms and yawned.

"Richard, I'm so tired, I think I'll head in," I said as I causally bent down to pick up my stuff. "See you later." Richard, almost falling back to the ground as he stood up said, "Let's go in." He said this as if he'd never heard the 'see you later'. My heart crashed to the bottom of my stomach and I began to feel sick for real. As I realized he planned to come with me. In a calm voice I said, "I'm really sleepy Richard. I don't think I want to sit up and talk tonight, so I'll see you later."

Richard looked at me, his eyes ablaze. With words spewing out of his mouth like flames, he said in a nasty tone, "What the hell did you say, you think you puttin' a nigga out now that I need you?

"Oh baby you can forget that, I ain't going nowhere."

What on earth was he talking about? "Richard, you've been drinking and I really don't want to talk to you anymore." I turned towards the door, and put my hand on the knob to go in.

Before I could open the door completely, my face crashed into it. Richard had grabbed me by my hair and shoved my face against the hard wooden surface. The door continued to swing open causing me to fall back on the steps. I could feel blood dripping from my nose as I came out of the shock of what had just happened.

But he wasn't finished. He then grabbed me by the shirt and began shouting, "Get up! That's what's wrong with all you 'hoes. A nigga mess up one time and you stinking heffa's want to put him out!"

I had no idea what Richard was talking about. I held my nose in an attempt to stop the blood as he pushed me up the stairs, leaving my bible behind on the steps. When I got inside, I sat in a chair in the corner and held my face.

For a week, I was held captive in my apartment. I was beaten and made to have sex with a man who I once considered a guardian angel.

Richard spent long periods in the bathroom doing what I know now was heroin. He would come out and beat me even more for getting out of my chair—at least that's what I thought was the reason at the time. I now know he beat me to instill fear. The kind of fear that, even when you can get away, you're too afraid to try; a fear amplified by low self-esteem and self-worth; a fear that gives power to those who actually have none—and eventually I submitted.

Richard started taking me back to the club I had sworn off. He would wait until he was completely drunk, then come over to the corner where I was sitting forcing me to dance. He was so drunk he fell all over me with each dance step. Everyone just looked on while he made a fool of me. He smelled so awful I had to force myself not to vomit. But I couldn't hold back the tears. I ran to the restroom, opened the door, and thanked God it was empty. I knew I had to pull myself together because I didn't want Richard to get upset and hit me in front of everyone. I dried my eyes and wiped the smeared mascara off my face. Just as I was leaving the restroom a couple of girls I knew came in. I said hello as best I could without crying again. As I walked out, I could feel their stares. I knew they were thinking, what a loser I had become.

As I came out of the restroom, I heard a loud crash coming from the dance floor. It was Richard. He had started a fight again and was being dragged out of the club, kicking and screaming.

I ran towards him, grabbing his arms from the bouncers. "Let him go, I got him." I pulled Richard up from the sidewalk. "Richard," I said in a soothing voice. "Come on, let's go." He calmed down almost instantly and we started walking towards home.

For the next five months, I would spend my life in this ritual of abuse. I did try to run one night. I ran to Sheila, the same friend I'd shared the secret about my grandfather with.

I sat in her house crying, not realizing I was scratching my pubic area uncontrollably as we talked. She watched me for a moment or two, and then asked point blank: "Girl, do you have crabs?" "Crabs?" I responded. "What's crabs?"

She began to tell me the many ways you could contract crabs, with the most probable in my case being sleeping with "a dirty nigga"—as she put it. She took me in her bathroom to look over my pubic area. "Yep. You got 'um."

She told me I would have to cut off all my pubic hair, but do it in the tub not standing up or on the toilet, so that the crabs would go down the drain, she warned.

"Okay," I said "Then I want you to put Vaseline down there." She explained that it could happen to anyone and that the Vaseline would kill them.

We sat and talked a few more minutes. We talked about how my relationship wasn't any different from most others. She too had been going through an abusive relationship with her boyfriend.

I was too drained from everything that had happened to begin thinking about where to run. That night, I headed home in a slight gallop. I had scratched myself until I bled. I did like my friend said, I continued to deal with Richard, thinking my relationship was no different from any other, and that in life you had to take the bad with the good.

On many nights I found myself at the club sitting at the bar reading my bible and praying to be saved from the hell I was in. On other nights, I would sit in the club drunk, but I kept on reading. Even when people started to talk and point. I didn't care. I just kept reading. I wasn't sure what was driving me; I just felt that if I stopped, I wouldn't make it.

"Okay, Richard, let's go." I'd say night after night, as the lights came on in the club.

"Okay," he replied, and we would be off on our merry way like a perfectly happy couple. That is, until Richard found something I had done or not done to fight about when we got home.

One night, while Richard was beating the crap out of me, I realized, no one was going to show up and save me, so I had better learn to save myself. That night I spoke to Richard in the same calming voice that had worked on Manuel the night Sharon was raped. I wasn't sure how long this little beauty-and-the-beast trick would work, but at least it kept him off me for now.

Richard felt secure in his relationship with me and would come and go as he pleased. He always made sure the rent was paid as I fed him what gibberish I could to stay alive. Every time Richard would leave, I would pray he'd never come back, and yet each night I would have his dinner ready just in case he did. I had become my grandmother.

Seeking out companionship wherever I could, I made friends with a girl named Deanna, who lived at the end of the block. She and I would sit in front of my stoop talking while we watched her children play. She had three in all, each had different fathers, and Baby Number Four was on the way. To me, she seemed to be at peace even though her kids were all under five and she had nothing of material value. I would go to her place to visit and just watch as she walked around, trance-like, failing to pick up the spilled cereal from the floor or wipe down the counter that was covered with the sauce from canned spaghetti she'd fed the kids the night before. Dishes were piled a mile-high in the sink, and the pungent smell of the dirty diapers laying on the floor next to a trash can that should have been emptied long ago, filled the room. But none of this bothered her at all.

We would sit each day doing nothing, as if she had nothing to do. With all that I had gone through, I had learned never to talk about anything too serious, but I just had to know. I wanted to ask how she did it. How did she keep from going crazy? Every night I would hear Deanna fighting with different men. They made so much noise you could hear the crashing sounds from my window. I figured the men must have been her babies' daddies, but that still didn't make it right.

The next morning she would appear as if nothing happened. She would sit on the stoop talking with me, never complaining. I never understood her but I knew that sometimes you could feel as if there was nowhere to go even if you could leave.

One evening, while Deanna and I sat in front of her apartment watching the kids, one of her babies' fathers stopped by with two of his friends. We sat drinking and laughing about any and every thing. It felt good to laugh genuinely again with people I didn't have to be afraid of.

It started getting dark and I knew I should be heading home, but I wanted to spend just a few more minutes just *being*, if you know what I mean. I knew I hadn't cooked Richard's supper and was already pushing it. As I got up to say my good-byes and thank the guys for the beer, I heard a car slamming on the brakes. We all turned towards the noise as the car door flung open and someone tried to leap out. The driver had to slam on the brakes to keep from hurting the guy. He started running in our direction. As he got closer, I could see his face. It was Richard! I panicked and tried to think of something to do.

He was yelling and screaming as he weaved through traffic. "Oh, ho I'm gon' kill you!" he screamed in the middle of ranting and raving about how he knew I was cheating on him.

I knew he wanted to start a fight so I tried to act calm. "Richard, what are you talking about? This is Deanna's baby's—" but he pounced on me before I could finish the sentence.

His fist struck me in my face, and knocked me to the ground. As I fell, I heard a tussling sound. One of the guys that had been sitting with us had grabbed Richard and was trying to keep him from kicking me in the head.

I held my arms over my face and tried to protect myself. I was shocked when I looked up and heard Deanna's baby's daddy tell his friend to let Richard go. "Yo, this that man's business," he yells, "This some bull. Y'all need to un-cuff that man."

Screaming again for them to let Richard go, he grabbed their arms in an effort to help Richard break free. They released Richard and he immediately snatched me up by my hair. "I'm gonna beat your ass."

I was embarrassed. I didn't know what to do. Richard slapped me and told me to shut up. My whole face hurt and my head was spinning. I took off running towards home, trying to dodge the bottles being lunged at me from behind.

When I reached my apartment, I ran inside and locked myself in the bathroom. I sat in the corner on the floor and listened to Richard take his anger out on the door. Trembling and jumping at each pound of his fist, afraid that one more blow might grant him entrance. I didn't know how much more of this I could take. I had seen women on television go through a lot less than I had break down. I sat with my back against the door and started rocking back and forth, which didn't give me any comfort, but it was what I had seen so many women do on television when faced with a similar situation.

Once the noise stopped, I opened the door and found Richard fast asleep. I tiptoed to my room and lay across my bed. I prayed he would not be there in the morning when I woke up, but he was.

The next morning, Richard was a different man. He sat quietly on the floor holding my legs. He told me how sorry he was. He said he had been out all day yesterday trying to get money for the rent. Richard said he had caught a ride home and was on his way to the store to get some beer to surprise me, when he saw me hanging out with all those guys. He couldn't help but lose it. I listened as the hurt from the night before resurfaced. Tears ran down my cheeks, as I helped Richard up and fixed us both some breakfast.

I wasn't allowed to visit my neighbor again unless he was with me. I did what Richard asked. I never visited Deanna again. Instead I suggested that she visit me.

Three weeks later, without any warning or reason that I could think of, Richard came home crying. He was high on something, but I didn't know what it was.

"Do you love me?" he asked, slobbering. Before I could answer he asked, "If you could, would you leave me?"

He spoke so calmly it spooked me. I had never seen this mood before so I wasn't sure how I should respond.

He asked again, "Do you love me?" "Yes, Richard. Why, what's wrong?"

"If you don't love me, it's okay. I'm leaving anyway." My heart lit up, but I tried to hide my excitement.

"You're leaving?" I sighed, trying not to sound too happy. "Well, you know if you ever need anything, I'm here. That was stupid! Dawg uh! Why did I say that?"

Richard looked up at me with tears in his eyes. "Oh you ain't gonna try to stop me, huh?"

I said, "Richard, if you want to go, go. I just want you to be happy." His tears, appeared to dry up instantly and was replaced by a strange look.

Richard appeared to be smiling when he said, "Oh, bitch, I'm gonna be happy cause your ass goin' with me."

It had never crossed my mind that he meant us. Richard got up, went into the bathroom, and stayed for about an hour. When he did decide to come out, he bent down and picked up a duffel bag he had been carrying, and said, "Let's go." "Let's go! Let's go where, Richard? I'm not dressed."

His eyes were fuming and he looked crazed. "I told you we are leaving. Now get your ass up and come on."

I walked down the stairs in front of him as he told me where to go. About twenty minutes later we arrived at an abandoned shopping center. We walked further and further back behind the buildings, only the light from a street light illuminated our way. Finally we stopped near an old wooden bench. Richard dropped the duffel bag to the ground and pulled out two ropes. A noose had been neatly made on each. I couldn't believe he planned to kill not just himself, but me, too.

"Oh, God!," I gasped as he threw the ropes over the rail. "Oh my God, Richard, what are you doing? Richard, you don't have to do this. I love you." I tried to hug him, hoping to calm him down, but it was too late. He was out of his mind.

Richard started crying and blurting out all sorts of crazy things about how he knew I really didn't love him. He continued adjusting the ropes with one hand, while pushing me off him with the other. I lay sobbing with my face in the dirt and pleading for my life.

I called on the one name that had always brought me comfort. "Oh, God, help me!" again I cry. "God, please! Jesus, Lord help me!"

I could feel Richard pulling at me and I tried to lay limp. I curled up to make it hard for him to move me, but a swift kick in my side forced me stand. Once on my feet, Richard said I had to go first because he knew I wouldn't do it if he went first.

I had stopped crying and words were coming out of my

mouth that I swear were not my own. "No, Richard. I don't want to leave here without you. Let's do it together if this is the only way you will believe I love you." I said, stunned by my own words.

We stood on the bench together with ropes around our necks. I had no idea of what my plan was, but that was where we ended up. I listened to all of Richard's reasons to die as I thought of all my reasons to live.

A small voice out of nowhere interrupted Richard's speech. "Hey, that's my bench," the voice said.

I looked down at a little old man who must have been hiding somewhere in the dark. The ropes around our necks didn't alarm him at all. He calmly took a seat at the end of the bench.

"You two killing yourselves, huh? Well life will sure make you want to die, won't it?"

Not allowing us to respond, he continued, "Each night I lay here thinking about the same thing and each morning I wake up happy to be alive. " He looked up at Richard.

"Son, you look like you've lived a long life. I imagine with each needle it gets a little longer. But what about you, little lady? What could you wake up and be tomorrow?"

"Sirrrrrr," I blurted out while crying. "I don't want to die!" The old man wasn't moved by my uttering and kept on talking. "I know, honey, and he doesn't want you to die. Do you son?"

Richard was yelling, "I don't need her. She can get outta here! I don't need anybody, I'm a man I can handle mine!"

The old man touched my leg and I knew it meant for me to remove the rope from my neck; as I stepped down slowly I let the rope drop from my hand.

The old man and I began to walk away taking a few steps at first, then speeding up as I urge the old guy too hurry before Richard came after us.

I guess I was running in front of the old man because when I reached the streetlights and turned around to call to him, he wasn't there. I hadn't been going that fast, I thought. "But you must have been," I argued with myself. "Or I would have noticed the old man when he left."

I'm really not sure what happened to the old man that night, I just remember feeling so happy to be free. I could have cared less what had happened to Richard. In my heart I hoped he would have the courage to kill himself.

I went home and sat in my favorite chair and began trying to wrap my mind around what had happened. I thanked the Lord for the person, whoever he was, that had rescued me. For a moment I allowed myself to think he was an angel sent by God. But I dismissed it, convincing myself that he was obviously someone in the dark watching the whole scene unfold, stepping out only after things had gone too far.

For the next few days I listened closely to each footstep that came in and out of my building. I followed every sound, trying to figure out where it would stop, wondering when it would be Richard's footsteps leading to my door.

I spent several days watching the news, awaiting any mention of a man killing himself, but no news came. All I could do to stay sane was to read my bible until I fell asleep. I had become too afraid to go to the church around the corner. I didn't want to come home and find Richard waiting to force his way into my apartment. I sat with my head by the window, listening to the songs that seemed to tell a story of a place with no worry. I wondered what that would feel like.

When I was finally ready to leave the house, it was because I had found all sorts of stuff Richard had hidden in the apartment. I found needles hidden in a little box under the dresser, which explained why he stayed in the bathroom so long. He also had several identifications, mostly of white people. But most importantly, hidden inside one of the papers, there was money, with which I needed to pay bills and get food. I knew Richard had probably beaten those people up and taken their purses but there wasn't anything I could do for them now, besides, I *realllllllly* needed the money.

Being out in the open made me realize what a basket-case I

had become. Although I hadn't heard from or seen Richard, I found myself jumping at every shadow, or seeing his face in crowds. I couldn't sleep and I had dreams of him leaning over me. I can't explain the relief I felt when I received word that Richard was in jail and probably wouldn't get out.

"Thank God," I said out loud, as my body took its first relaxed breath in a long time.

However, I was surprised that months later I was still having flashbacks; sometimes I thought I saw Richard, but I would quickly dismiss it by reminding myself he was in jail.

My neighbor had finally had her baby and couldn't wait to get out. She wanted me to go with her to a club that had just opened on the West side. I told her how I felt about hanging out in the Spanish bars but she said this was a black club so I agreed to go.

I went home to get dressed. And then walked back down to her house when I was ready. It would take us about forty-five minutes to walk to the west side if we didn't catch a ride, so we bought two forty-ounces of Colt 45 to drink as we walked and talked. By the time we reached the club, we were both feeling the groove and couldn't wait to hit the dance floor.

She was right about the club being nice and so were the men. Deanna knew everybody, and they were all treating us to drinks to celebrate her new baby. I was feeling good because I hadn't danced like that in a long time. It was my night and I felt like all eyes were on me again. The place was packed, disco lights twirled as the music blasted, and it felt good.

"Uh-uh," I said to my dance partner as the music slowed and I began to walk off the floor. "I don't dance to slow songs."

He kept pulling my hand in an effort to persuade me to stay. I pulled away gently breaking his grip, giving it just enough of a tug to say that no really does mean no.

Looking out toward the crowd as I head back to my seat, I could have sworn I saw Richard. My heart rate sped up as my eyes searched the area where I thought I had seen him. He wasn't there; I rushed over to my table and told Deanna who I thought I had just seen.

She was drunk and refused to take me seriously. "Girl, that nigga is in jail. If he was out he would have been over here by now beating your ass," she said laughing.

I convinced myself she was right. If Richard were in this room, I would know it by now. I tried to have a drink and relax, but it wasn't working. Some guy came up behind me, he put his hand on my shoulder in an attempt to ask me to dance. I jumped so hard my leg hit the table, spilling everyone's drinks.

"I'm sorry!" I said. "You scared me."

"Baby, if you that scared of the nigga, you better go home." The other guy at the table said jokingly. "I don't want your husband tripping on me."

"I'm not married," I replied, upset at his remark. "But you're right; it's time for me to leave." I looked at my friend. "I'm leaving, girl, are you coming?" I asked as I got up from the table. "Yeah, here I come." Once we were outside, I felt better. I could see the people around me and I no longer felt closed in. I tried to calm myself as we walked, taking in deep breaths and hoping the nightair would calm me. I stopped abruptly, grabbing Deanna's arm I pulled her back. "I think I saw a shadow of someone up front."

"Girl you are tripping. What did that nigga do to you?" she said shaking her arm loose from my grip.

I stayed silent, keeping my mind on what's going on and looking back at any sound as we started walking again. We were almost three blocks from the club when Richard stepped out from behind the bush holding a machete. He was high and looked as if he'd been sleeping in the gutter.

He looked at me with a smile and said, "Guess who's back from the dead?"

Everything happened so fast, I don't remember what happened to Deanna. I remember screaming for help, but no one came. I was trapped, and had nowhere to run but home, so I kicked off my heels and took off. I ran as fast as my legs would carry me, but somehow I never seemed to get more than a few feet ahead of Richard. I was getting tired and it started to rain but I knew I couldn't stop.

I ran towards a porch with lights on, and begin knocking frantically while calling out for help. I knocked as hard as I could but instead of someone opening the door, they turned the lights off. Fearing no one was going to help me, I ran like I had never run before. But, when I looked behind me, it looked as if Richard was walking. But I knew he couldn't be because he was now right behind me. The rain was coming down hard, I was drenched, and my mascara had blurred my eyesight, but I kept moving. I could hear Richard screaming out that he was going to kill me as I turned the corner to my street. I ran even faster trying to get to safety. I was only a few feet away from the hedges that separated my building from the house next to me, but before I could dash for the steps, something inside me said, "No! Don't go inside!"

I looked at the door that would lead me to safety, but made a split second decision to duck down behind the bush instead. I knew this would be the only time Richard would lose sight of me. I lay on the ground, crouched between the building and the bushes in the rain, while listening to Richard beating on the door of my apartment and yelling, thinking I was inside. Everything suddenly went silent and then I heard something I couldn't believe. Richard is inside my apartment!

"But how?" I thought, crying even harder. "Is there nowhere I can hide from this man?"

When Richard realized I was not in the apartment, he went crazy. I heard glass breaking and things being thrown against the wall. I listened to crash after crash until there was silence. Even though the noise stopped, I didn't move because I was terrified. "What if it's a trick? What if he's still there?" I wondered to myself.

I heard sirens in the distance and soon saw blue lights

everywhere, but still I can't move. Someone had called the police. Thank God. I heard the CB sounds coming from the window in my living room. I knew Richard couldn't still be there. I got up and walked up the stairs and through the door, crying, soaked from head to toe. I broke down when I saw my apartment. Richard had cut up everything. The couch, the chairs you name it. There was water all over the floor because he bust the toilet. But the worst damage was done to my bedroom. Richard had turned everything up side down. There was writing all over the walls, which said if he couldn't have me, no one would.

My pictures had been slashed. I was now truly a complete wreck and each sound drove me closer to the edge. I was afraid for my life, even in a room filled with officers. One of the officers said he needed to ask me a few questions. He wanted to know if I had any idea who would have done such a thing.

I shook my head no.

"Are you sure?" he asked disbelievingly.

I nod my head yes.

"Miss, you do understand that whoever did this intended on killing you had they found you here?" The officer said, in hopes of coaxing me into giving him the information he needed.

Hearing these words made me sob even harder as I buried my face in my hands.

"Think, Miss. Are you sure?

"Yes, I'm sure." I said, feeling I couldn't possibly tell on Richard.

"Girl, you know who did this. Officer, she knows it was this crazy nigga right there in that picture," my neighbor said as she walked through the door pointing at a huge picture of Richard and me.

"Do you know his name?" the officer asked my neighbor.

"Yes, it's Richard Coggins," my neighbor replied. The officer radioed Richard's name into the station and found that he had an extensive record of violence. The officer also found out that one of the women he had beaten wound up in the hospital with a severe concussion.

I was shaking. Just thinking about what Richard would do to me for turning him in had me terrified. I knew he would kill me for sure.

A female officer walked up to me, she introduced herself and said she worked in the Battered Women's division. She said I should see a doctor or get some counseling, to make sure I was okay.

I agreed.

She took me to a hospital on the East side of town. The emergency room was on an upper floor; unlike the emergency rooms I was used to. The officer rung the bell and the door buzzed and swung open. We walked up to a window and I heard the officer say my name while whispering the words 'nervous break down'. Everything else about that night is a big blank.

The next thing I remembered, it was morning and my good friend Colette, who lived next door to my grandmother, and her mom, were leaning over me as I lay in the bed. I was a little drowsy but I recall them bringing a pastor to pray for me. Collette saw the police at my apartment that night, but she didn't come in. With all that had happened since I moved on my own we had grown apart. She had been faced with Richard's fury herself and promised she would not have a part in my killing myself.

Colette didn't know what I had been through. She had heard Richard had taken me through some bad times but had know clue what was really going on.

She leaned over talking to me as if I were a child.

"Do–you–know–who–I–am? Can–you–hear–us?" she whispered looking as if she half expected an alien to come out of my mouth.

I looked at her and smiled as tears rolled down my face. "No, I don't. Should I?" I asked. I pretended not to know them the whole visit because I didn't want to relive the horror of what had happened.

Colette, who knew me as well as anyone, looked at me and placed her mouth close to my ear. "I know you're faking it." She was right, but I wasn't going to let her or the doctors make me leave, because I had nowhere to go.

The next morning, after taking my medication, I walked down to the breakfast room to sit while thinking things out. I was feeling pretty weak so I held on to the wall, as I slowly dragged my hands against its coolness. I looked around at the others on the ward with me. I tried to imagine what brought them to this place, I wondered if they, too, were faking it. The more I observed them the more I realized they were not. Some of them sat talking to themselves. Others talked to people who weren't there. I felt sorry for them. Even though I didn't know their stories, I knew what it was to miss someone. I myself had often pretended I was talking to my mother when I was feeling especially sad.

The experience was too much for me and I became so emotional I couldn't speak up when the orderly pushed the breakfast cart away without calling my name. I'm not sure why I just stood there in tears, leaning against the wall like a baby, instead of saying something.

A nurse who had been watching me came over to comfort me. She put her arms around me and slowly walked me back to my room.

"I'll order you a special breakfast with anything you want, okay? Then you and I will sit and talk about how you ended up here," she said gently rubbing my back.

I gobbled my food down as I told her my whole life story, including the fact that I was faking and really didn't belong on her f   l   o   o   r   .

She didn't say much, she just gathered up my tray and told me to get some rest.

"I'll be right down the hall." She added as she closed the door.

Those were the last words I heard before drifting off to sleep, feeling safer than I had felt in along time. The medication made me sleep through the day and when I woke up the shift had changed. Once again, I was alone. I remember wondering why it seemed, in life, you are always starting over, identifying yourself and telling your story over and over again to prove you are who you say you are, hoping people will say, "Oh, she's not like the rest. Her situation is different."

'Different', hmm—there's the sympathy word I'm looking for. It means you slipped through the cracks and this horrible thing shouldn't have happened to you.

Well, I had decided that I wasn't going to give my story all over again. And I didn't need to be different because in actuality, everyone is different. We all have a different reason for ending up in the same place. I looked at the orderly who again pushed past me without offering a meal, but I said nothing. I sat there watching television in the TV room, looking at the people going back and forth down the corridor until it was dark.

I thought I heard Richard's voice and I wondered to myself if I, in fact, was really sicker than I thought. But it was real. He was standing at the desk asking for my room. I walked to the open doorway and I heard the male desk nurse asking Richard questions.

"Are you family?" he asked "Yes." Richard replied, lying through his teeth. "Good, because she hasn't had a visitor today."

"There she is," the nurse said as he pointed to where I was standing.

"Janice, look who's here." Tears fell down my face as the nurse walked him over. "Enjoy your visit," he said and walked away.

Richard held my hand as he stared at me with a worried look in his eyes. "Are you okay? How are you feeling?"

"I'm fine. I just want to get some rest."

"Yeah, you do need some rest. Let's get your stuff so we can go."

"I'm supposed to stay here," I said shaking as I took a seat.

"Get up right now, don't make me stomp your your face in the ground right here," Richard said as he twisted my wrist so no one could see him.

"What,?" he said looking down at me. "You thought I wasn't going to find you? You know yo' girl would turn her mama in for a dime bag.

We walked to my room and I got dressed. I couldn't believe Sheila had told him where I was. My tears were now coming down in streams as Richard made his threats. We walked back down the corridor to the nurse's station where Richard told the man I wanted to leave. I remember trying to act faint pretending my legs had given way, dipping down just a little bit. Then allowing my hand to shake as I sign the papers for my release. I hoped someone would say I was too sick to leave. But no one did.

I blurted out in a high pitched voice as if I'd just remembered. " Oh, I'm scheduled for some tests in the morning and, the male nurse interrupted me cutting me off before I could finish. "Young lady, these doors open both ways and we can't keep you here. You don't need to worry about the tests because they're just routine."

With tears in my eyes, I signed the voluntary release and walked out with the man who put me there. Weeks went by before I was actually back to normal—by that I mean strong enough to think clearly. We were staying with a friend of Richard's, who shared Richard's feelings on violence. He took every opportunity he could to beat his own wife. I knew I would never make it and I sure as heck had to find away to get away from Richard the first chance I got.

First, I would need a plan. My options were slim and I had grown tired, just tired of it all. I just wanted to be somewhere where I could relax without worrying about food or clothes or sanity. I just wanted to be a kid, a kid whose biggest care would be what if the guy at school didn't like her. I didn't want to go to another friend's house, or another hallway. No way! Especially friends that always seemed to disappear after a week or two. So what could I do? It hit me, I remembered Marvin's daughter. She seemed so happy the last time I saw her. That was it! That's what I would do. I would go to a foster home.

Janice E. Sullivan

Chapter Ten
A New Beginning

———•••••———

This morning was different. At 16 years old, I was waking up for the first time in a long time looking forward to the day. After making sure Richard was gone, I got up. I washed my hair, picked it into a soft, even afro, and then got dressed. I smiled slightly at the thought of today being the day that I would get a new home. I opened the front door and looked around carefully before stepping out. The coast was clear. I darted out the door and up the street, making sure to take precaution. I took back roads and looked around constantly. My heart beat steadily, my palms had a slight sweat and were flushed and clammy as I prayed to make it to West Genesee Street, which was a few miles away. That was where the Family and Child Services division was located. I knew my whole life depended on my not getting caught. It was terrifying: Richard had proven that he could always find me. He threatened constantly that although I couldn't see him, he could always see me. My pace quickened with each thought. I was determined to get to what I considered to be safety.

When I got to Family and Children Services, the brownish brick building looked cold and uninviting. It wasn't at all like what I had thought it would be. I expected it to have a warm, welcoming look. When I entered the doors, the room seemed even colder than it had appeared from the outside. There was a small waiting section with maybe ten chairs in it. Behind that area was another sitting area, only this one was larger than the first. There were also a couple of offices with huge pane windows that allowed the person on the inside to be viewed. The big area had several kids in it. One of the boys was in handcuffs, the other in bandages. I recall there being an infant on a worker's desk and a couple of kids who looked as if they may have been mentally challenged. I wasn't sure what to do. This was not at all how I had rehearsed it in my mind. I took a deep breath hoping to put my fear aside and walked further into the second sitting area. I had made up my mind; I was determined not to leave. There was no way I was going back to Richard or out on the streets.

I wasn't sure who to talk to, so I stopped a person rushing by.

"Sir, excuse me, Sirrr!" I exclaimed a little louder. Realizing my first attempt was far too faint. "Thanks," I said as I gained his attention. "I need help."

"What kind of help do you need?"

"Sir," I said, becoming overwhelmed, as crocodile tears streamed down my face. "I need a home."

His face softened. "Yeah, I know, honey. Unfortunately, parents can seem very mean at times, but I promise, by tomorrow you won't be mad anymore."

He gave me a sucker and suggested I watch television for a little while, and then go on home. He then turned and walked away.

I sat there feeling helpless and sad. "I don't have a home," a voice echoed inside of me. "I don't have a family and I'm not mad." It continued. I cried until my nose began to run. I sat there looking at the drips, thinking of them as the desperation in me. I refused to wipe it.

A middle-aged black woman came over to me.

"Heyy! Stop that! You're too big to be acting like that. Look at these other kids, and you're crying like you've just lost your best friend. Here, wipe your nose" (Her real reason for coming over, I'm sure).

She handed me a piece of tissue.

"Look how they're looking at you."

I looked around slowly at everyone looking at me. I was 16 and older than most of the kids in the room, but I felt just as afraid and lonely as they did. I didn't care if they stared.

"Who brought you in sweetie?" I gave her a blank stare. "Honey, what worker brought you in?" she repeated, now just a little disturbed. "No one, I came on my own." "What do you mean you came in on your own?" "I don't have a home, so I came here to sign up for one." I said as I continued to wipe my face.

"Ooh, Honey, you can't stay here. This is a place of business. It doesn't work like that at all You're going to have to leave."

"Ma'am please, I don't have a home, and I have nowhere else to go."

"Honey, I understand, but there are procedures. Plus, with you being your age, you most likely won't even get a home. There may be room in a youth house but I wouldn't want to send anyone there that I didn't have to."

She stopped talking and took the seat next to me.

"Look, why don't I take you home and talk with your parents to see if we can work things out?"

"Okay," I replied, thinking when she walked away, I would just find someone else who was willing to help me.

"Give me a minute. I was just about to sign out for lunch."

She stepped over to a desk about five feet away and returned back to me much quicker than I wanted. I heard her say to one of the other workers on her way out that she was taking another one home, if anyone was looking for her.

The worker she had addressed yelled back, "Okay, but isn't this your day off?"

"Yeah, like there is such a thing around here." She responded as we whisked out the door.

That ride for me was like the last mile. So far, I had not been clear on whether my life was really a tragedy or if people encountered this stuff all the time. Let's face it, most of the relationships that I had witnessed in my life all consisted of some form of abuse. Maybe I *was* uppity and wanted too much. Maybe I had let my fairytale-mind blow things up to this big dramatic, never-ending script.

I needed to know.

If I had made more of it than I should, I would own up to it, pull myself together and deal with the hand God had dealt me. I wanted her opinion. I felt she would know. After all, she made this kind of decision every day. She said her name was Mrs. Green and that I could tell her anything so I did.

I began telling her every ugly detail of my life, one tear at a time. Before I could finish she had pulled over to a phone booth to make a call. When she got back in the car she asked if I thought my grandmother would sign papers saying she didn't want me back in her house.

I was sure she would so I replied, "Yes."

We were both quiet the rest of the ride. When we arrived at my grandmother's door, Mrs. Green stood in front of me and knocked. The lifeless atmosphere could almost be felt seeping out once the door was opened.

"My name is Mrs. Green and I am with Child and Family Services."

"Come in. How you doing, Ma'am?" my grandmother solemnly offered.

"I'm fine," the caseworker replied as she looked around.

"The reason I'm here, Mrs. Seals, is because Janice came to our office today and said she has nowhere to go. Are you her legal guardian?"

"Yes'm, I am. My daughter, her momma, is very sick and just can't keep the kids anymore."

"Ma'am, I'm not concerned with that. I just want to know if you would be willing to sign these papers stating that you will not allow your granddaughter to return to your home."

"Oh yes, Ma'am. I'll sign 'um."

And with that the caseworker whipped out some papers, got my grandmother's signature, and then we left. On the ride back she told me she hadn't figured out what to do yet, but she would find way to work it out. Tears of relief rolled down my face.

She looked at me and smiled as she reminded me not to get too excited because beds were limited, and most of the halfway houses were for delinquents with a history of violence. I don't feel that would be the best thing for you, she sighed, but it may have to do for right now.

I just nodded and thanked God for this woman, who wasn't supposed to work that day but had decided to come in to complete a backlog of files, was determined to help me.

When we got back, I overheard the complaints from her co-workers for bringing me back. "There is just no room," her supervisor said.

"We have a list of children a mile long and not one available placement."

As Mrs. Green walked back over to me I could see the despair on her face. She looked worried but still managed to give me a reassuring smile. The time went by very slowly that day and the closer it got to dark the more I began to think I would have to go to the halfway house. Deep inside, to me it really didn't matter because any bed was better than no bed at all.

An hour or so later the worker motioned for me to come into her office so she could explain what was happening. By the look on her face I already knew. I interrupted her before she could speak.

"Thanks, I know you've tried Mrs. Green, but you really don't have to worry, I'll be fine. I've been through worse. And every time God has worked it out."

"What do you mean?" she asked.

"Once, when I was very ill, God promised me I would be okay. And that he would be by my side always. Maybe this is supposed to happen like this. Maybe this is the life he has for me."

"No, Baby, it's not, Mrs. Green replied, her sadness showing in her voice. God is a caring God and things will be okay!" Her phone rang breaking our moment.

"Excuse me," she said as she picked up the receiver.

"Hello." Oh, hi, how are you."

Her face lit up as she listened. "Uh-huh, yes, wonderful. You don't know just how timely this is." She looked up at me and smiled. It turned out the call had been from a foster parent, whose biological daughter had just left for the Air Force, so she decided to take on another child. She wanted an older girl child so she wouldn't have to change her daughter's room around or worry about it being destroyed. This was the agreement between her and her daughter. When Mrs. Green hung up that day she said we were in luck. But I knew that luck had nothing to do with it. I knew I had been saved by grace!

I will never forget the day we pulled up at my new home. It was big and beautiful, with a little white fence to protect the grass from passers-by. As we walked to the door, I recalled trying to put on my best win-you-over personality so my new family would like me. Walking through the door for me was like an audition.

Ma, as I learned to call her, looked me up and down and smiled.

"Girl you need a perm," she said before sitting down with the worker to discuss me.

She was right, my hair had dried to a tiny nappy ball by the time I reached her house. I smiled a half-shy smile and sat where I was asked to sit.

When they were finished, the caseworker told me she was leaving and was confident I would enjoy being here.

"Mrs. Wheeler's one of the best foster parents that we have and she has had over 500 foster kids." She said as we stood at the door saying our goodbyes.

I soon found that Ma had a very quick tongue and often used it when she was upset. She swore a lot, and called us out of our names. I ignored it for the most part because to me it was still a great place. I went about my business of settling in and made friends with Ma's oldest biological daughter, "Triple D", who was about twenty-eight. Triple D wasn't her real name, but that's what she preferred to be called. Turns out it was her stage name.

She was a call girl and dancer by night and a medical secretary by day. The two other foster boys that were there when I arrived often alluded to the fact that there was something more between them and Triple D than I knew. I watched carefully as I always had and realized quickly that they weren't lying. I didn't try to judge or ask questions. In fact, I really didn't care; I just wanted to fit in so I wouldn't be asked to leave.

On many occasions I would accompany Triple D to the places where she danced. She said I was her costume girl, but I spent most of the night running back and forth for drinks for her and the other ladies in between acts. It wasn't difficult and Triple D did take care to keep all the grubby old men off me. Her mother knew what she did for a living and was not pleased, but there really wasn't anything she could do. So there I was, hanging out with Triple D and the pimp I soon found that she had. I was often made to shoplift for her when were supposed to be shopping for me with the check that had come in from the state.

When we would arrive back home, Triple D would pull out the few items I received. Flashing them before Ma erased any question of what we had really been up to. We would all sit around the table laughing and joking about the things she and her sister had gotten away with as kids.

"It was a good thing I didn't catch you," Ma would joke as we all sat down for dinner.

Listening to all their stories made me realize I wasn't so bad after all. The only difference with Ma was, no matter what they did, she never asked them to leave.

Ma was a woman who had plenty of brass. She knew every trick in the book and could pull it out and show it to you. I loved hanging out with her and her friend Joyce, who to me was just like family. They took me shopping with them as well, but they did not say it was for me. So when we walked into the store I, of course, who had learned not to expect anything just stood there waiting for Ma to get whatever we came for.

I must have looked silly because Ma, in her oh-but-so-jazzy

way yelled, "I gotta drive you here and try the damn clothes on for you, too?" "No Ma'am," I answered. "What do you want me to get?"

She asked, "Well, what you have?"

"Nothing," I replied.

"Then get what you need." She responded now irritated.

I didn't need to be told twice. That day we shopped for everything from bras to socks. By the time we left the mall I felt like a new person. Although I, myself, had made a profession out of getting my clothes at one time, this was different because shoplifting didn't make you feel like you were one of the people who had the right or deserved nice things. Instead it made me feel like a fraud because the people looking on would only see the pretend me, the 'boosted' me that I was able to conjure up.

I had come to believe long ago, that no one really wanted to see the real you—no, not the tattered and torn you—but they wanted to see the you that was easiest for them to swallow. No one wants to know the truth, because that would mean he or she would have to do something to help.

It is a fact that people would prefer you keep your misery to yourself. Don't believe me? Well, the next time someone asks you how you are doing, just start to tell them about the bad day or week you're having and watch their whole countenance change. Nope, I wasn't a fraud this time and I was happy to carry my arm-full of bags across the parking lot, like I had seen so many other girls do before.

Our next stop was the beauty parlor for my first perm. I had been wearing my hair in an afro, since my mom wasn't around to plait it. And on some days it was a challenge even for me to comb. I'd say the perm was a good move indeed. It made my hair appear to grow two inches longer as the stylist combed it out.

I was now ready for school. Ma had done such a wonderful job with me. I looked like I had never known a day of trouble. I took to my new life well. It had been over a month now and Richard hadn't even crossed my mind. He, as far as I was concerned was on the other side of the world.

I knew he would never have a clue of where to find me. No way, not out here—it just wasn't the area you'd see him, or expect to find me. I relaxed, and went about my business of starting a new life. I made friends here and there, and hung out with the popular people. Ma's place was the hangout; everyone loved to come to her house. We had a huge family room downstairs that was just "the most" (slang for "gorgeous"). Everyone loved it and got a big kick out of Ma, who always knew just when to interject one of her little digs. She'd be walking around upstairs in the kitchen as if looking for mischief.

"Okay, this ain't a hotel!" she'd yell down the stairs. "If you want a snack, you better come get it."

Then, when we came up the stairs, she would be sitting there, fanning her hands as if to dry your newly polished nails, saying, "Ooh, y'all getting a snack? Get me one too, please. My nails are wet."

Everyone would burst out laughing, realizing we had just been tricked into fixing her lunch.

She could be kind when she wanted. But she had an alternate side as well—the side that made her beat me with the broom for sneaking on the phone at night or run through the house yelling obscenities at everyone after she had drunk too much. Yep, Ma had her ways, but, for the most part, I'm glad she took me in. I learned a lot, and grew into the next part of the person I was to become.

It is true: your yesterday does not have to be your tomorrow.

I, for whatever reason, cannot remember the circumstances or the events surrounding the day I left Ma's.

I believe it was because I had turned seventeen.

I tried to recall that day on many occasions. However, I always came back to the same thing: I can remember completing the tenth grade, because I had to go to summer school for English in order for me to move on to the eleventh, and then that's that— I can't remember anything else. The next thing I knew, I was in my own apartment, which just so happened to be in front of the very garage in which I had spent so many lonely nights after my grandfather had put me out of the house. I can't even remember why I didn't graduate. I have thought about asking my foster mother what happened many times. But I always let the notion go. I feared she would say I had done something bad that I couldn't remember and was asked to leave. This would force me to face the fact that maybe, just maybe, I was the horrible person I was made out to be by my grandfather. In a future conversation, Ma would tell me that I was the last girl she ever took in.

Chapter Eleven
God Has a Plan

The leaves are falling from the trees, which can only mean winter is approaching. My friends and I will no longer be able to sit on the stoop and socialize. The days have become long and boring and I have nothing to do and too much time on my hands. I feel a great emptiness and my mundane life forces me to question my purpose. It's hard for me to believe this is all I am to become.

I reflected back on a conversation Colette and I had had, that day we both agreed on one thing: that we wanted more out of life. We had too much responsibility for girls our age. At twelve years old, we were tired and felt as if we were carrying the weight of the world on our shoulders. Colette was responsible for watching over a younger brother and sister, managing the bills, and cooking and cleaning while her mother worked at night. And I was trying hard to hold on to what family my siblings and I had left. We carried more hurt than we were willing or able to verbalize, and we both lowered our heads as the weight of the conversation sat upon us.

We knew all about our mothers, and, following their path, our lives didn't seem promising. Although I remembered my father, I didn't know much about him, or what life would have been like had he stuck around.

It was on that day with Collette that I decided to find out who my father really was and what part he played in who I had become. This seemed like as good as time as any to take that first step. So, I went to work doing the research it would take to keep a promise to myself I had yet to fulfill. It took two weeks to track him down, and another week to get up the nerve to make the call.

I was finally on the phone with the man who fathered me.

He still lived in the same place on St. Simon's Island as he had when I was a kid. The conversation started off slow and then I just blew up. I started yelling and screaming at the man I wanted so much to get to know and love again. Tears ran down my face as I listened to all the remorse and regret that rolled out of his mouth. His words were like a song I once loved and couldn't get enough of, but now held no meaning. I had been through too much. His words just didn't have the effect on me they would have had in another place and another time.

My father told me he had always loved me and had no idea what I had been through. As he spoke I could hear the sadness in is voice, but it was too late. The remorse and sadness wasn't enough. All the pain and hurt I had carried for so long came blaring out of my mouth as I refuted what I, at that time, could only label as lies.

"How could you not know?" I yelled. "You're my father. It's your job to know!"

He offered no reply—only silence.

That day I spent so much time yelling and being hurt, I never heard my father hang up. It wasn't until I came out of my rage, did I hear the dial tone thumping in my ear. I didn't try to call him back. I had tried and it just didn't work out. I found comfort in believing he was no good anyway.

As if the conversation with my father had never occurred, I began preparing for an evening out.

"Screw um," I said to myself as I applied my eyeliner with a shaking hand.

I really would have preferred to cancel my blind date, but I couldn't do that to my girl. Jasmine was one of my best friends from the projects, and she had gone through too much trouble to make this night happen. Although she was my friend Marsha's aunt, she was the same age as I. Marsha's grandmother waited twenty years after having Marsha's mother before giving birth to Jasmine. Marsha and Jasmine had grown up more like sisters than niece and aunt. Jasmine was married to Kevin, who lived six doors down from me when we lived in the projects, and was like a brother to me. On many occasions he begged me to run away from my grandfather. He and Clint, another close friend of mine, would point out abandoned houses they had scoped out for me to live in, and promised to bring me food. However I knew better; those two could barely sneak extra desert out the house, let alone a meal. Yet, I loved them both dearly for trying to help. Kevin and I had the kind of friendship that would allow us to go ten years without speaking, and then one day bump into each other and just pick up from wherever it was we had left off. We had all lived in the Bricks so I knew there would be no need for pretense to night; they knew all about me and I knew all about them.

There was only one thing that could rattle me that evening, and that was Kent. Kent was the one guy I had a secret crush on for most of our school years. I must have dropped a thousand books in front of him and he never once picked one up. Now, at his request, here I was, getting ready to have dinner with him.

The blind date was Kevin's and Kent's idea. They had both joined the Marine Corp after graduating from high school. They were fortunate to have been stationed together. The next thing I knew, Jasmine was planning a dinner for four upon Kent's and Kevin's arrival back to the States.

I asked Jasmine a thousand times if Kent knew it was me he was meeting. She said yes and that he remembered me very well. I just couldn't believe it. How could he remember me when he never spoke? Well, regardless of how this evening would turn out, I was determined to look and feel good. I rolled a joint to help me mellow out and finished getting dressed.

I was careful to look good, but I didn't want to look like I was trying to impress. Besides, I only had to walk across the street to get to Kevin's and Jasmine's place. I walked out of the house and crossed the street feeling great. I knew what I would talk about and how I would act. Kevin had chosen to get out of the Marines but Kent had two more years left on his tour, and was only home for a short time.

As I approached the walk that lead to Jasmine's door, I noticed a guy getting out of his car. He was heading in the same direction. I turned my head, pretending not to see him behind me. It was Kent. As we neared the door of the hallway, I knew I would have to acknowledge him, because there was only one door.

As I reached for the doorknob, a man's hand hurriedly reached out ahead of mine in an attempt to open the door for me.

"Kent," I said in my most surprised voice.

"Yes."

"How are you?" I said trying to contain my smile.

"I'm fine, and you?"

"Great," I replied.

So far, so good, I thought.

"Well isn't this funny?" I said smiling. "I didn't know you and Kevin were close."

"Yeah, Kevin and I served together. It was kind of do to a need."

"A need?" I asked.

"Yeah, I needed to eat, and Jasmine was one of the few wives who came over the water with her husband, so I would go over for dinner at least once a week. One night she told me you wanted to meet me, so I told her okay. I told her, when we get home, let's do it, so here we are."

Those words hit me right in my vanity.

"Meet you!" I snorted. "Jasmine told you I wanted to meet you? Oh, no, I didn't want to meet you! Kevin told me you were asking about me."

We must have been a little loud because Jasmine peeked her head out the door. She smiled, and said, "Oh I see you two have met."

I gave Jasmine "the look," but before I had a chance to say anything else, she opened the door, grabbed my hand and pulled me in the house.

"Hey, you're here now, so you two stop."

I went in but I was determined not to have a good time. I tried hard to keep my game face on. But as the night went by, the combination of good conversation, mixed with food and alcohol, made it hard not to relax. Kent was amazing! He was funny, a gentleman, and smart. I understood why so many girls had a crush on him when we were in school. You just couldn't resist his strength masked by his kind-mannered personality.

We had both forgotten the ugly scene outside and were laughing our heads off. We made silly jokes and talked about different events from our youth. By the time the evening was nearing an end, I had really begun to like Kent. I smiled girlishly, not sure if he liked me. I really didn't want the night to end, nor did I want Kent to excuse himself first, which to me would be a clear indication that he wasn't interested.

I stood up and made my announcement.

"Well guys, I had a very good time tonight, and I thank you for having me. But it is getting late, and I know you have to get up early, so I'll say good night."

I reached over to extend my hand to Kent.

"It really was good seeing you again. I had a great time."

As I held his hand, my heart and my mind were going in circles.

"Oh, say something. Please," I thought. "Don't let me leave. I know you had a good time too."

I let his hand go and headed for the door.

Kent called to me in a voice that may have been the best thing I'd ever heard.

"Hey, Jan, if you don't mind, I'll walk you out."

"Thanks, Kent, but I only live across the street." I said wanting to play a little hard to get.

"Well then, I'll walk you across the street." He said insistently.

"Okay."

Once we were outside, we seemed to forget that we were

133

both supposed to be on our way home. I didn't want the night to end, but more importantly, neither did he.

"Would you like to go for a ride?" he asked.

"I'd like that very much."

We walked over to Kent's car, got in, and were off. As we pulled out, I saw Jasmine's head sticking out of her window. We drove off, headed to the lake by the park. We sat and talked until the wee hours of the morning, arriving back at my apartment just before dawn. Kent walked me to the door and I invited him inside. We sat on the sofa and talked some more. I placed my head on his shoulder and we both fell asleep. Later that morning, Kent thanked me for not making him leave. He said somehow, he felt as though he couldn't be away from me, but he didn't know how to say it. I admitted that I had the same feeling as we made plans to see each other again. We spent all our free time together. Kent loved my free spirit. I told him of the far away places and things that I wanted to see and do. He was the first person I could share all of me with. I even told him about my past.

Kent came from a loving family, so it was hard for him to believe all that he was told. I wanted him to know just how lucky he was, explaining he should never take it for granted. In the three weeks we spent together, Kent made me feel like anything was possible. I hated that our time together was approaching its end. He had to report back to the base on Monday and today was already Thursday.

I had taken so much hurt and disappointment in my life, that I made it a rule not to expect anything more than what was offered. I told myself, "At least you had a good time, so just be thankful and move on." But I wanted more. To avoid breaking down or being hurt when Kent came to say his goodbyes, I left my apartment that day and stayed gone until late that evening; I didn't want to be there when Kent came.

I knew he would have to pull out Friday morning and I just wanted him to go. By the time I got home I was mentally drained and really needed to lie down. I walked in and turned on the water for a bath. I fell across my bed, and lay there wishing I could get in the tub fully dressed. While I was laying there contemplating throwing myself in the tub with my clothes on, I heard someone knocking at the door and calling my name. I couldn't believe he was at my door so late.

I thought, "Why doesn't he just go, already?"

When I opened the door, Kent grabbed me as if he hadn't seen me in years.

The words "I love you and I can't leave you here," rushed out of his mouth. "I'm not sure why, but I just know I can't leave you."

I asked, "What would we do? Where would I live?" I tried to be the voice of reason.

His only answer was, "I don't know, I just know that we will be all right.

"Do you love me, Janice?"

"Yes, I do Kent."

With all the love my eighteen-year-old heart could hold, I agreed to go. I spent the whole morning packing and making arrangements. Since welfare would still be paying the rent, I gave the keys to my apartment to my play sister, Colette, and asked her to check on the apartment every now and then. I needed to have a place to return to just in case things didn't work out with Kent. I wanted to believe this was a new beginning, but I couldn't help but think that, surely, something would go wrong, or Kent would change his mind, and I would be stuck on the stoop with everyone else, forever.

Kent came to pick me up and we headed to North Carolina where he was stationed. On our way, we stopped in Philadelphia to pick up Davis and Williams, two of Kent's Marine buddies.

We all swapped stories that day on our long ride south. Davis, which was his last name, wanted to marry some girl who couldn't stop cheating on him. And Williams, well, he wanted to get out of the military and "find himself." Me? Well, I needed to know who I was. I wanted an identity. As for Kent, he wanted a family like the one he experienced as a child.

Everyone took turns talking and driving. When it came to my turn, I figured, okay, how hard could this be? After all, I had stolen Colette's mother's car more than a few times. I climbed in the driver's side, turned the key, and pulled back on to the road. "So far so good, just keep straight," I thought.

When I saw the signs hanging over the highway, I did what came natural. I slowed down to read them. There was no way I could have read all the information at the speed I was going. I think it may have been the third or fourth sign that gave me away, prompting the boys into kidding me about being sure I had a license. But, just like the backboard supports the rim, Kent stood by my side. Well, that is, right up to the point where I missed a turn and swung around at about 60 mph to make it, losing, what I think, was the muffler.

Kent simply smiled and said, "My turn," and took the wheel.

He drove the rest of the way to Camp Lejeune. I had never been on a military base before, so I was psyched. It was still the weekend, and Kent had promised we would look around once we were settled. Our first mission was to get a room at the base hotel. Each one was like a little apartment. They had everything. Dishes, pots, a refrigerator—you name it. I tried to tell Kent it was too costly, but he wouldn't listen. He said there was no way he was going to put me in a room off base by myself. Of course, by the end of the week, he realized I was right.

To save money, Kent decided I would sleep in the barracks on the weekends, after his roommate left on furlough. That first Saturday went fine; all of Kent's friends came by the room to meet me, complimenting Kent on his "good find," as if I wasn't in the room.

Each day Kent and his buddies would trail off to formation and I would start having that empty feeling again. It was as if my life started when he was in my presence and ended when he wasn't.

About a week after our arrival, Kent was gone for what

seemed to be an extremely long time. It normally would take about a half hour for his squad to perform roll call, but it had been over two hours, and he wasn't back yet. Restless, I figured I would walk around to see what was happening on the base. It was daytime so visitors could be on the base without being escorted. I walked for about ten minutes before it dawned on me that things were a lot further apart than they looked when we were riding in the car. So, back to the room I went. When I returned, I found Kent, along with Williams and Davis, sitting on the bed. I made a joke about their long faces and no one said anything.

"Hum, this must be serious." I said jokingly.

Davis and Williams stood up, trying to give a little smile.

"We'll catch you later, man." Davis spoke first.

"See you around," followed Williams.

They placed their caps back on their heads and walked out the door.

When the door closed, Kent looked at me as the guys had.

"We have to leave for Okinawa, Japan," he said.

"What? When?" I asked filled with excitement, thinking he meant us.

"In the morning," he answered.

"Stop playing, Kent. They wouldn't tell you like that, and then we're just supposed to up and go."

Kent took my hand and pulled me toward the bed.

"I guess you could stay with Irene," he said ignoring my last remark.

"Who? You mean the girl I met two days ago?" I answered, my surprise at his comment being very apparent in my voice. "Right." I responded in a sarcastic tone, pausing now to look at Kent, as he sat on the bed with the broad muscular frame that always seemed to boast of his strength, now slumped in a state of surrender.

I became quiet as I realized that Kent wasn't kidding. And that the "we" he had indicated earlier didn't include me.

"Well, do you want to go home?" Kent said, partially yelling. "Because I have to go, and there isn't any time to find you an apartment or even a room." Kent jumped to his feet, angry at the situation.

I didn't say a word. I just sat there listening in disbelief. I wasn't sure what I would do, but back to the stoop was not an option. I would feel too much like a failure. The past month had been the best time of my life.

"What about your father?" Kent asked.

I think this would be as good a time as any for you to go home and deal with your past. Your father would love to have a chance to tell his side of the story. I know we talked about us one day going together, but maybe it's meant for you to go alone."

Home wasn't a big word to me since I had had so many places that I had called home—none of them ever really being my home, just places I was allowed to lay my head for whatever period of time I could. Now Kent was talking about going back to the very place that had thrown me away. Immediately, I thought up twenty reasons why not to go, the biggest being the last conversation my father and I had, which ended with me yelling and blaming him for all my troubles. What could I possibly say now that would take all that back?

Kent said, "Let me handle it. If I'm going to marry you, I should at least ask your father for your hand."

"So—ah," I started, in response to Kent before realizing what he had said.

"What did you say?"

"I said, if I'm going to marry you, I might as well ask your father for your hand."

My face lit up. I had to force myself not to scream.

"You haven't asked *me* yet." I said getting smart.

Kent, without saying a word, kneeled down and took my hand in his. He looked in my eyes and asked, "Will you marry me?"

I smiled a great, big Kool-Aid smile and screamed, "Yes!"

Kent remained on his knees. "Will you marry me today?"

"Today!" I shouted. "You mean, *today*, today? I mean, yes, I will, but can you get married in one day?"

"Here, you can, he said, grabbing my hand and leading me towards the door. "Let's go and call your father."

I stood outside of the phone booth as Kent talked to my dad. I could only hear bits and pieces, but the one thing that sticks in my heart, even today, was Kent's response to my father asking him why today? Kent's reply made me know that everything was going to be all right and, for once, I knew I would be safe.

"Mr. Sullivan," he said, "I don't know if you've ever been afraid of losing the one thing that's right in your life, but that's how I feel about your daughter. " Whatever my father said made Kent smile and then they hung up.

"What did he say Kent? Why didn't he ask to speak to me? "I knew he was probably still mad, but I don't care. "It's fine". "I'll be okay here while you're gone."

"No, you won't. Mr. Sullivan said for me to put you on the bus. He has been waiting his whole life to have his little girl home again. He thought he had lost you forever when the phone got disconnected the last time you called. He said he sat by the phone waiting for you to call back, but you never did. He told me he knew exactly how I felt and gave us his blessing. He sounds like he really loves you. I don't know what happened between your parents, but at least give him a chance."

"Heyyy!" I said, thinking back on Kent's earlier statement. "Why did he say put me on the bus? I can just as easily drive there."

"Oh, nooo, you *definitely* can't drive," Kent said while laughing as he took off running so I couldn't hit him for cracking on my driving. As I ran behind Kent, I ran saying a silent thank you to God for bringing this wonderful man into my life.

Chapter 12
Someone to Love

Before leaving for Brunswick, Kent and I drove all day looking for a place to tie the knot. Without any luck. We didn't know that we would need blood work as well as witnesses before we could get married. We were running out of time and Kent was insistent on not going to Okinawa without getting married. Out of frustration and desperation, that night we made our own vows to each other and swore that no matter what, we would always be Mr. and Mrs. McFadden. Then we fell asleep in each other's arms.

With a smile on my face, I gazed out the window as the greyhound bus headed towards Brunswick, Georgia. My thoughts were only of Kent and the new life we would share. For once, everything seemed right in my life and I didn't want to think of anything else.

No matter how hard I tried to think only of Kent, I couldn't help wonder what seeing my father again would be like. Would he like me? Should I hug him? What if he doesn't recognize me? A tear rolled down my cheek as the questions ran through my mind. Suddenly, overcome with anger and defiance, I wiped my face and reminded myself that they owed me. As far as I was concerned, my whole family left me to die and I wasn't going to go begging and acting as though I needed them. All I wanted was a place to stay until Kent came home, and then I would be outta there.

I placed my head against the window to take a short nap but was awakened by the drivers voice announcing my stop. As the bus swung into the terminal, I looked around the parking lot to see if I could spot my father. I was nervous and I wanted to prepare myself for my first real contact with the man that, for the past 14 years, had been only a memory. When I got off the bus, I saw him sitting in his wheelchair, waiting for me to step down. I wondered if he would recognize me, so I looked the other way. When my feet touched the ground, I heard him yell, "Janice!" as he rolled over to me with a smile so big, it made my eyes fill with tears. I managed not to let one tear fall as he reached up to hug me. He then took my bag, placed it on his lap and led the way to the car.

Our reunion was totally different from what I had expected. On the ride home, my father asked a million questions which included where I had been and why I never came home. He told me about the many times he had traveled to New York looking for me, but no one knew what had happened to me. I couldn't believe it! I explained to him that I never knew he had ever tried to find me. In fact, I hadn't seen my mother, or anyone else in years. A tear fell from my father's face as he grabbed my hand and said, "I was told, that you had become uncontrollable and had run away. No one knew where you had gone."

The sadness in my father's voice made me cry. I tried to keep my own voice from cracking as I asked, "Who? Who said that?"

"Your mother."

"My mother! You've seen my mother?"

"Yes, she's here."

"Here? What do you mean here?"

"Your mother lives here in town with your brother and sister."

I didn't ask any more questions because too much was happening too fast, and each time I tried to speak, I'd get a lump in my throat. My father sensed my hurt and didn't ask any more questions either.

We rode for a few more minutes deep in our own thoughts before pulling into the driveway of a small house made of cement blocks.

"Who lives here?" I asked, "I'm tired, can't we just go to your house?"

"Yes, we can, Honey, but I just thought I would stop by so

your mother could see you."

"My mother!" I squealed. "She lives here?"

My father, who was already blowing the horn replied, "Yes, she does."

The door to the house swung open, I could see a woman's frame that was not much different from my own standing in the doorway.

"There's someone here I want you to see!" my father yelled as he beckoned her to the car.

My mother came towards the car staggering most of the way. She didn't look like the strong, vibrant person I remembered. She was dressed in an old worn housedress, her hair was a mess. It was obvious she had just gotten up. She came around to my side of the car to give me a hug. My father obviously hadn't told her I was coming I could tell she was genuinely surprised to see me.

"Oh, my God! I never thought I would see my little girl again! When did you get here?"

"Well, not too long ago actually. My father just picked me up from the bus station." I said coldly.

"You have to come inside and see your brother and sister," she said rushing back towards the house.

"Oh, and you gotta meet your step dad too," she added as she tripped over a small root, but quickly regained her balance.

"What's wrong? Why are you staggering like that?" I asked as she tried to lead the way to the small gray house.

"Well, honey, your mother isn't doing too well. The doctors have me on all kinds of medication that make me very drowsy. But I still want you to come in for a minute."

She didn't say "Welcome home," or "Where are your bags?" Nope, she said, "Can you come in for a minute?" As I walked through the door, I took a long look around, not recognizing my mother in the layout of the house at all. Instead, the room before me was dimly lit, the badly-worn furniture that was now covered in sheets had been ruffled from the previous sitter. There was colorful plastic foliage covered in dust on each table and the gray cement bricks that made up the walls were bare. There was no warmth or care, just space. My mother had always been a very proud and neat woman with good taste. But here she was living in this little two-bedroom cement house. I wondered what had happened to Mr. J. D.

I looked over in the corner and saw Dedra and James, my sister and brother. Until that moment, I had no idea what had become of them. When they realized who I was, they were very happy to see me. Five years had passed and I had changed a lot. I was a woman now, on my own and about to be married.

I took my attention off them for a moment and looked at the man who was now married to my mom. I couldn't see what she could possibly see in this man. I exchanged a few pleasantries with him and prepared to leave. I gave one more hug to my brother and sister, told them I would see them later, and left.

Going over the bridge from Brunswick to St. Simon's Island was beautiful. I loved the way the water shimmered when the car lights hit it. And the smell was a mixture of salt water and oysters. It brought back memories of my great uncle Buddy, who was my grandmothers' brother. He would take us kids to the beach to gather oysters during low tide. He'd crack them open right there on the spot for us to eat.

As we drove the long road draped with moss-laden trees, I couldn't help but think of the many occasions I rode up and down this same street with my face pressed against the car window; looking out with tears in my eyes, not sure what was going on as my parents screamed back and forth at each other.

My father drove in silence as I marveled over the town where I grew up. The island was only ten miles from Brunswick, but by the time we reached the house, I was completely worn out. I just wanted to take a hot bath and go to bed.

When I entered my father's house, I couldn't help the shock on my face as I looked around at the condition in which he was living.

This was not the nice, neat place I remembered.

Sensing my discontent at the condition of his home, my father looked at me with a sad, but hopeful grin. I could tell he hoped my disappointment would not keep me from staying.

He rolled his chair around towards me while explaining how it was just him and he really didn't use much of the house.

"You can change anything you want. Without a woman here, I admit, things have become a little run-down."

"Oh, I'm okay. I just need a moment to get used to things, that's all."

I could see my reaction had hurt him, so I pretended to be excited.

"Hey! Where's my room?"

My father rolled his chair through the kitchen to another room, and pointed towards a door.

"It's right there where you left it."

As I opened the door that led to my old bedroom, I couldn't believe my eyes. The room was filled with stuff that obviously hadn't been moved in years. It was my stuff, just like the day I left it, over fourteen years ago.

My father rolled over to me and gave me a hug around the waist.

"I know," he said, still sensing my amazement at his living conditions. "Tomorrow we'll clean it up the way you want it. Let's just get some sleep tonight."

I gave him a big hug, because all the hate I had held onto for so many years couldn't add up to the loneliness I saw here now.

The bathroom consisted of a bathtub, sink and toilet awkwardly positioned on an unvarnished wood floor. The light switch was a long string, hanging down from a naked bulb.

That night I bathed quickly and fell asleep on the sofa in the living room.

Morning came and I really didn't want to get up. I felt something crawling down my leg, so I shook my foot lightly still dazed from sleep. I shook my foot for the second time, but this time I remembered where I was. I jumped up, screaming and yelling for help. My father rolled in the room just in time to see me beating my own leg, as the big brown water bug flew away.

He came over and shook my covers, while laughing.

"Oh, Lord, honey, I thought something was wrong. That's just a little cockroach. It won't hurt you."

From that point on, I had the willies. I constantly felt something crawling all over my body and things did not get any better. It was one thing after another. The water tasted like eggs. Every ant, beetle, and roach had our address. Within a week, I was completely covered with bites and forced to finally make a choice between keeping the window open and being bitten all night by creatures, or closing the window and suffocating from lack of oxygen.

By this time, I wasn't coming across as the world's greatest daughter or houseguest. I had taken every opportunity to make sure my father knew I wasn't happy with the living conditions.

I mean, come on! The house had been the same for over sixty years. He was born in that house, so I didn't feel I was telling him anything he didn't already know.

Kent called around the second week of my stay. I couldn't wait to hear his voice. When my father yelled from his barbershop at the front of the house, to pick up the phone, I barely gave Kent the chance to talk.

"How are you, my princess?"

"Oh Kent," I replied as I began rambling on about the conditions. "I can't take it. Please, can I come there?"

"I really wish you could, baby. But, it can't be that bad."

I was about to reply when I heard the voice of a man in the background.

"Charles, can I get a quick cut?"

I pulled back the curtain to the window in my room, which looked directly at the shop. There was my father holding the phone with his hand over the receiver. My mind instantly flashed back to an incident that happened years ago. A time that now seemed like deja'vu.

I was around five years old. My mom, who had left us children with my father, was calling to see how we were doing.

"Mom," I said in a low voice, afraid someone might hear me, "Please come get us. Dad drinks all the time and he tries to hurt Jr. I'm frightened, Mom. I want to go with you."

There was a loud sound in the background then just like now; it sounded like the bell that hung over the door in the barbershop. I pulled back my curtains and saw my father listening in on our call.

"Mom," I said slowly, "Dad's on the phone."

"Janice! Janice, are you there?"

"Yes, Kent, I'm sorry." I said shaking off the old memory.

Disappointed that I could not leave Brunswick as soon as I would like, Kent and I finished our conversation and I hung up. I leaned back on the bed and thoughts of Kent were replaced with the memories of the day my mother took us off the bus, leaving my father and everything else we had behind. I realized now, recalling everything my father had said since I returned, that he would have never let us go without a fight. He loved us. And I had always loved him too.

Neither my father nor I mentioned the call, but I could tell he heard my complaints. After that, I tried to settle in and make the best of it. I reacquainted myself with some of the girls I grew up with, as well as a bunch of my cousins, who actually remembered the day we were taken off the bus.

I instantly became fond of my cousin, Arrie, who had returned from California two years ago. We spent hours laughing about nothing, just passing time on an island we had both outgrown. My dad thought having Arrie and me hang out was just the greatest thing. He said that even as kids we would always have something to laugh about as we ran in and out of his shop.

Arrie told me how lonely my dad seemed to him. He said he had watched the life drifting out of my dad long before he left for California.

"He's a new man, cuz. I hadn't seen Uncle Charles like this in years. Welcome home," he said as we sat on the wooden beam outside the shop. "You know, for a long time, no one knew if Uncle Charles would get over that day your mother took you guys off the bus. Every day after that, Unc would just sit out in front of the shop and look out for the school bus as if he expected y'all to get off. He drank so much, that some days he wouldn't be able to open the shop. Eventually, his customers were forced to go into town for a cut."

I sat listening to Arrie with my mouth open as he filled in the blanks from my past. Hearing how my father would boast about me day in and day out, as if he had been in contact with me all the time, was hard to believe. Could it have been that while I was on the streets ready to give up, it was my father spending each day speaking positive affirmations over me that kept me going?

I learned from Arrie that my dad had the tub and sink put in once he knew I was coming. This made me feel awful about the way I acted upon my arrival. Talking with Arrie made me feel closer to the man I called my father. I made my mind up right then that if God had given us another chance, I was going to take it.

From that day on, it was my dad and me. We did everything together. We were seldom out of each other's sight. When I got a job at a resort on the island, he'd take me to work at 6:30 in the morning, go get my breakfast, then watch me eat. Then he would return at noon with a full-course lunch for two. At quitting time, he'd always be outside waiting on me. For a while, I thought it was sweet because I couldn't see that what he was going through was fear-based. Once I figured out what was going on, I couldn't let him continue to do that to himself. He had to know and trust that I would never leave him again. The bond we shared was a blood-bond and it was strong.

Although the day would come when I would have to go, I still wouldn't be leaving him, only his presence. He was my father;

and no distance could ever take that from us again. I was in his life to stay this time.

Over the next few months, the Island seemed to come alive. My father and I spent days together, just doing fun things. We gave some of the best cookouts you'd ever attended. Everyone hung out at the shop just like old times. The friendships I made would stay in my heart and life forever. It was wonderful how life had opened her arms up for me and all those around me. I was now truly different. I was ready to take on the world with a smile. There was a life in me that I had never known, and it made everything around me that may have once been in black and white, take color.

My father's business picked up. His old friends, who had left, came back. My dad had awaited this moment for a long time; he was ready for the new business once again, with me, his daughter, by his side. He taught me how to cut on the days I wasn't working, forcing his oldest friends to be my guinea pigs. Although reluctant, the men would sit with their hearts in their hands as I performed an old-fashioned cut and shave, switch-blade style.

My dad never let anything slow him down. In fact, it was my father who taught me how to drive, helping me get my license. I would have never in a million years believed that this day would have ever come. I spent years crying inside, wishing I could be like a normal kid. And here God had held onto all of it for me, until I was ready. And I finally was. I wanted to drop all the hate and give each of my parents a chance to clear the slate.

One at a time, I talked to each of them about what actually happened. My mom gave her side of what happened as we sat in the laundry house one day folding her clothes. I thought it strange that this was where our conversation would take place. This was the very same setting that carried the deepest hurt between my mom and me as the wounds of her not letting me attend my recital when I lived in Palm Beach was still alive and well in my mind. She sat beside me on the bench. Each of us folding pieces of garments as if they were pieces of our lives, as she told her side of what life was like for her back then.

To my surprise she started out with words that would hurt any child.

"I never wanted kids," she began. "I spent my childhood raising seven sisters and brothers while your grandma ran out with different men. I was stuck with the cooking and cleaning, and a lot of times, trying to fend off her dates. It was horrible for us. I did all I could do, but I wasn't able to protect them. I was just too young. By the time I decided to run off, my younger sister who was twelve at the time was pregnant by her father, and nothing was done about it. Of course she wasn't allowed to have the baby, but all of us girls had suffered from the same abuse. Between the eight of us we had four fathers, or should I say five, on the days Mama was mad and told the truth."

She stuttered over her words, trying to pick them carefully.

"I just wanted to get away so I ran to the first man who had really showed me what love felt like." Charles was such a kind man. I fell in love with him instantly. When he asked me to marry him, I said yes. At the age of six-teen I had no idea of the commitment or sacrifice it would require.

I became pregnant with Junior a few months later. It was unplanned and I didn't want the responsibility. I just wasn't ready after what I had gone through with my own family."

I nodded my head as she continued to talk.

"Your father, on the other hand, was happy and couldn't wait. For a while, things were good. We moved into his parent's old house and settled in, raising a family I wasn't ready for. When we got married, I thought it would be just us two; laughing and having fun like when we first met. I tried to be happy, but I wasn't.

"Soon after that you were born," she said with a sigh.

"And although I loved you with all my heart, I felt trapped. I had spent most of my childhood raising children, and I was just tired. I just needed a break, some time to just get away. But your father wouldn't hear of it; he thought a mother's place was home with her kids at all times. He became more and more possessive; he questioned me all the time about my whereabouts. I knew being in the service was taking a toll on him, but he was a responsible man and would do whatever it took. I got sick with you more than I ever did with your brother. Your aunt, my sister-in-law at the time, would stay with me to make sure Junior was okay.

"I could tell your father had started drinking heavily. Every time he would call from the base, he would be in a rage, spouting out names and accusations. I knew then I wasn't going to stay with him, but at that time, I had nowhere else to go.

"One weekend, while your father was home, he was drunk and started arguing with me because I had been gone all afternoon. It was raining pretty hard that night and the winds had blown several branches down. One struck the light pole outside of the house, causing the lights to go out. Your father, not wanting the huge tree branch to rip the wires apart, got the ladder and went out to push the branches out of the way. He was drunk and I tried to tell him to leave it alone, but he wouldn't. He climbed up the ladder to the top of the pole as he had done many times before, but this time, when he touched the branch, a flash of lightning jolted the branch and your father, throwing him to the ground.

"I heard the yell and ran out. Charles lay on the ground, unable to move while his legs and the branch were all ablaze. I ran to the pump for water and when I came back, Charles was unconscious. I called for help. When the ambulance arrived, your father still could not move. Charles's legs and back were injured. He was paralyzed from the waist down. His legs were burned so badly they had to be removed. Your father died that night, right before my eyes, as he received the news that he would never walk again.

"After that he became unbearable. He would throw things and go into rages of self-pity. He wouldn't let me help him. He would lay there with you and Junior thrown across his chest, not saying a word. He was in a great deal of pain mentally and physically. His medicine was strong and there were times when I would give him more than he needed to keep him asleep so I wouldn't have to deal with the rage. No one knew what I was going through each day. I can't explain it without sounding selfish, but I wanted my life back. The only time I could relax was when all of you had been put down for the night. That's when I would slip off with Marvin. I had met Marvin long before I left your dad. He'd come to Brunswick a couple of times in search of work. He told me about Belle Glade and said he would be there if I ever decided to come. I never wanted to leave my children, but I knew it would kill your father if I took you with me. So I waited until Charles was able to get around by himself. You were probably four or five when he opened the shop and started to cut hair. He was always good with his hands. You and Junior were his little helpers and everyone was happy but me. I was twenty-three with two kids and a husband in a wheelchair, paralyzed from the waist down. I wanted out.

"One night, as I put you kids to bed, I decided to leave. And I did. I told myself you'd be better off with your father."

She paused as if not wanting to go on.

"Please finish," I pleaded.

"When I got settled," she said with another long sigh, "I told your aunt where I was. She would call me and tell me how you kids were doing. That's how I knew Charles was out of control. She told me how Charles would get drunk and roll around in his wheelchair looking for me with you on his lap and Junior hanging onto the back of his chair. I knew I would have to come back one day to get you and your brother, but I must admit, that day on the phone, I wished with all my heart, that you would have told me you were happy, and didn't need me. I knew I needed more time. I wasn't ready. I just wasn't ready."

My mother lowered her head as if reliving that day all over again.

I sat running what she was saying through my mind, yelling on the inside.

Looking up again, and recomposing herself, my mom began to tell the rest of her story.

"The day I took you off the bus, was something I just didn't want to do. But you were my kids and I had to do something. That's it. I don't know what you want to hear, but that was it."

Her attitude changed, she was now defensive and short.

"I moved here and there until I got sick. Eventually, you kids went to stay with your grandma."

When she finished, I was angry inside. She had sent us to the hell she herself said she ran away from. I didn't question her like I thought I would. I had given her the chance to say she was sorry for all she put me through. I didn't interrupt her—she could have said how much she loved me, or explained why she never came back, but she didn't. To her, it was cut and dry, but not to me. I had endured the kind of hurt that would last a lifetime.

As I left the laundromat that afternoon, my feelings toward my mother were no different from before. I still carried a deep emptiness covered with abandonment and neglect. I had waited my entire life for her to explain why she never came back for us. I had desperately hoped that it wasn't because she did not want us.

I swore that day I would never be like her. I drove away thinking how grateful I was that Kent convinced me to come back to Brunswick. I had finally begun to shed the emotional weight I had carried for so long.

Janice E. Sullivan

Chapter Thirteen
Packing The Wrong Baggage

—••◆••—

The one thing that kept me going was the fact that when Kent returned home we would be married. I loved him deeply and we were as close as two people could be. Because of him, my life had changed.

I wanted to be a good wife and give Kent the best home ever. But deep down inside me, I knew, just like my mom knew, that I didn't want children. I was too afraid I would be like her. The thought of the commitment and responsibility it would take to raise kids overwhelmed me. I knew I had already made Mistake Number One. I should have shared with Kent what my mother should have shared with my father years before. Neither of us wanted kids. It was too late now, I could only hope that Kent would settle for making the best home we could, for my brother and sister whom I had planned to move in with us as soon as I was able.

Kent promised to return by February, and I couldn't wait! But I could tell my father felt just the opposite; he knew Kent's return would mean my departure since Kent and I would have to leave for Jacksonville, North Carolina a few days after his arrival. I did all I could to comfort my father. I assured him repeatedly that I would visit often. Yet it seemed to do nothing to lift his spirits.

As promised, Kent arrived in late February to pick me up. He was pleased to see how beautiful and mystic the Island really was, compared to my initial description. He spent a few days taking in the small town that was filled with history and then managed to ply my father with so much attention that it put his mind at ease before we left for North Carolina. As we drove off the Island, I knew everything was going to be all right. I had my husband-to-be at my side and the father I had always wanted just a few hours away.

That following month on March 15th of 1983, Kent and I exchanged our vows. We stood in front of a judge and two strangers that were being released from an overnight lock-up we quickly inducted as witnesses, officially making me Mrs. Janice McFadden. A few months after that, Kent's tour of duty ended and we returned to Syracuse. Kent didn't get a job right away, so we had to move in with his parents just to make ends meet. It was tough at first, plus my talents were limited. I hadn't done much in the way of work. I was finally able to get a job working at McDonald's as a cashier. I had to be at work every morning by 5 a.m. I liked what I was doing; it was fun and I worked hard to be the best cashier I could. A few months later Kent also got a job. He was offered a position as a line engineer with Chrysler Corporation, which gave us the income we would need to strike out on our own.

It seemed as if nothing could go wrong. We were happy, and fate was finally smiling down on me—the young girl who had been thrown out on the streets five short years ago.

One day to my surprise my owner/operator called me into his office.

"Janice," he said, "You're a hard worker. You're not like the rest of them. You're different. If you keep it up, you'll have a bright future here."

He leaned back in his chair while tapping his pencil against his chin, as if thinking of what to say next. Then he said, "I know you'll do a great job, congratulations."

I wasn't sure if I had just been promoted or not. In fact, I really didn't understand what had made me different, but I was so proud I wasn't like the rest of them. I ran home and gave Kent the good news. And we celebrated, hoping I understood what "Congratulations!" meant.

The next day, my supervisor sat me down to discuss my new duties as swing manager, erasing all doubt I had been promoted.

Within four months we moved into our very own apartment. Our first set of official furniture was a pair of milk crates, cleverly designed as end tables, tucked neatly at each end of a box couch that I had found on sale. But we didn't care, it was ours, and it was a start. We lived in that apartment for just over a year, saving every dime so we could buy a house on the east side of town. During those days, it was uncommon for a black couple in their early twenties to purchase a home, but with all I had gone through, I had to have a place that truly belonged to me. I also kept another promise I made to myself, and that was to complete my GED. I attended night school at the Syracuse University Equal Opportunity Center, and in a matter of months, I was given the certificate that put me in a position to obtain my second promotion as assistant manager, which was a salaried position.

Kent and I were focused; we were determined to have the home and life we had both dreamed of. Kent worked hard and put in extra hours whenever he could. And when the opportunity opened up, he started working the night shift because it paid more. We did whatever we could do to make a good life for ourselves. Working at night created a whole new atmosphere for Kent. The big thing on the night shift was drinks afterwards. Everyone knew where the Chrysler men hung out after a hard day's work. The words 'premium pay' just seemed to bring the woman out in droves, each one of them hoping to snag themselves some security. Because Kent worked at night, he too would often have a few drinks with his friends after he got off work.

One night, as I lay in bed half-asleep, Kent came in drunk. As I lay on my stomach he knelt down on the edge of the bed beside me. He leaned over me and kissed my cheek as he often did. This night however, he continued to kiss me and began fondling me. He rubbed his hands up and down my breasts and hips, which made me uncomfortable. The smell of alcohol on his breath made me gag. I became sick to my stomach as memories of my grandfather flooded my mind. The man leaning over me was no longer Kent. I was overcome with the horrible vision of my drunken grandfather with his hands all over me. I pushed Kent away, screaming and kicking. He jumped up startled by my reaction, but was too overcome by alcohol to ask what was wrong. Instead, Kent backed away in an apologetic, boy-like manner. He drifted off to sleep fully dressed in a chair on the other side of the room.

After that night, I became what I now know as frigid. I denied Kent his spousal pleasures and made up excuses, so he—my husband—wouldn't touch me. On the rare nights when I had no choice and all my excuses had run out, I would lie motionless, with tears running down the sides of my face, asking God to help me.

Our relationship began to deteriorate. Kent would blow up at me and leave the house, sometimes for hours. I didn't want to lose my husband. I loved him and missed our closeness. We didn't talk anymore when Kent came home from work, instead he would come to bed and just turn his back to me.

I tried everything to change how I felt about having sex with my husband. I even tried having a few drinks before Kent got home to loosen myself up. It worked for a while, but Kent soon became tired of coming home to a wife who smelled of more alcohol than he did. I didn't know what to do about my marriage, which was falling apart. I couldn't tell anyone how I was haunted by my childhood molesters each time I tried to make love to my husband.

The more I felt Kent slipping away, the more I wanted to go home to my father. And, when I should have been working on saving my marriage, I was planning how to escape before I was asked to leave. I had become so conditioned to people asking me to leave that I created a condition I called "hurt-myself-before-someone-else-could." Kent never had a clue that I was really crying out, and not walking out.

Strapped with more emotional baggage than any one person should carry, I headed for St. Simon's Island, to the one guy, who would love me unconditionally: my dad. He had become the best thing that ever happened to me.

Being home made me feel free. I didn't have to pretend anymore. To me there was always an aura of constant pressure when Kent and I were together to be the perfect couple. Our friends would brag about how wonderful our marriage was and how they wished they had the kind of relationship we shared. It put us both in an awkward position. Our friends had no idea what life was really like. They, like most people, wanted what was put before them and not the truth.

After a few days of lying around doing nothing, I felt it was time I get out. I decided to ride by my mother's house to check on my brother and sister. When I arrived, I saw Dedra sitting on a curb along the side of road. It was dark and I was surprised to see her sitting all alone. As I got out of the car, I could tell something was wrong. She looked up with sadness in her eyes but was relieved to see me.

Reaching my hand out to help her up, I said, "Let's go get something to eat."

I asked her several times what was wrong but she just kept shrugging her shoulders. I suggested we sit and eat outside so we could both let the breeze blow against our skin. The breeze that was blowing that night blew in a way which made you feel as though you could actually feel the darkness.

As I reveled in the small-town beauty, I looked across the table into my little sister's tear-swollen face. I saw in her eyes what I had wished someone would have seen in mine years ago.

I looked her straight in the face, and asked, "Is someone touching you?" I didn't wait on her response. I could tell when she looked down, her eyes filling with tears, just what her answer was. "Who is it?" I asked calmly, taking the time to explain how it had happened to me too.

I was pretty much prepared for anything but my mouth fell open as she said my mother's husband. She began telling me how he would come into her room at night, penetrating her while he covered her mouth with his hands. My heart swelled as it filled with hurt and anger. I wanted to kill him. She grabbed my hand begging me not to say anything.

"Of course, you're kidding right? I'm going to talk to Mom first and then put his ass out!" I yelled.

She told me she had never said anything because she felt my mother wouldn't believe her.

"Most of the time Mom is drugged up. She would swear he was right next to her," she said in a dry tone.

There is no way this could be happening. I had already lived this nightmare. This time I knew what I was going to do: I would go to my mom and question her about my suspicions. I wouldn't say a word about what I had been told. Then my mother and I would join forces, doing all we could to get him locked up.

"Unbelievable!" I yelled as I slammed my mother's bedroom door. I walked out of the house, shaking my head in disbelief. I stood there on the porch, frozen, unable to cry, hoping she would come after me. But she didn't. My mother, like most women, was in denial. She didn't want to hear anything I had to say. She defended a man over her child, just as her mother had. My blood ran cold and my heart raced with hurt. I wanted so badly to react to all I had learned from my baby sister. But I wasn't sure what to do. I wanted to yell and curse at my mother, but I didn't. My upbringing had taught me to never disrespect my parents, even if they were wrong. So I did nothing.

I drove back to my dad's home in disbelief that my mother had taken a position of denial instead of packing his bags and throwing him out like I had rehearsed in my mind over and over again as a child, when I wished she had been there to protect me. When I reached my father's house, I lay across the bed, called my husband, and cried, never saying why.

My father, as usual, would roll into my room to question me when I came from town to get any news he could about my mother. I could never understand why he loved her with all his heart still. It amazed me that even now, he would take her back after all these years. What kind of love could outlive all the pain she had caused him?

That night, I told my father there was nothing to report. I was just really glad he was my dad and then I gave him a hug, and drifted off to sleep.

My few days with my father went by too fast. I knew I had to get back to work, and, face the husband on whom I had walked out. Before leaving, I would have to make one more stop. That stop would be my mother's house, knowing she wasn't at home, and hoping to find her husband.

When I arrived, he was there as usual, just sitting around waiting on my mother to come in from her second job to fix him dinner. I could tell by his reaction that he was surprised to see me. After all, I did know my mother's schedule. But I was there to see him.

"Coming in!" I yelled through the screen as I pushed the door open. I didn't give him a chance to say anything.

"I came by because I needed to see you. I'm not going to mix words nor waste my time listening to your trying to deny what I am about to say. I know you've been molesting my sister, and frankly, if it were up to me, I'd kill you. But because you people are all mixed-up in the head, my only concern is getting my brother and sister the hell out of here. Until then," I said, putting my hand in my pocket and gesturing towards a knife.

"I promise I will kill you if you ever touch my sister again." His response, or lack of one, was admission enough for me. My emotions were mixed, and all pleasantries escaped me, I got back in my father's car and we drove in silence to the airport.

I couldn't wait to see Kent.

Tonight, I would be the wife he wanted. Kent's not being home when my friend dropped me off, would give me just enough time to prepare for our special night. I got all dolled-up, in one of my sexiest nightgowns, and waited. I sat there that night until daybreak, but Kent didn't come home. Finally, frustrated and angry, I grabbed my jacket, got the car out of the garage, and headed for any of his friends' houses, who may have known where he was. Of course, like men, each had their own rendition of how they had just left him and he should be at the house by now.

Desperate, I even went by Ann's house. It had been rumored that she was Kent's new sidekick. He had been seen with her frequently, from what I heard. There I was at another woman's door, asking her if she had seen my husband. I knew things had become distant between Kent and me, but I didn't know how much until I pulled away from another woman's doorstep.

After that, things never seemed to be the same. We both went on doing our own thing, coming and going as we pleased. Not taking the time to communicate with each other, about what had gone wrong. I remember the night that may have been the end of our relationship. Kent was to pick me up from work. I sat outside in the rain, waiting on him for hours, and he never came. I took a cab home, only to be locked out, I climbed onto the roof, hoping the office window would be open, but it too was locked.

I began to sob. I remember thinking to myself, just as I lost my footing and fell to the ground, "How did we get here?" What had gone so wrong? I sat there on the ground, soaking wet from my tears and the rain, trying to compose myself.

I needed to get away. I wasn't going to let him come home and find me like this. Hurt, wet, and crying. No way! I decided to go to one of my friend's houses, attempting to stay out longer than Kent. I tried to show him what it felt like to worry, while, I sat back and had a few drinks and God knows what else.

My soul was empty and I didn't know how to fill it.

One night turned to several. Soon our life felt like one big contest of who could commit the most hurtful acts. Our home was filled with a constant trade of words that would slash clear-through to the bone, causing irreversible damage. In my attempt to win, I recall going to work on many occasions so drunk from the night before, that I would literally fall out on top of my desk. A wastebasket would be positioned on the floor beneath me as I puked. My co-workers never questioned me, nor told on me. Instead, they would always come to my aid, opening the store and bringing me everything from Alka-Seltzers to club soda in an effort to try to get me in a condition to work by 10 a.m. This was when our corporate office, which was located in the same mall, right next door, would open.

Mentally shaken and beaten up from the night before, somehow, I would make it through another shift.

It was during this time that I decided to talk to Kent about having the kids stay with us, thinking this might bring us together again, and give him a family. He agreed, not having much to say one way or the other. I was just happy he'd said okay. I felt in my mind that if we could just get through the next couple of months, we would be okay. I knew having the kids living with us would give us something other than our own problems to focus on.

Janice E. Sullivan

Chapter Fourteen
Forsake Not Your Spouse

My father was so happy to hear I was coming that he paid for the plane tickets that Marsha and I needed. I could have paid, but I just couldn't see putting anything else on Kent, plus taking Marsha was my idea. I wanted her to see why St. Simon's was so special to me. None of the friends who had grown up with me in the projects could imagine living the type of life I told them about. Marsha would be my confirmation that I was somebody.

That day, when we boarded the plane, I'm sure Marsha's own motive wasn't just being a good friend as well. Yes, she understood how important it was for me to finally be bringing my little brother and sister home with me. However, she had never flown nor had she been to an Island, so the reward outweighed the sacrifice, by far.

Marsha couldn't wait for the doors to close. We would only be on the island for three days, so we'd have to rush around if Marsha was going to see all the sights. I sat quietly watching her gaze out at the clouds, as I planned how to make this the best trip possible.

When we landed, my father was there to pick us up. While he drove us home, he asked both of us a lot of questions. Marsha liked him right away and he seemed to like her. As we pulled up to my father's house, I could see a beautiful light-green Monte Carlo, with a white vinyl top. I assumed it belonged to one of my father's customers. But when my father turned to me, giving me a great big smile and said it was for me, I couldn't believe it. My dad had bought me a car!—not just a car, but, my *first* car. I just couldn't believe it. He always had a way of turning all of my missed moments into memories. Here I was grown, married, with a home of my own. But I had just received my GED and he was determined to make it special. My father was always trying so hard to make up for all the years of fathering he had missed, and I loved him for it. He was truly my hero and I was "Daddy's Little Girl," no doubt about it.

Marsha fell in love with St. Simon's on the first day. I think looking out of the windows of my new car had something to do with it.

"This is my car," I told Marsha, as we drove around. "Sure Kent and I have a car, but this is *my* car."

I couldn't wait to tell Kent. I knew he would be equally surprised. Kent was always blown away at how my father treated me, and so was I. He just had so much love and understanding for me, even when I sometimes didn't deserve it.

Our time on the island was passing quickly; we barely slept. I wanted to show Marsha the world through my eyes, so I made every moment count.

When it was time to leave, it became clear to me where my need to make everything perfect came from: my father. Before we left, he had one more surprise. Not only had my father purchased the car, but he intended to ride all the way back to Syracuse with us, just to make sure I got home safe. If I never received another thing from him in life, that day would have been enough.

When we pulled up in my yard Kent marveled at my new automobile. He was impressed. Kent and my father made small talk as he unloaded the car. My father respected Kent and wanted us to do well. As I reached the doorstep to the house I looked back at Kent who had reached around to grab my father, attempting to assist him inside. Instead of allowing Kent to lift him, my father shrugged Kent off. He stated he would not be staying. My father asked Kent to take him to the airport; he didn't even get out of the car. Of course, we argued with him, trying to convince him to stay at least one night, but he flatly refused. He said he only came to make sure I was safe and had to get back home for his dialysis treatment.

I had come to understand and know my father; I knew the real reason he would never come in was because he didn't like feeling helpless. He didn't want Kent to have to carry him in the house or from room to room once inside. I understood how he felt. I gave him a great big hug and kiss, and thanked him once again for all that he had done for me. Then he and Kent were off to the airport, where my father would have a four-hour wait for his flight.

Once everyone settled in, I realized how right I was about having my sister and brother come live with us. It was great. Although they were now teenagers, they still listened to me. I was glad I could take part in showing them a new life. They enjoyed the school they attended, and both began working at McDonald's part-time. Kent even spent more time around the house. And I started cooking again. We had never had kids, but the math was simple; you can feed and clothe two 'way cheaper than four.

The time rushed by. We had gone through two birthdays, taught James how to drive, and decided that Dedra, although fourteen, wasn't cut out for working just yet.

We were approaching another holiday season and I felt we were finally going to be okay. The holidays were my favorite. I had spent many years envisioning the day when my family would be gathered around the table laughing and talking as the sound of holiday music filled the air.

This was the one time cooking became a family chore. It was tough getting them to see the vision, and although Dedra and James complained, in my heart I knew they would always remember the Christmas cookies in their holiday shapes that had to be just right.

A new year had just begun and I was enjoying my life, which was finally coming together. However, the spirit of gift-giving would have to extend just a little longer. My mother would be celebrating her 42Nd birthday on the 16th of January, and the kids wanted to get her something special. She had asked me to buy her a coat on a couple of occasions but her request was not a priority for me, so I never did. Now Dedra was pushing the issue, and I had promised that she and James could send the coat as their gift if they paid half. We spent hours running around the mall looking for what had to be just the right coat but never found it, and I was exhausted. I couldn't wait to get home.

"Phew!" I said, sitting on the sofa, finally just me, the television, and a big bowl of butter pecan ice cream, when the telephone began to ring. Don't answer it, immediately popped in my mind.

"Ugh," I moaned, picking up the phone with my mouth filled with ice cream. "Hello", I said as irritable as possible.

"Mrs. McFadden?"

"Yesss."

"This is Sister Demery from your mother's church."

"Uh-huh," I replied.

"Listen, I have bad news, your mother collapsed at church tonight. She has been rushed to the hospital. I think you may need to come home."

"What? What do you mean collapsed?"

"She was playing the drums as she always did, then all of a sudden fell to the floor. At first, we thought she was in the spirit, but when she didn't move, well, we called your grandmother."

"Is my mother okay? What'd she say when she got up?"

"Honey, she never got up. When the ambulance came, she was rushed off to the hospital, and that's all I know. Your aunt Kati—"

"Who?" I interrupted. "I don't have an Aunt Kati."

"Well your daddy's sisters asked me to call you."

"My father was there?"

"No. We had to call Harry too."

"Harry? Ma'am, that is not my father. Is there anyone there who knows where they took my mom?"

"Yes, Baby. I'm trying to tell you they took her to Brunswick Memorial."

Click immediately followed. As fast as I could, I dialed the number to the hospital.

"Come on, pick up!" I thought as the phone rang for the fifth time.

"Isn't this a hospital, for Pete's sake?"

I was cut off by the voice on the other end. "Brunswick Memorial."

"Ma'am, my name is Janice McFadden and I'm looking for my mother who was just brought there," I screamed.

"Calm down, Mrs. McFadden. What's your mother's name?" I quickly gave her my mother's name.

"Yes, your mother is here."

"Well, is she okay?"

"She's with the doctor and, well, right now we don't know much. She was breathing on her own when she came, but they are moving her to life support."

"Oh, God!" I screamed.

"Please, please no! What do you mean life support? What do you mean?" I repeated, crying hysterically.

"Ma'am, I'm gonna see if I can find one of your family members who can probably tell you a little bit more than I can."

And almost comically, just like the news reporter who always seems to interview the one brother with the gheri curl bag over his head, she found Pat.

"Oh, no, oh, no!" Pat was yelling and crying in between big gasps of air.

"Pat, Pat please, I need you to calm down and just get somebody else to the phone. Who is there with you? Where is my brother?"

"He's in the back—Um-uh, um-uh."

"Get him, please."

"Hello." I hear my brother's voice come through the phone.

"Junior, what's going on? Pat has me all scared. What happened to Mama?"

"I don't know. They say she just fell out at the church. When

When I got here she was in a coma…

As the word came out of his mouth, he began to break down.

"A coma," I said. "How could she be in a coma?"

"Look! I don't know what's going on," he yelled. He was crying again and not making any sense. "I don't know. I don't know, Jan." He repeated as he continued to sob into the phone. Then there was silence on the line.

"Hello, is this Jeanette's daughter from New York?"

A woman with a very strong voice said as if taking over.

"Yes."

"Well, I'm a good friend of your mother's and right now, baby, it doesn't look good. They cannot get her to wake up. The doctor said he believes it was an aneurysm, but he can't be sure until they run more tests. Are you coming home?"

"Yes."

"Where are her other two kids?"

"They're here with me."

"When you coming, baby?"

"Tomorrow." I replied.

"Okay, I'll let your brother know. He just can't talk right now." Then she hung up.

I sat on the couch with my head in my hands. Why am I so upset? Why do I have to come home? Why do they expect me to just be there for her? What if I had never found her? I was going through a lot of emotions all at once. But I knew the worst would be trying to figure out how I would tell Dedra and James, who after everything, still felt my mother was a good mother, that we may lose her.

I called the airlines.

"I need three tickets, please, for tomorrow to Jacksonville, Florida." I waited for the agent's response.

"Credit card please," came across the phone.

I gave her the needed information.

When Kent came home, he agreed that we should go to

Brunswick. I told Dedra and James our mother was sick and we had to go home for a little while. They were used to my mom and all her medicines so neither thought much of the trip. Not to mention, it was their first time flying and they were excited.

My older brother, Junior and his wife Sharon, who I hadn't seen since our incident with Manuel and Raphael, picked us up from the airport, along with, of all people, Pat! By the time we got to Brunswick, I was furious. From what I gathered from her, my mom fell out in church and lay on the floor for about twenty minutes when blood started running from her nose and mouth. It was at that time they called my grandmother, who by her account had found Jesus, and finally got the nerve to leave my grandfather

and Syracuse. Pat said she showed up with her oil to pray, as my mother lay there sprawled out on the floor.

"Thank God someone finally had the sense to call the ambulance." I added lashing out.

When we arrived at the hospital, we gathered in the waiting area near the intensive care unit. We were waiting to find out from the doctor when we could see our mother.

When the doctor finally came over to us, he said, "I want you to know that your mother has suffered what we call an aneurysm of the cranium. In some cases, you can operate to remove the blood, thereby giving the patient at least a fifty-fifty chance of recovery. But," he said, looking at us while choosing his words carefully. "Your mother's case is inoperable. The aneurysm is right on the brain, so there is no way we can get to it without causing more damage to her. In my professional opinion your mother has already expired. We're keeping her alive by life support. Without it, she would stop breathing. Her brain has, already, stopped functioning."

My mother's younger brother and my one-time molester, was now very upset himself, he intervened in the conversation. With a low and strained voice from in back of the room he said, "Sir, I was told she was breathing on her own when they brought her in."

"She was, but once we examined her we had no other choice than to put her on life support. You can go in two at time to see her, if you wish. But she won't know you're there, nor will she respond. I'm sorry; I know this is a tough blow." He said looking down briefly.

The doctor asked, "Can I please speak with the person who is going to be in charge?"

"That's her daughter right there," Dutch said, jumping in again.

'She's the one in charge." He said pointing at me.

"Yes sir," I said, taking the role just given me.

The doctor drew me away from the rest of the family.

"I didn't want to say this in front of everyone because I know these are difficult times, but your mother at this point will not recover. It is in my professional opinion that we should remove the life support."

"Remove it! What do you mean remove it? You just said she can't make it without it." I said surprised at his remarks.

"Yes, but I also said she doesn't have any chance of coming out of her coma. At some point you're gonna have to consider the people who are still here, along with what you'll take them through, if you drag this on. I know it's a lot to deal with, so just take your time and consider what I have said. If you need me, the nurse knows how to reach me."

As I walked back towards the waiting group of family and friends, they rushed over to hear what the doctor had to say. I explained to them what the doctor had explained to me.

I looked into their faces and declared, "I'm not signing it." I turned away from them and walked towards my mother's room with Dedra, James, and Junior following close behind.

We completely ignored the doctor's request of two at a time and all went in together.

Being inside the room was a lot tougher than I ever thought. I had never had anyone close to me die. I looked on as they all leaned over the bed, crying and grabbing any part of my mother they could hold. I was unsure what to do or how to react. I slowly eased over to her bed and rubbed her leg, letting her know we were all there.

It was too much for my oldest brother who had always been a momma's boy. He became hysterical and started hyperventilating, and then he passed out as he tried to get my mother out of the bed. This made Dedra and James all the more terrified, causing them to break down.

So here I was, in charge of the life of a woman, which until a couple of years ago, I had no clue how to contact. Someone else should be handling this, not me. But, of course, the family thought I was the most educated and could understand what the doctors were saying.

It was only two days into the New Year, and I already wished it were over. We spent most of the days at the hospital, leaving in shifts to shower or change. During the next couple of days, I watched a father that I loved dearly, suffer. He hurt as if he were still married to my mother. He posted his wheelchair outside her window, waiting on every chance he could to get inside, just to be near her. It tore me apart to see what everyone was going through. I wondered should I have been acting differently. Why didn't I feel anything? Why were my emotions so non-existent?

That night, when things had settled down, I went into my mother's room just to sit. As I sat there in the dim light, listening to all the sounds of her equipment, I began to cry.

Why couldn't you love me? Why didn't you once come for me? I waited for you. I was your little girl. These thoughts haunted me as I was now almost bawling, but I never said a word.

I picked up her hand and looked into her face. I could see the years of worry locked in the crevices of her tiny wrinkles. I explained that I knew it wasn't easy for her, and how, in some sense, she and I were more alike than different. To me, my mom had spent her life chasing happiness, and I had spent mine waiting for it.

I stood up and straightened my clothes as I wiped my face with the end of my shirt.

"We don't want you to go, but I understand if you must."

I gave her a kiss as I prepared to leave the room. On the way out, I whispered, "Go and find your happiness, Mom, you deserve it."

As I walked down the hall I was stopped by the doctor.

"Has your family considered what we talked about?"

"Yes, we have and, no, we're not." I said walking away.

When I got back downstairs to the cafeteria, I was a lot stronger. I looked around the room and realized that everyone was tired and they needed someone to lead them. Everyone was afraid to be the first one to go home to get some sleep.

On, January 4th, at 11 pm, I stood in the back of the room and did what I do best, I took control of the situation.

"Okay. I just left my mother's room, and she is doing fine. I talked with the nurse and she promised to call if she wakes up. So right now the best thing we can do is go home get a good night's rest, so we are all thinking clearly tomorrow. Those of you who have jobs, go on to work tomorrow. You need to take care of your families. Anyone else like me, who doesn't have to work, well, I, along with my sister and brother, will be here around ten. So come on, let's get up and I'll see everyone tomorrow."

They all got up dragging themselves out slowly, allowing their relief to show on their faces briefly.

The next morning everyone came back. They started filtering in around nine and those that worked, well, they took an early lunch to be there. It must have been around 1:00 pm when the nurse came in and announced that my mother had expired. We all jumped up and ran to my mother's room. When we reached her, my mother was lying there stiff, cold, and dark. Everyone was hysterical but me. In my eyes, something was wrong.

There was no equipment at all in her room, no monitors, no life support. The tubes in her arms were gone.

"Nurse, nurse!" I yelled as I walked over to her.

174

"What happened to my mother's equipment? Why is all her stuff gone? I didn't sign any papers."

"I know, the doctor's on his way now to explain."

When the doctor arrived, he spoke calmly, "Your mother's heart stopped and there was nothing anyone could do. Due to the size of the family, I had the nurses remove all the medical apparatus before I had them inform the family. It would allow you to pay your last respects a little more comfortably." As he spoke, he did not look at me.

In my mind, I knew what had happened, but how do you prove it? My inner voice said, "Not now—this isn't the time," so I walked away. My family needed me and I had to be there.

It was like a scene from a movie. We had never lost anyone close to use before and emotions were high. I tried as best I could to comfort Dedra and James, but I couldn't come up with any words remotely close to what they were feeling. I remained the strong person everyone assumed I was and immediately started making plans to have the funeral home pick up the body.

The hardest thing I have ever had to do, I did that night. I watched my father cry like he himself had been given a death sentence. He was completely out of control. I became frightened for him, begging him to please calm down because I wouldn't know what to do if something happened to him.

Afraid to let myself feel anything, I tried to make light of the situation.

"Hey, come on, I said in a jovial manner, you guys are acting like someone just died. You're gonna get us thrown out of here. Let's let the doctors do their job. You know mom wouldn't want us to cry."

My brother Junior turned around with saliva coming from his mouth, crying like a four-year-old child. He looked straight at me and began yelling.

"How in the hell do you know what she would have wanted? You ran off?"

"Ran off!" I said pausing, as what he had just said kept

ringing in my mind. I caught myself; I didn't even reply because I knew this was harder on them than it was on me. I had dealt with the hurt of absent parents all my life.

That night, we all left the hospital, each person going his or her own way. That was January 5th. It would take until January 10th to bury my mother and, of course, I would have to pay the bulk of the expense. Thank God that what we couldn't pay, the funeral director let us owe.

Many of my mother's friends gave what they could in the way of donations or food for afterwards. Harry, her so-called husband, did nothing and said nothing until it was time to decide where my mother would be laid to rest. He, all of a sudden filled with grief, just broke down, reaching out for me as if he thought I would embrace him.

I stepped back without acknowledging his attempt at compassion. I looked at the funeral director and said, "My, mother will be buried on the island. My father has a plot there for our family."

Harry immediately recoiled like a snake and said my mother was his wife and that she would be buried next to him.

I stood up, smiled at the funeral director, placed the paperwork on her desk, and advised her to call me, for the final proof on the obituary.

"You have all the information you'll need," I said. Then I turned and left without another word.

The funeral went off as planned. Friends and family from all over came to my mother's homegoing. The church was filled with well-wishers, and others were still coming, even after the funeral had started. Sitting up front made it hard to see everything, but I was able to catch a glimpse of Marvin as he entered the church. There he was, as big as day, walking down the isle with Aunt Carol and his new family. I hadn't seen him since I was a child. Somehow, the sight of Marvin brought up all kind of emotions that I wasn't aware I had. I burst into tears, heading towards the center aisle where Marvin was about to sit. I ran to him with my arms stretched out, looking for the man I grew up with, to comfort me.

Instead, he pushed me back.

"Hold on, Ma'am, I think you got the wrong person."

Just then, my baby sister, Dedra, who was behind me said, "Daddy, that's Janice."

He gave me a quick pat on the back and moved on to his children. That day, I felt another form of loneliness that I hadn't felt before. The man I knew at one time as a father had pushed me away for reasons unknown.

It hurt.

After the funeral, there was so much commotion at the house I could barely think. I went outside just to sit so I wouldn't have to tell one more person, "I'm okay, thank you."

While I sat listening to the after-funeral chatter, Pat, who had gone door-to-door collecting what she could for the cause, sat down beside me. Although she always had good intentions, she was one of those people who never missed anything and had the worst timing for bringing things up. I could tell by the look on her face, that she had something on her mind.

She plopped down next to me with a big sigh. "Well, she gon'."

She said in her down-home voice. "I sure am gon' ta miss Julissa."

"Yeah, me too," I replied.

Then the real intention of her sitting next to me came out.

"Yeah, Julissa shol' would have like ta hear that. You know, ya momma never thought you loved her."

"What? Okay, Pat," I said rising halfway up.

"Nah, cuz, I'm serious. She use to always say you never once stayed with her when you came ta town. I mean she use to cry, cuz."

"Well, she never asked me to stay. And besides she had a house-full of people."

"I know, but you still could have stayed with her sometime.

She thought you felt you was too good."

"Well, why would you tell me this now? Why didn't you tell me when it would have made a difference?" I was now annoyed at her presence.

"'Cause, 'cuz, I don't think you know that you were your mother's favorite child."

"Huh?" I said, now really about to blow my stack.

"No, I'm serious. She use ta brag 'bout her daughter in New York all the time. I knows 'bout yo' big house and new cars—how you was the boss of all them peoples. She even had a a'bum with a picture of you she carry 'round that say 'my favorite photo my daughter', with a picture of you."

"Well, she never acted like it," I said as I stood up again.

"My father always picked me up, so that's where I stayed. And that's that, so excuse me please." I was now walking through the door of the house, thus ending the conversation with Pat, but walking dead smack into another. Harry and his family were making plans for my mother's possessions.

"I'll take this. I'll take that," is all I heard as I entered the kitchen.

"Shelly can have her clothes," shouted one of Harry's relatives.

"Who?" I said in a loud enough voice. "No, no, no, no! No one is taking a damn thing out of my mother's house! My brothers, sister, and I will decide what goes where! No one else will!"

I paused and looked around.

"The car is going to Dedra. Junior will pick up what he wants tomorrow. The only thing I'm taking is her dishes." I said forgetting the "we will make the decision" statement I had just made.

"Hold on. This was my house and she was my wife and I have something to say."

"The only thing you have to say is 'bye and you are lucky your not saying it right now. You need to have your stuff out of here by tomorrow or I will throw it out."

Harry tried to argue, but he was no match for me, especially with the memory of what he had done to my sister still fresh in my mind. The thought of it coupled with the few drinks I had already had brought out a mean streak in me, and anyone who knew me knew I wasn't the weakest link. I meant business. I threw him and his whole family out. As far as I was concerned, he had done nothing but brought hurt to our family anyway. I escorted them to the door, once again trying to protect the ones I loved.

As I watched Harry and his family pile into their cars, I looked over in the yard where a crowd had gathered around my eldest brother, Junior. He was upset, and everyone was trying to calm him down. Not knowing what was going on, I walked over only to find out it was me that had him so upset.

Directing his anger at me he yelled, "Who made you the boss? You always just take over. You just show up and think you run everything." He was yelling through slurred speech so I knew he had had too much to drink. "You ain't nobody! Momma always liked you best anyway. I don't care what you did, you got everything anyway."

What the hell was he talking about? He was always the favorite. Hell, she kept him. I wanted to scream back at him. But I didn't. I just went back into the house.

As I watched everyone clear out, I poured myself a drink. I sat there until everyone was gone. I sat there and had drink, after drink, after drink, while going over everything that had happened.

"This is crazy," I thought, "If they only knew."

Looking at the bag of stuff from the hospital that belonged to my mother, reminded me of all the work that still had to be done. I pulled off the tag that sealed the bag tearing it wide open. There, lying on top, like it had been set there on purpose, was the little photo album Pat had told me about with a picture of me on the cover.

I cried that night for all the things my mother and I never said or settled. Eventually, I drifted off to sleep for the first time in my mother's house, since I was eleven.

The next morning I woke up feeling renewed. I wasn't going to fall into a bunch of regret, nor was I ready to forgive the woman who was my mother. The hurt was too deep.

I began preparations to close down the house and head home so I could concentrate on building a new life for my sister and brother, a life that would be full of love and good times. But, first things first, I would have to contact a lawyer because I was more than sure Harry would try to fight me on my decision to completely cut him out.

Although I felt overwhelmed from just thinking of what was ahead, I felt comforted knowing that soon my husband would be arriving to be by my side. I got up, got dressed, and headed to town. I stopped at the phone booth to call my father so he would know what to tell Kent when he arrived.

"Dad", I said as I heard the receiver being lifted from the holder. "Dad."

"Hello," my father answered in a shallow voice.

"Dad, are you okay? You don't sound very good."

"I'm just not doing too well this morning. I just ain't feeling my best." "Did you have a good time with your father last night?" he said sarcastically.

"My father? You're my father. You mean Marvin? I didn't even see them after they left the house. They went straight back to their hotel. Anyway, I called to let you know where I was going before you got all sentimental on me."

"I just wish it was me, is all."

"Wish what was you?"

"Well, I wished it was me who had died and not your momma. She was a good woman. With you leaving, and her gone, I really don't—"

"Uh-uh, stop right there. You're just upset."

I knew why my father was hurting. I more than anyone understood how tough it was to spend your life feeling sorry that things hadn't gone the way you hoped. But I imagine it must hurt worse when you've lived your life thinking one day things would change, thinking one day, the person you loved would one day love you again, then have to accept that it will never happen, because that person was gone forever.

I think my father had held on to the hope that my mother would come back to him, and now that hope was gone. I couldn't handle his pain so I tried to cheer him up.

"You need to get up right now! Get yourself dressed so you can meet your favorite daughter in town for lunch after your doctor's appointment. Better yet, I'll come by the dialysis clinic so you can brag on how cute I am. Now give me one of those Charlie-Brown smiles and get dressed."

My dad did his best to sound cheerful and hung up.

I arrived at the dialysis clinic late but, of course, my dad's car was still there. I headed inside where I was sure he would be waiting like a little kid, wanting everyone to see him get treated like a baby. He loved to hear the nurses say how much I loved him or how close we were.

Once inside, I walked over to the counter where my father usually sat if I were late. There was a new nurse on duty and I wasn't familiar with her so I asked,

"Excuse me. Where is Charles Sullivan?"

"Are you here to pick up his car and belongings?"

"No. He's supposed to meet me here."

"I'm sorry, what'd you say your name was?"

"I'm his daughter, Janice. Where is my father?" I demanded.

"Well, we called his brother, your uncle, I guess. His name was on the card in the case file of who to call if something should happen. We informed him that Mr. Sullivan suffered a heart attack during his treatment."

"Oh my God!" I yelled. "Oh my God, please, where is my father?" frantic with tears running down my face, I ran toward the door as she called out behind me that he was taken to the hospital.

At the hospital, I wasn't very pleasant. As far as I was

concerned, these were the same people who killed my mom.

I wanted to see my dad. When I got there, he was already in a room. I stopped, took a few minutes to thank God he hadn't taken my dad too, then asked for his doctor.

"Well, Mrs. McFadden this has been quite a haul for you, I hear. I was told you just lost your mother."

"Yes sir." Tears were again starting to roll down my face. "How is my father doing?"

"We have him on a bed of ice right now to reduce his fever and hopefully make him comfortable. He has a lot of bed sores."

"Bed sores, what bed sores?"

"Your father has several sores on his backside and lower buttocks, which is common in paraplegics, because they're constantly sitting. Left unattended they can become infected, as his have. But right now, that's not my first concern. Your father suffered a loss of oxygen to his brain during his heart attack, and, right now, I'm not sure just what the damage is. At this point, he seems to have forgotten everything up to today, but he also is having a hard time remembering events that may have just taken place. Let's go in together. It's time for me to check on him anyway. And, Mrs. McFadden, please remain calm. We don't want to upset him," he said, cautioning me.

As we walked over to his room, a nurse was walking out.

"Don't tell me, you're his daughter from New York. He was afraid no one would pick you up."

"Well, yeah, I am from New York but I've been here. My mother just passed, so I've been taking care of things."

"I'm sorry. Maybe I misunderstood what he was trying to say."

The doctor stayed behind to discuss a few things with the nurse. I walked over to my father's bed on my tiptoes, thinking my footsteps might startle him. As I looked over in the bed at my dad, tears began to well up in my eyes again. He looked so defeated. I immediately wondered where did all the gray hair come from? It was as if it had appeared overnight.

"Dad," I whispered, touching his hand.

His eyes opened slowly, followed by a big fat grin that made the tears just fall from my eyes.

"Hey, Ma'am, how are you? Can I please have some water? They said they were going to bring me some water."

"Daddy, it's me, Janice. Don't you recognize me?"

"You know I use to fish. You wanna go fishing with me and my daughter. She's coming, you know."

I began to break down so I ran out. The doctor suggested we give it a few days because sometimes things come back gradually. I didn't call my brother at work because there was nothing we could do at this time. Plus I didn't want him to leave work again after missing so many days already.

Instead, I went to the hotel where Marvin was with the kids and told them what happened. At this point, I wasn't feeling very strong or ready for a confrontation, but, of course, what I wanted never seemed to matter.

Marvin had plans of his own. He was leaving that day so he could get back to work, and had planned to take his kids with him. He said while my mother was alive, he, of course, would never have interfered. But with her being gone, it was time he did his part. I asked the kids what they thought. And they both wanted to go with their father.

Here we were with Marvin, choosing again, but this time my mother wasn't one of the choices. I gave my sister the keys to my mother's car and was done with it. I gave them both a hug and then I left. For the next six months, my life would drag by slowly. Kent stayed for as long as he could, which was two weeks, then he returned to Syracuse. Dedra and James called and said they had arrived safely; they were now full-fledged residents of Baltimore, Maryland.

Each day that I went to the hospital, was a repeat of the one before. While sitting with him, my father would tell me how his only daughter from New York was on her way to get him. Although my father never fully recovered from his heart attack and didn't recognize me, he never forgot who I was. When he did recognize me, it was as if I had just arrived. Everyday was as if I had just arrived in town. My father would beckon for me to get his clothes so we could go out on the town and celebrate my arrival—again.

At times, he would even try to get up, forgetting he couldn't walk. I never understood how serious his condition was. I sometimes laughed or played into his desire while my friends were there because it seemed so funny. I remember egging him on many times, asking what color he wanted as we looked at his pretend closet. The one person he loved enough to remember was mocking him. I was too afraid to face reality and not strong enough to show the true fear I felt.

The doctors said there really wasn't anything more they could do for my father and he would be released at the end of the week. He would either have to have an around-the-clock nurse or be placed in a home. My first thought was to take him back to New York with me.

I told his brothers of my plans and that I could take care of him.

"He doesn't want to go to a home," I explained to them. He has begged me not to."

"With no insurance and with Charles bein' in the condition he is in, there is no way you can give him the care he needs," said his eldest brother.

"His doctors are here, so he will be able to continue his treatment. And I feel that is the best thing for him at this time," said the other brother with finality.

"Well, if I can get a nurse to take care of him, then the best thing is for him to be with me," I replied in the same tone and walked out the door, headed for my father's room.

As I entered his room, I sat down and just looked at him. He was like a baby. He had a great big grin on his face, as if he hadn't a clue to what was going. I pulled my chair close by his bedside and just lay my head on the railing. I held his hand as tears streamed from my eyes yet again. I knew deep in my heart I couldn't take care of my father, but I also knew that he seemed to understand every time I mentioned taking him to the nursing home. He would grab my hand and say, "Daughter, please, if you put me there, I'm going to die. Please, I'll die!"

He would just keep going on and on until I promised I wouldn't do it. I couldn't help but think how terrible I would feel watching him look at me as they rolled him into the nursing home. A place where I promised he would never have to go.

I loved my father. I loved him more than anything. I held him close, wanting everything to be as it was. As I held him he twitched slightly, indicating the sores on his backside and legs were still painful. His diabetes had gotten worse. Looking at his raw flesh made me ill. I couldn't see how such a little sore could become so—

"Oh my God!"

I flinched at the realization of what I had just thought rounded home. One night, long before my father's attack, he was lying in his room complaining of not feeling too well. He asked if I could lotion the bed sores on his back and legs. He said he just hadn't been able to lotion himself and his skin was in bad shape.

As I turned my father over to lotion him, I couldn't do it. Just looking at the then-tiny sores all over him with the dry, drawn skin scared me. I told my father I couldn't do it. I apologized to him and went to my room.

Why didn't I see past myself and clean out those now infected sores?

I knew then and there that I had been kidding myself about being able to take care of him, or anyone else for that matter. At that moment, I convinced myself the best place for my dad was a nursing home.

I had already deserted him when he needed me to take care of him. Now I was betraying him by allowing him to be put in a nursing home.

"Today's the big day, Mr. Sullivan," the nurse said as she drew back his curtains, preparing his room for his departure and the next patient's arrival.

"Am I going home?" he asked as he looked at me with little boy eyes.

It was obvious that he didn't remember anything about what we had discussed all week. How he wouldn't put up a fuss and that this was the best thing for him. I hoped when it was time he would accept his fate and go without putting up any resistance, which would make it easier for me.

"Yeah, Dad, remember? It's time to go to your new home. You're gonna make a lot of new friends and have a bunch of pretty girls waiting on you hand and foot. You'll like it Dad, you'll see."

"Neece," he said, using a very old nickname for me.

"Please, don't leave me! Don't put me in that home. I'm gonna die if you leave me, Neece. I'm gonna die!"

"Father," I said now trying to be stern. "You have to go, and I have to get back to New York. I promise you everything will be okay, and you know I will come to see you so much you won't even know I'm gone."

With that, the nurses came in and plopped him in his chair. They rolled him downstairs, where my uncle and brother were waiting so we could all introduce father to his new home. The drive was quiet; I felt uneasy, almost like an intruder as I climbed in my uncle's car so I could be with my father. I looked out the window, carefully scanning my father's surroundings. The outside was nice enough, but the inside was a whole different story. I wasn't pleased at all. So much so, I almost couldn't go in. It had a smell that made me sick. The smell seemed to be a combination of old age and cleaning supplies.

Since my uncle had made all the arrangements, I hadn't seen the place before. But seeing it now for the first time made me realize what a sad place this would be to spend your last days. But there was nothing I could do. I had to keep reminding myself it was for the best.

Once outside the doors I felt better and somewhat relieved. We had finally come to the end, settling on that which was best for everyone, including my father. I took a deep breath. I couldn't wait to settle back and get some rest on my flight home. I was anxious to see Kent for the first time since my mother had passed almost, seven months ago. Boy, what a year this had been so far.

When the plane landed in Syracuse, I felt great. I hadn't realized just how much I missed being home. The sun was shining brightly and people were bustling around. Compared to Brunswick, Syracuse was the big city.

Kent was parked outside waiting in front with the T-top off. The car was shiny and clean. He jumped out to give me a big hug and kiss. I could tell he missed me and I had missed him too. We decided to drop my things off then go hang out for a while just riding and talking. When we reached the house, I asked Kent to grab my bags while I ran in to give my father a call. I just wanted to make sure he had settled down and let him hear my voice.

I dialed the number, smiling at my husband who, through all of this, had been so great. He'd paid for most of my mother's funeral, welcomed Dedra and James into our home to live with us, and then traveled back and forth to Brunswick without ever saying a word.

"Hello? Hi, I'm Janice McFadden. May I please speak to my father, Charles Sullivan? He checked in this morning and I just want to make sure he's all right."

"Ma'am, please hold."

"Hello," a male voice said.

"Hello. Hi, I was holding for my father, Charles Sullivan."

"Yes ma'am, Mrs. McFadden. I know. Uh, I'm the doctor on staff at this time and, well, uh, ma'am your father passed not more than an hour ago."

"NO!" I dropped the phone and Kent picked it up. He said a few words to the doctor then hung up. He picked up the phone book, called the airline and made reservations for me to leave the following morning. He then sat back down quietly and held me in his arms as I cried hysterically, repeating what my father had tried to tell me over and over again. My father's bowels had backed up in his stomach, poisoning his system and killing him. I felt someone should have seen this; how can you not note that someone hasn't defecated in days? He should have been checked.

The guilt I felt that day over what I had done to my father would follow me all my days. This trip, I would be gone for over a year. Kent would travel to Brunswick three times in an attempt to bring me home, after he had received several calls from so-called friends. They expressed their concern about how I spent most of my days drinking and that I had lost the job at McDonald's that my boss in New York had arranged for, because I was too drunk to go to work.

I wanted people to just leave me alone, while I called myself "working things out." I had betrayed the one person that loved me the most, and the pain and guilt was far too much for me to handle.

Each time Kent would come to get me, I would say I wasn't ready and would send him back home. Although I loved Kent, I just couldn't leave the one place that would always be home to me and the only place I could still feel the presence of my parents in the air. I just couldn't go back yet. Kent would stay a few days hoping I would change my mind then leave telling me when you're ready let me know. I'll be at home waiting.

It seemed as though I would never be ready. Syracuse was the furthest thing from my mind. So much so, I had even begun sleeping around, letting each day fall where it may as I smoked my weed and enjoyed a few hits of white powder.

I remember, like it was yesterday, that awful night Kent would come for me one last time. Kent showed up at my brother Junior's house unannounced. Sharon, my brother's wife, had called him, informing him I was seeing someone and she felt he should know. But I knew her real motive, even if my brother couldn't see it. She would have loved to get her hands on my new friend and she thought Kent was her answer. When Kent pulled up, the sun had gone down, the night air was still warm, and a perfect breeze was gently blowing through the trees.

The tape player was up loud, playing one of the latest slow jams. Both of the coolers were filled with Golden Champ ale and Rum 51. We were all playing spades and laughing as I passed a joint. My new friend, Darrell, was there, along with several others. I had met Darrell through Pat and he was a nice guy. We could relate to each. Neither of us knew where we should be next in life. He understood me when I told him that at one point I was so sure of everything I wanted out of life, but now I just wanted to do nothing—no responsibilities, no questions, no pretending to enjoy a touch that made my skin crawl, just nothingness, that's what I wanted.

I must say I was surprised when Kent walked in, but not happily so. I gave him a mechanical hug then went back to the game. After about an hour or so of watching my friend, Darrell, and me, I believe Kent had taken as much as he could take. He peered over his glass and looked at me as he drank down the last of his rum.

"Let's go," he said, grabbing my arm.

"Okay, Kent, just let me finish this hand."

"No, we're leaving now!" Kent put his hand around my arm a little tighter and pulled me to my feet.

I knew my husband well enough to know when he meant business. Although he wasn't hurting me, Darrell reacted nonetheless and stood up as if Kent was the one out of line and I was his woman.

Kent dropped my arm and pushed Darrell in the chest.

"What's up? You got something to say about me talking to my wife?"

"Nah, man," Darrell said, backing his chair back. "I'm sorry, man. I didn't know you were her husband. I was just trying to make sure the lady was all right."

"Well I have an idea who you are, sitting here all night making eyes at my wife, I think me and you need to step outside!"

As Darrell walked towards the door, I jumped in front of him. I told Kent to go on because he had been drinking and didn't know what he was saying. That night was the first time Kent had ever put his hands on me. Everyone including my uncle and brother, watched as he pulled me outside for the first physical fight we ever had. Kent kept hitting me with tears in his eyes, asking how I could turn on him with another man. He left the next day without as much as a word.

Chapter Fifteen
Hitting Rock Bottom

———••◆••———

Since Sharon and I had had a knock-down, drag-out fight for telling Kent about Darrell , I moved in with my Uncle Dutch and his new wife Pat, my mother's old friend. She felt she was looking out for me. She had no clue her new husband had spent years molesting me. However, I held no grudge against him. In fact I had chalked his behavior up to being just as confused and screwed up as the rest of my family.

I spent most of my of my time hanging out with Sharon's younger sister, Veronda, who was all grown up now. We would spend all day sitting around my uncle's house, waiting on nightfall so we could head for the club to eat blue crabs and talk some man into buying us drinks.

In spite of the beating I got from Kent when he heard I was cheating on him, I continued sneaking around with Darrell when his fiancée wasn't in town. I knew when she came to town, he would always leave me for her, but I just didn't care.

Darrell and I began spending more and more time together, but we both knew it would go nowhere. We'd ride around, talking late into the night and listening to Kenny G's latest hit 'Songbird.' It became our theme song. Listening to that song really put us in the mood. It seemed to say so much without having any words to it at all.

One day we bought a fifth of rum and headed back to my uncle's house to hang out. We sat up until around 2:00 a.m., watching movies, and waiting for my uncle and Pat to come home. We always waited until they were fast asleep before we would dare do anything. They finally came in around 2:45 a.m. and, as expected, went straight to bed. Darrell and I couldn't wait, with all the rum we had consumed, it didn't take long for us to start grabbing each other, and eventually exhaust ourselves. We were sound asleep in the middle of the living room floor, with our clothes thrown around, when I was awakened by the sound of my uncle snickering, as he headed back to his room where I heard him wake his wife so he could drag her to the living room to spy on us. I was so glad that I had awakened when I did. I quickly placed a blanket over both of us and pretended to be asleep when they poked their heads around the corner. I could tell they were disappointed that I wouldn't be the brunt of their morning joke.

That morning I sat thinking about my life. I knew that not only was I letting myself become someone that deep down inside I knew I was not. I had also begun to do things that I would have detested in someone else. I was spiraling towards rock bottom and not sure I could reverse my descent, but I knew I had to try.

That afternoon, Darrell stopped by to tell me that his fiancée was in town. He said he needed to spend some time with her, but promised to come by later that night. In anticipation, I showered, put on one of my long, colorful loungers, and waited. I anxiously listened for Darrell's car to pull up in the driveway, as I drank rum sizzler after rum sizzler, while trying to shake the emptiness I felt inside.

It was after midnight before I heard tires roll across the gravel as Darrell pulled into the yard. Feeling especially empty and lonely, I rushed to the door to give him a great, big kiss. But instead of receiving me into his arms, he stopped me and pushed me away.

He pointed towards his mouth and said, "No, not now. I've been with Darla and we were oral, but I had to see you."

"What?" I thought, not sure how to respond. This nigga must be crazy. I know he didn't say what I thought he said, but nonetheless, I was glad he had stopped my attempt to kiss him.

"Why would you come by here like that?" I asked.

"Well, I knew I could only get away for a minute, but I just had to see you. I told Darla I was going out to get us something to drink and eat. We're going to spend the weekend at the hotel."

"Who made that decision?" I asked. "Never mind," I said as I turned him towards the door. "Don't even answer, just go."

As Darrell pulled off that night, I could hear "Songbird" playing on his radio. The song that had brought us together, was now the song of our separation.

That night, I hit rock bottom. The only thing I could do was cry out to God as I drowned myself in sorrow and self-pity—only this time, He didn't answer. I prayed, I cried, and I yelled out on my knees, begging and pleading. I needed to feel him near, comforting me, but for the first time in my life, I could swear I saw Him standing with His back to me. I was dealing with so much guilt, and had done so much wrong, I thought I would never be forgiven. That fear kept me on my knees for hours, crying, pleading, and begging Him not to leave me. It must have been just before daybreak when I felt God's peace come back into my life, instructing me to go to back Syracuse.

when I got up that morning I called Kent; without any questions he wired me a bus ticket.

I was headed home.

Janice E. Sullivan

Chapter Sixteen
Unfinished Business

When I got home, my old job was still waiting for me, just as my boss had promised it would be. Everyone was glad to see me and life was just as I had left it. Kent never mentioned or questioned me about what had happened that night in Brunswick, nor did I question him about what he had been doing in Syracuse. We just kind of picked up where we left off, which meant nothing had really changed.

We still had a horrible sex life and our communication had basically stopped altogether. We were in a place in our lives where we no longer valued what we had had together. The only thing we could do was to try to coexist. It was a long road back, but such a short distance to stray. We tried, and I feel we wanted to love each other, but we just didn't know how.

One night, my girlfriend, Jasmine and I decided to go to a club, just to get away. Jasmine and her husband, Kevin were having their share of marital problems too. They were on their third child and still living with Jasmine's mother.

Kent had already left for the evening with a few of his friends. He had also taken my brother, James, who after finding out his father only wanted him and Dedra for the Social Security benefits, had decided to move back in with us.

When Jasmine and I entered the club, to my surprise, James, Kent, and his buddies were sitting at a table. We acknowledged each other, but chose neutral corners. After a short time James came over to me and asked for my keys to the car. He wanted to pop in at another club further down the street.

Although "The Lions Den" was one of the most popular clubs, it could still be one of the more dangerous, depending on who you were.

For Jasmine and me it was like home. The club was located just a few blocks from the projects where we grew up. So I guess that made us one of the Colliones, the gang that ran it. Kent, on the other hand, grew up just over the tracks in Pioneer Homes, run by a gang calling themselves the Duces. Although the Colliones and Duces considered themselves rivals, most of them had gone to school together, dated each other's sisters, or played on the same boy's club team. So no one ever worried about any major conflicts, but, like most gangs, you could always count on the one or two clowns who just couldn't let go of what they felt represented who they were. It couldn't have been more than about fifthteen minutes between Kent and my walking back over to our individual corners when I saw a big fight break out in the middle of the floor.

I turned to Jasmine, "I don't believe this," I said shaking my head, realizing the party might be over before it even got started.

Jasmine, who was facing the crowd, started screaming at me as she tried to talk over the blaring music. But I could hardly hear her. Jasmine suddenly grabbed me by my arm and swung me full circle.

"Janice, that's Kent!" she yelled,

I turned quickly to see my husband fighting off five guys, alone. I dropped my drink and ran over to try to break up the fight. I recognized a few of the faces of the guys that had attacked Kent. They were the same kids that used to come to our house to play with my brother James when we lived with my grandmother.

Not one of Kent's friends was anywhere to be found. Kent had boxed while he was in the Marine Corp and was an excellent fighter. He was doing a good job of protecting himself, but there were just too many of them. I tried to do all I could to get Kent away from them. Two of the guys had broken bottles, and were swinging them wildly as the others rushed Kent. I continued to yell into the crowd, punching and beating anyone who came close to my husband. One guy was swinging inside the huddle on top

top of Kent with the broken bottle he held in his hand. As Kent bent down to protect himself from the blows, I could see a pool of blood all around him. I kept swinging my way through the crowd of guys hovered over Kent as we tried to make it to the door. When we finally reached the exit that led outside, I remembered: the car was gone! Blood was dripping from the cuts on his body but Kent managed to stagger into the small hall that was between the exit and the entrance. I stood between Kent and his attackers. I turned to those who were still following us and shouted, "Whatever it is, he is my husband, please stop!" I began yelling at them and pushing them away.

"What are you doing? He is my husband!" I screamed again.

Because they knew me, they would not return my pushes.

Jody, the leader of the group, knew me better than any of them because I babysat him while his dad worked as a day laborer with Marvin in the strawberry fields outside of Syracuse.

This boy was trouble since he was six.

Now angry, I looked Jody in the face and said, "Enough, Jody! He's had enough."

He replied like a child as he said, "Okay, but your husband started it."

Once everyone retreated back to the club I stood helplessly looking around for James or anyone who had come with us, but there wasn't anyone to be found. Kent leaned on me as I tried to get him as far away from the club as possible before something else happened. When we reached the sidewalk, James drove up. Seeing all the blood on Kent, I guess he forgot he was driving and jumped out of the car, which hit the curb and almost ran us over.

"Please help me," I said as my brother grabbed Kent's arm in an attempt to hold him up. "I have to get him to the hospital."

On the ride to the hospital I tried to do all I could to stop Kent's bleeding but I couldn't. He was going in and out of consciousness and I didn't have a clue as to how to save him.

When we reached the hospital they rushed Kent to the emergency room. After receiving thirty-two stitches across his face the hospital released him. When they rolled him into the lobby, both his eyes were swollen shut, and he had several other lacerations, but he was okay. I told Kent I was going to get the car and to wait for me. When I pulled up he was sitting on the hospital steps crying. It appeared to me that his tears were more from hurt pride, than pain. I tried to comfort him. He wanted revenge. I had to talk him out of getting his father's gun and going back to the club. "I understand how you feel". I said sitting down next to him. "How do you know what I feel!" he blasted. "They didn't attack you. You're their friend, right?"

"Kent, they are not my friends!" I yelled in disbelief that because I didn't get attacked they must be my friends.

"Yeah? Then why aren't you cut up? Why don't you have any bruises?" he said sarcastically.

Kent was right, I wasn't hurt. In fact, if not for his blood on my clothes, you would have never known I was involved at all.

When we returned home I helped Kent get in the bed and he immediately fell off to sleep. I placed my head on his legs, had a silent cry, and fell off to sleep as well.

A few hours later I awakened to a knock at the door. I peered out the window to see Wil, one of Kent's best friends, and two other guys still getting out of the car. I watched the two guys walk up the walkway sheepishly, with their heads down, apparently dreading the moment they would be face-to-face with the buddy they had abandoned at the club as though they never knew him. They had all been friends since childhood, and had been stationed in the same battalion in the military.

Whatever happened to 'No-man-left-behind'? I thought. This was their motto even as kids.

I told Kent they wanted to see him, but he didn't want to see anyone. I could almost feel his hurt and humiliation as he looked up at me barely able to see. His eyes filled with water as he mumbled the words, "I just want to rest."

His buddies stood anxiously on the front porch awaiting Kent's reply. I went back to the door and cracked it just wide enough to deliver Kent's message. I had to listen while each one gave his excuse as to why he had not come to Kent defense.

"Man, I was in the restroom. I didn't even know what had happened," said one.

"I had just walked to the other side of the club. By the time I realized what had happened, I couldn't get through the crowd" said another.

Although I found their excuses nauseating, I said, "It's okay. He'll be fine. He just wants to rest." Then I closed the door, indicating I wasn't interested in anything else they may have had to say.

For days, Kent refused to see anyone. The whole situation had deeply affected him. He wasn't the same confident man I had known and married. Although I was with him, he had shut me out.

Everyday I asked myself what I could have done differently. Why didn't I just drop my purse, jump in, and defend my husband tooth and nail? I had been a fighter all my life. As a youth, I had fought just about every guy in the neighborhood. I knew I could have done more; why didn't I?

From that night on, Syracuse no longer felt like home. I couldn't look my husband in the face, without feeling guilty and unworthy. I wanted to run.

Eventually, the things that seemed so important to me, had no real meaning or importance. The job, my friends, the home that I once cherished so much, none of it mattered. Things were no longer working between Kent and me; I just wanted out.

I had spent my life in search of real love, only to get it and then realize that I didn't want it anymore. I had become complacent, and no matter how hard I tried, I could not lose the feeling of emptiness in the life I was leading. No matter where I was—at work, out with friends, or just sitting in my own living room—I just couldn't *feel* anymore.

Syracuse was the only future I had, but I was ready to make it a part of my past.

As usual, I kept these feeling to myself. I lived each day pretending nothing was wrong. I could only hope that God would hear my heart and rescue me from this emptiness.

One day as I lay on the sofa, I received a phone call from my mother's sister. I was shocked to hear from my Aunt Cynthia, but pleasantly surprised just the same because she had never called before. She told me she had someone who wanted to speak to me.

"Who?" I responded.

She continued to tease me, "Who have you asked about every time you came home?"

My throat tightened as I thought about the first name that came to mind. My heart began to flutter and a smile came over my face, but I played it cool.

Sighing, I calmly asked again, "Who, girl?"

"Silk."

"Who?" I said, now confused because it was not the name I expected or one I recognized.

"Oh, I mean, Mike."

"Mike?" I said, the joy, now being heard in my tone. "Don't play," I said, "I thought he had disappeared and no one knew where he was."

"I know but—" my aunt was cut off mid-sentence and a familiar voice came on the line. "

Yeah, little Nigga, I was missing till I heard you had been in and out of town."

"Mike! Oh, my God! Where have you been! I've asked about you so many times. The last thing I heard you had been sent away and we moved to New York."

"Yeah, well, I try to keep a low profile. The only reason I am here now is I thought you would be here. Plus, I'm thinking of moving Mama here. So, what's been up? I hear you all grown up now and done got married."

"Ah, man, I can't believe you're in Brunswick," I said ignoring his statement about my marriage." I was there for about a year after my parents died," I continued.

"Yeah, I heard. I'm sorry I missed your mom's funeral," Mike said solemnly.

"It's okay. I'm sure she knows if you could have, you would have been there."

"So why didn't you ever move back home?" Mike said changing the subject.

"Uh, for one it's too hard to find a job. Either you have to be a maid or lucky enough to land a job at one of the plants, that's it. And, believe me, I'm nobody's maid."

"So, when ya coming back?" Mike said ignoring my last comment.

"I don't know. I hadn't planned on returning anytime soon."

"Well, plan. Don't worry about money, you just get here. I can't wait to see you."

His words were smooth, but carried an undertone.

"Yeah I can't wait to see you, either," I replied, before hanging up.

I sat in the chair for a few moments, trying to figure out what it was I was feeling. My heart was racing and I had a strange desire to be home right then.

"Wow," I thought. Where could this be coming from? And why on earth had I spent so much time asking about the man who had molested me when I was five?

Even back then, I never hated him, but to have these feelings just from hearing his voice had me confused, to say the least.

I wasn't clear on what I was feeling, but as each day went by, I became more and more excited about going home. I acted out how I would respond when I saw Mike again. I didn't want to be too melodramatic, nor too aloof. I did want him to see how sophisticated I had become, and that I had really been taking care of myself. I wanted to have on the perfect outfit, and have my hair done just right. But I knew I had to deal with Kent first.

What excuse could I possibly have to justify going home again? I decided to just tell the truth. My cousin, whom I had not seen since I was seven or eight, wanted me to come home and help his mother get settled in her new place. Everyone knew I had a flair for decorating, so I would be the perfect person. More importantly, he was paying for it, so it wouldn't cost us anything. Kent's response wasn't what I thought it would be. He didn't ask any questions. He simply shrugged his shoulders and said, "Go."

I went straight to the phone and started dialing, looking back at Kent for a final approval.

"Are you sure?" I asked.

Kent looked at me and asked, "Are you?"

I nodded my head yes, while dialing the airline to make my reservation.

The following week, I was on my way. I had arranged for my brother to pick me up in Jacksonville. When I arrived in Brunswick that night, I learned that Mike had left shortly after he spoke with me and he had not been back.

Everyone just wrote it off with, "Girl, that's Mike. He just pops up for a day or so, and then he's gone."

My Aunt Cynthia tried to explain how Mike had been that way all his life, here one day and gone the next. "The only thing he has ever been attached to is his daughter and his mother," she paused, then added, "And you, when you were a child. He wouldn't let anyone touch you either when he was around."

I was furious, I sat there listening to them cover for a man who obviously didn't value either of them or their time. I didn't care how he had been all his life. All I knew was he hadn't given me the money back for this trip, and I wanted it.

We sat up that night, drinking and talking about Mike, AKA "Silk," the name everyone seemed to prefer to call him.

I found out "Silk" had been in and out of jail most of the time due to drug abuse and crimes he committed to support his habit. Except for weed he has been clean for a few years now, Cynt said as she spilled her guts over gin and juice. I discovered most of Mike's past relationships had been abusive and violent.

Mike undoubtedly, was bad news. But no matter what she said, I could only see the Mike I remembered, the Mike who had looked after me as a child. I knew if he had had someone with him who cared, he wouldn't have gotten himself in so much trouble. My heart went out to him. I also knew his mother's controlling nature played a major part in his drug use. She pushed away anyone he appeared to care about, so he would only have her to depend on. She behaved like some jealous girlfriend.

The next morning, I got up, got dressed, and went to see some childhood friends. Both of my sisters-in-law, Sharon, who was married to my brother, Junior, and Veranda came with me. Sharon and I had put the whole Darrell episode behind us—letting bygones be bygones, just as we had done with Manuel and Raphael as kids.

It was a beautiful day so we all decided to head over to Cynt's house first. As we got out of the car and headed up the walk, Cynt was standing at her door looking out.

"Girl, where have you been?" she said, looking at me as if we had an appointment.

"Oh, I got people to see. You are not the only person I know," I said jokingly.

"Well, I had a surprise for you, but you done missed it now."

"Oh, well," I exclaimed, feeling my oats.

"Oh, well nothing, my Nigga," I heard a voice say as a man from behind Cynt pushed her aside.

It was Mike! Silk! Whatever he called himself! It was him! I ran to the door as he stepped out, jumping into his arms, delighted to see him. He swung me around with one arm locked around my waist, slowly letting me down in a manner that was more than cousinly.

"Well, I see you made it," I said, standing back, looking Mike up and down with a cattish grin.

"What do you mean I made it? I'm the one that told you to come."

"Well, you need to be here when I arrive next time," I said

with a smile.

That day, Mike paid for everything. He bought crabs and alcohol like it was a big celebration. If someone wanted something he would say, "Ask Janice." If I said, "Yeah, that sounds good," then he would give me the money and say, Give them what they need." He made it clear to everyone that this was only happening because I said so.

As night turned into early morning and the drinks had diminished, I decided it was time to leave. Veronda and Sharon had both left an hour earlier, but Mike had insisted that I wait until he was ready to leave because he wanted to drop me off. He said first he had to take care of some business, but would be right back for me. He must have been gone for two hours or more before I got fed up and decided to take a cab.

Just as I was dialing the number Mike walked in.

"What are you doing?" he said.

"Look, I'm tired. I'm just gonna take a cab. You guys go ahead and do whatever, but I'm gone!" I said, angry at how long it had taken him to return.

"What! Didn't I say I would take you home?"

"Yeah, but you also said you would be right back."

"Okay, Man, let me take this girl home," he said to no one in particular as he snatched up the keys he had just laid on the table.

"I told you I can take a cab, Mike."

"And I told you I was taking you home," he stood holding the door open for us to leave.

That should have been my red flag right there, but of course, I ignored it.

On the way home we talked about what we had been doing with our lives, pretending that it mattered, knowing that it didn't. There wasn't any small talk that he and I could have come up with that night that would have covered up the obvious physical attraction we were trying to ignore. It was as if we were on a first date rather than one family member dropping off the other.

When I got out of the car, Mike gave me a look that puzzled me. I couldn't put my finger on what it was that actually bothered me about the look, so I let it go.

After an awkward silence he said, "See you in the morning," and pulled off. I, on the other hand, stood there in the street thinking about what I already knew in my heart: that I would soon be having sex with my very own cousin—again!

I anticipated how he would react now that I was a big girl, and able to take all of him just like he had said I would. I wish I could say it was the alcohol, but it wasn't. I had the same feeling now as I had had that day in my living room in Syracuse when Aunt Cynt put Mike on the phone. I knew then that when we got together again, it would be more than cousinly.

I went into my brother's house, plopped on the sofa and fell asleep content, and with a smile on my face.

The next morning I got up and began getting dressed so Sharon, Veranda and I could hit the streets. As we were getting ready to leave, Mike pulled up. Veronda, who, unbeknownst to me at the time, had eyes for Mike, announced his arrival in such an excited voice, you would have thought he was some kind of a celebrity.

"Here come Silk! Here come Silk! Let's get him to buy us some beer."

Before Mike could step out of the car, she was there to greet him.

"Hey, Silk, what's up? What you got?" leaning carefully over the open car window so to expose what lay inside her low-cut top. Mike, ignoring her, attempted to open his car door and get out.

"What you mean, 'What I got?' What you got?" he snapped.

"Nothing now, but if you give me some money, I can have some beer."

Ignoring her response, he started walking towards me, as I also headed towards his car.

"What's up? Oh, you were just going to leave like that, huh?"

205

"Nah! I didn't know you were swinging by. I thought you meant you would catch up with me later. Everybody always saying how busy you are. They never know when you're gonna pop up. So I figured, sooner or later, I would catch up to you."

"Well, just 'cause I'm too busy for them niggas don't mean I'm too busy for 'Pretty Good'."

We both broke out laughing as he called me by my nickname from years past.

"Come on, you hanging with me today."

He told Veronda I would catch up with her later at Cynt's.

"As we drove off," I asked, "Where we going?"

He answered, "Nowhere really. I just wanted to get you away from that ho'."

"Mike, why would you say that about Veronda?"

"Man, you know that girl sleeping with old men for money."

(I gave a slight chuckle.)

"I heard you were trying to get some of that yo' self'" I said, laughing, as he turned the corner.

"Man, please, I was trying to get that ho' down on her knees, if anything."

"Mike!" I yelled, surprised by the candid remark.

"Whaaaaaat? I was!" he said laughing.

"Anyway, where are you headed? This roads leads to 95 South."

"Nigga, I know where the highway goes. We gon' run down to Daytona for a minute. You cool?"

"Yeah, I'm fine," I said.

The ride to Daytona took about three hours. Mike met up with a few friends, stopped off to see his daughter and, of course, her mother, who had left Mike years ago after several broken arms and legs.

I still remembered E, which is what we called Mike's daughter, although she was a lot bigger now. She still reminded me of the fat, chocolate baby I used to carry around on my hips. Her mother, Betty, didn't recognize me until Silk explained to her who I was. For a second, she had a strange expression on her face, but it vanished as she rushed over and gave me a hug. Something about her hug was odd and forced, as if she wasn't really hugging me, just going through the motion. I was relieved when Mike said, "Let's go." I got the impression from the way Betty kept staring at Mike and me that either there was something that I didn't remember and she did, or there was something she knew that we both thought she didn't. Either way, it was weird and uncomfortable.

We left their house and headed back to Brunswick.

"You're finished?" I said surprised, as we headed back to 95 North after only being in Daytona less than two hours.

"We drove down here so you could see a couple of friends for ten minutes?" I asked.

"Nah, we rode down here so we could just get away; the friends were just a part of what was happening."

"Oh," I said laughing at how cool Mike thought he was.

We rode along not saying very much. Then Mike pulled off at a restaurant so we could get something to eat. We ate, talked, laughed, and reminisced about how, as kids, he always got us in trouble doing things he knew we weren't supposed to do. We laughed about the time my hand was cut trying to jam it up the coke machine trying to pull out sodas because his hands were too big.

He smiled as he looked at me. "My Pretty Good." He said leaning back in the booth. "I can't believe it's you."

"Yep, all grown up and in the flesh," I taunted.

"Come on let's go," Mike said standing up suddenly. "We gotta get back."

We made one quick stop to the liquor store and jumped on the road, drinking and laughing all the way. By the time we got back to Brunswick, it was starting to get dark and people were already hanging out, getting ready for the weekend. We headed straight to Cynt's.

Mike had bought enough alcohol and weed to keep

everybody happy. He passed the bag to me and announced he had to make a few runs, but would be back.

The whole time Mike was gone, people knocked on the door, asking for him.

Cynt was constantly yelling through her window, "He'll be back. He had to make a run."

An hour later, sure enough, Mike popped his head in the door. He asked me to fix him a Hennessy and coke and was gone again.

I asked, "Cynt, what does Mike do?"

She just looked at me sort a matter-of-factly and said, "He'll tell you. You know how he is when people discuss his business."

"Oh, Silk don't play that shit at all; he'll bus' 'em in the mouth," one of Cynt's friends replied from the corner.

"Girl, that boy ain't gon' hit nobody," I said. I looked at Cynt again and asked with some frustration,

"What is he doing?"

Cynt said, "Unh-uh, I ain't got nothing to do with that man's business."

After and hour or so, Mike again peeked his head in the door. This time he gave me a small bag and said, "Count this and keep it for me." Then he disappeared again.

I opened the bag and there was several hundred dollars neatly folded. I counted the money, folded it back up, and put it in my purse. Mike would return every other hour, giving me wads of money each time.

"You must be Silk's woman?" asked Cynt's friend who was still sitting in the corner watching everything like she was paranoid or had a complex.

"No, I'm his cousin," I answered, disturbed by her presumption.

"Oh, no disrespect, Ma'am, it's just, Silk don't trust anyone. And I ain't never seen him give anyone his money."

"I know that's right," Cynt chimed in.

That night, I left Cynts' house with a purse full of money,

still unaware of what was really going on. You see I had smoked weed and snorted a little cocaine, but only on a small scale. Maybe I thought it was weed he was selling. I can't say for sure. But at the time I didn't ask Mike where the money was coming from, nor did I ask why, when he stopped by someone's house, he would park around the corner and leave me in the car. At the time, I believed he didn't want any of his women to think I was his girl.

Each morning, before I could barely get out of bed, Mike was at the door ready to plan my day.

One morning he said, "Come on, you goin' with Me."

"Where are you going, Mike? I ain't trying to ride back to no Daytona," I said

"Get up and come on! I ain't say we was going to Daytona." "You ain't say it last time either," I argued as I got in the car.

Mike pulled up to my great-grandmother's house. She was 103 years old and still had all her faculties. She also had the family trait of always trying to be comical. While she and Mike exchanged quips, I stepped outside for a minute to take in the fragrance of all the beautiful flowers surrounding her house. I had just opened the door when an old friend, whom I had met during my first few visits, pulled up. He had heard I was in town and had stopped by my brother Junior's house to see me. They, in turn, told him he could probably find me here.

Now I knew he was lying, because I didn't even know I was coming over here. But if he felt it was important enough to lie so he could get to see me, what the heck.

"Let's take a spin around the block," he said.

Without a moment's thought, I jumped in and we took off. With all the catching up, plus the stop at the liquor store, the ride around the block took a little longer than I thought it would. When we returned, I could see Mike's car was still there, but this time he wasn't lurking around outside like he was my keeper. I thought to myself, good, he hasn't come out yet.

Once I was in front of the car, I could see that the windows had been rolled up and the doors locked. I stepped out of the car, waved 'bye to my friend, and went in the house. I looked around, but saw no sign of Mike. My niece, who was really a cousin that called me auntie because of the age difference, told me Mike had taken off on a bike. He threw his keys against the couch and asked her to tell me, "I got the wrong Nigga."

I picked up the keys not sure what Mike's remark meant and left. It didn't take long to find him. He had only ridden around the corner to Cynthia's house, whom he seemed to favor when it came to just hanging out.

I pulled up slowly beside Mike, "Need a lift fella?" I said jokingly.

"Nah, give that nigga you left with a ride."

"Okay, don't say I didn't ask," I yelled as I sped off. I parked in a spot a block or so ahead of Mike. I went my way, and Mike went his, I was completely blind to his display of aggression and control.

I received several warnings about how Mike doesn't play, from most of the folk that hung around him.

"You're the first one to get away with talking to him like you do," one guy said, with two or three others co-signing his statement.

To me, in my mind, I felt it was because of who I was to him when we were growing up.

"Y'all treat him like he all that. Running around here 'Yeah, Mike', 'Hi Mike', 'What you say, Mike'? Pleeeeease! He is just another man! Y'all just don't know how to deal with him," I said, enjoying my sense of power.

Later that night, before leaving Cynt's house, I went out to the backyard where Mike spent most of his time. Since I had his keys, I wanted to let him know I was leaving. As I stepped out of the door, I saw a small crowd around a body on the ground. The body was that of a woman and the man standing over her was Mike. He was yelling and making a big fuss about something, but I couldn't tell what.

The woman was holding Mike around the ankles as he kicked

her. She begged and pleaded for him to stop. I had been there before and knew how it felt not to have anyone to help you.

Mike was pointing a gun at the woman on the ground as he continued kicking her in her side. He made it clear that he would shoot anyone who tried to stop him, so no one did. Not paying any attention to the threats, I ran up to him and demanded he stop. Without even looking back, Mike swung the gun around and struck me across the face with his forearm. I stumbled and fell to the ground. The light shone on my face identifying who I was, as he now stood over me with his gun pointed in my face.

When Mike saw it was me sprawled, on the sidewalk he blamed the girl.

"See what you made me do? I'm should kill you," he said, landing another blow in her side with his foot.

I was so afraid, I started crying, screaming and pleading at the top of my lungs for him to stop.

With the gun still pointing at the woman's head, Mike slowly turned back to her and pulled the trigger. The sound of the gun made me curl over, and cover my face. I lay there too scared to look at what I knew would be a dead woman. When I opened my eyes, I saw that Mike had only shot at the ground next to her.

"If you mess with anything that belongs to me again; I promise you next time I won't miss," Mike said as he gave the girl one more kick before coming to help me up.

"Come on. Mike said in a calm voice as if nothing had happened. What you doing out here? Didn't I tell you I never wanted you anywhere around me when I'm out?"

"Yeah, but I was just coming to tell you—"

Mike cut me off as he held me by one arm and opened the door to Cynt's house with the other.

"We're gone," he said, closing the door behind him. The expression on Cynt's face said loud and clear what she was thinking. I believe she knew what was about to happen even before I did.

That night, I slept with Mike. I felt in my heart that we had

211

a bond no one would ever understand. Mike said, I was special and he needed me.

The next few days would be almost too good to be true. We spent every moment together laughing, or riding along the coast of Florida's most popular beaches. We stayed in fancy hotels, went to theme parks, and took late night strolls along South Beach in Miami. It was like heaven. A world totally different from what I could ever imagine had been opened up to me, and I wasn't going to let it go.

I could sit down at the finest restaurant and order anything I wanted. Mike spared no expense when it came to me and it didn't take long for people to start questioning our relationship. Although we tried to keep things under wraps when we were in the presence of family or anyone we knew, it didn't work. It wasn't long before I could feel the stares and prying eyes. We tried hard not to let anyone in on our little secret, especially since I would be leaving in a few days and all this would be behind us—or so I thought.

My plan was to get on the plane and head back to Syracuse with the details of my affair with my second cousin tucked deep away in my mind, never to surface again.

Instead, when I returned home my head was still full of memories of the most wonderful week I could have ever hoped for. I walked off the plane towards the luggage area with my face carrying the most pleasant of grins. People all around were smiling and waving as if my whole expression was due to them.

Seeing Kent, of course, swung me back into reality. He lowered his face towards mine to extend a welcome home kiss. Reluctantly, I leaned my head upwards, giving only a peck to the husband I hadn't seen in a week.

I put my arms around him and gave him a quick hug.

"Well, I've only been gone a week and it feels as if you've gotten bigger. Your shoulders are huge," I said in an exaggerated tone.

"Nah, that nigga you was with was just skinny," Kent said without looking back as he walked slightly ahead of me with my bags.

I didn't respond. I surely didn't want to spend the ride home disputing my whole trip. So I said nothing. As far as I was concerned, I was back and it was business as usual.

The next morning I got up, got myself ready for work at McDonald's, and resigned myself to finishing the life I had started.

Chapter Seventeen
One Decision Away

A week went by, then two, and I was miserable. I couldn't get the thought of all that I had done in such a short time out of my mind. I would go into work and find myself going through the motions, not really caring about what was going on in the store. I just didn't want to be there. Then I would go home and have the same exact feeling about a place I once considered my little haven.

Mike said he was miserable too. We spent hours on the phone whenever we could. He would call me at work during my slow periods. Then he would call again when I got home, always having Cynt ask for me in case Kent answered.

Kent wasn't stupid, he knew. He saw all the calls coming in from Georgia and began asking questions. I, of course, claimed it was Cynt but he often questioned the validity of what I said even though he was never home. He tried to make me think the only reason he wasn't there was that I never paid him any attention when he was. We had a two-way street of blame and neither of us was afraid to cross it to get to other side. We spent whatever time we could with whomever had distracted us from our once so-important marriage. When Kent wasn't picking an argument so he could storm out of the door, I was, so I could call home.

One night, while talking to Mike, I told him that I was tired and just couldn't take anymore; I wanted out of New York, and out of this life. "I'm unhappy, and I miss you so," I said.

I knew I was only talking out of frustration, but Mike immediately took me up on my comment.

"Then come home," he said.

"What?"

"You heard me, Janice, come home."

"I can't. I couldn't just leave Kent. He is my husband, and we have so many responsibilities here to cover. I just couldn't do that to him."

Mike replied in a dry voice, "Stay then," and hung up.

I awoke the next day, planning "fifty ways to leave my lover" (taken from a very popular song in those times). I dragged all kinds of reasons and excuses around in my head. I dismissed them for either being too strong or just a flat-out lie, until finally, I just decided to tell Kent the truth.

I was very unhappy, I felt we had grown apart and I had outgrown whatever it was I was meant to do in Syracuse. I felt there wasn't anything left for me here and my heart longed to be home. That was it, just the truth in a nut-shell. It wasn't that I didn't love him because he was truly my soul mate. I just didn't know how to hold on to what we had.

Somehow, cruel word by cruel word, all the love we had and everything we shared, slipped out the doors without being noticed, until all memory of who we were together and what we once stood for, was gone.

Mike had it all figured out. He wanted me to come right away. I refused to leave bills that I had created on Kent, so Mike sent money to pay off whatever I owed. So I did. My next worry was how to tell Kent I was leaving him. How do I tell the man I love that I just didn't feel loved and wanted to leave? I decided to do it on that Saturday. I took Kent out for dinner, informing him that I wanted to talk about something very important to both of our lives. Then I laid it on him.

His response caught me off guard. I never expected Kent to say how much he loved me or that I was all he had. No, I expected him to concur with my findings and we would leave the table shaking hands, realizing it was for the best. Instead, my husband offered to relocate, change jobs, and sell the house, whatever we had to do to work out our problems.

That, for me, was not a part of the plan. I became stern and contrite, saying, "It's just not in the cards for us. And before we become one of those couples who hate each other, I would prefer to leave now, still loving my childhood sweetheart—but not in love," (which at that time to me was a feeling you were supposed to feel forever). I didn't have a clue about the real commitment it took to be a wife. I had spent most of my life running, and my mother who was the only example I had, was on Husband Number Five when she passed.

By the end of dinner, we both had cried until we just couldn't cry anymore, finally agreeing that I was right. Kent said he would never give up on me or our love. He said he knew I was leaving because I had to. He understood I had to do it for me.

I only told a few close friends I was leaving and, of course, none of them took me seriously. They couldn't see or understand why I was walking away from my home, career, and husband just like that. I tried to explain that it wasn't "just like that," as they put it. I had been unhappy for quite some time.

As I listened to their statements of concern, I could tell that, for the most part, most of them were just concerned about the possessions I had agreed to leave behind. I left with only the things that would fit in my luggage. I let Kent keep the cars, the house and all that was in it.

I remember telling my play sister Colette, as she made clear her concerns about my leaving,

"If it was meant for me to have, I'll have it again."

She continued to talk as if I hadn't said a word, giving me all the reasons why she thought I was a fool. I hadn't told her about Mike and I decided, for the sake of argument, not to.

I listened to her go on that day, but remained unmoved, as I snapped pictures of the home and life I was leaving behind.

There was only one other task that troubled me, and that was making sure that the woman who was to succeed me was deserving of the man she would get. I asked Kent boldly and openly who he had been seeing. At first, he denied even the thought but eventually opened up and told me about a woman who had been pursuing him. But, of course, there had been no reciprocation on his behalf.

I said, "Call her!"

"You're crazy," Kent said startled.

"Call her," I repeated. "Tell her you want to take her to the Library (this was a nice supper club). Then go out and buy a huge bouquet of fresh flowers. Wear your black-and-gray suit, the one that makes you look like God's gift to women." I said smiling at him like a friend, rather than a wife. Kent reluctantly did what I asked. He made the call and spent the evening getting dressed in a slow and melancholic manner. When he was finished, I took a moment to look at him, giving him the once over. I reached up to fix Kent's collar. I was unable to control the tear that had found its way to my eye. I leaned over and gave Kent a kiss as I whispered the words "I love you" in his ear, because I really did; I loved Kent with all my heart.

I watched him get in the car that night through our living room window. I wondered how I could feel so much love for Kent but be so unattached.

As his lights grew dimmer and harder for me to see, I let the curtain close slowly and began packing for my trip.

It would be Fred, one of our long time friends, that would take me to the airport this time—not my husband, who had made this trip many times, standing by my side, no matter what I was going through. Fred drove slowly never saying a word to me other than the general complaints about the traffic. I hoped so that he would at least try to hear my side. I needed him to say what I was doing was okay, that I wasn't a terrible person and everyone understood, but he didn't. Instead, he threw my luggage and me out on the curb and drove off without so much as a hug. January 1989 would be the last year I would call Syracuse New York my home. I was twenty-seven. Within three months of moving to Brunswick with Silk, which was what he now preferred to be called, I had moved into a luxury condominium, filed for divorce, and started taking treatments at a fertility clinic. I knew the request for a divorce would hit Kent hard, but it was not my intention to hurt him. And I certainly wasn't going to tell him of my decision to have a family. But Kent received the bills from the fertility clinic; he couldn't believe that after just three months, I was planning to have a child—something I wouldn't even consider with him—and was asking for a divorce. I was torn up inside. I had no idea that the hospital would send the bills back to Syracuse! I should have changed the address on my insurance card—but it was still covered by Kent. That day the words would once again cut too deep to pull back.

I hung up, and sat there going over all the conversations Kent and I had shared about my reasons for not wanting to have kids. And how ironic it was now for me to be seeking help to conceive, because of damage that was caused by the abuse I endured as a child, with the man who may have caused it. After just a few treatments, Silk and I found out it was hopeless—the damage was severe. The doctors said it would be a simple outpatient exploratory examination, but when I awoke, I found that not only had I been admitted, but I had gone through a four-hour operation. "Irreparable damage to my left fallopian tube, with massive scarring," is what I was told when I came through. Mike had given the okay for the removal. He said the doctor explained to him that since I was already sedated it would be best—in regards to the cost factor to perform the surgery while I was already on the table. I didn't know enough to be angry back then; I didn't realize that my rights had been violated.

It should have been my decision! Everything was happening so fast. At some point, I felt sure of myself and knew what I was doing; but on the other hand, I was scared, and thought this whole thing was just one big mistake. But, I knew there was no turning back. Our relationship was out of the bag and all bridges that led to a possible retreat had been burned.

I, myself, was glad our relationship was now public knowledge; I was tired of all the stares and accusing eyes that seemed to be on me constantly. I needed to show people that our relationship was real and not just some sordid, dirty affair, so, We went shopping! What better way to make myself feel better?

Picking out the things for my new home was fun. Silk had given me carte blanch on everything, sparing no expense, so much, so that even the sales clerk at one of the furniture stores nicknamed me "Gold Finger." He said he hadn't seen a finger quite as powerful as mine, and he was right. Whatever I pointed to as we walked through the store, Silk would say, "She'll take it." We ended up with a sum of about $20,000 that day, just for starters.

The clerk was elated. He raced around the store like I was a Rockefeller—or, in my case—Rock-a-Sister. Once finished, he asked me my name and information to get the paperwork started. By the time we reached the office to complete the bill of sale, his manager had taken over, inviting us to sit while he finished the details. He drummed steadily away at his keyboard, only looking up to smile. With his last stroke, he pushed his chair back, sat up, and looked me in the eye with an 'I know you just didn't waste our time' kind of look.

So I asked, "Anything wrong, Sir?"

"No not at all. If you have at least $15,000.00 down," he replied while standing up and closing the folder he had been working on.

"Well, what about my credit? I know I have A-One credit."

"Let's see," he said as he looked back at the paperwork. "You have no job; you're new to the area. What credit?" he said smartly.

At that point, Silk, who had been wandering around, made his way back to me in the office. "Hey, what's the hold up? You know I have things to do."

"The hold up, Sir," the manager replied, "is about twenty thousand dollars. How will you be paying that?" he said and walked past us to assist someone else.

"Oh, this nigga got me fucked up," Silk said, following behind the white sales manager.

"My Nigga, didn't I say I had to go?"

"Yes, you did. And I said we need twenty thousand dollars."

Silk reached in his pouch, which to me resembled a purse, and pulled out more wads of money then I had ever seen. He placed it on the counter, looking at the manager without blinking.

As we left, I could tell that for the sales clerk, this was more than a commission. His smile showed he was genuinely happy that someone of color finally stopped the obvious disrespect his boss must have shown many of his patrons that were of color, times before. He stood proudly, holding the door for us to leave, giving Silk an under-handed slap five. I too enjoyed shutting down the manager's attempt at belittling us. This was refreshing to me and gave me a sense of importance that I hadn't felt before. I thought, So... this is what it feels like to walk in a store and demand respect. Not for who you are, but for the weight of your wallet.

That night was the start of a new era. "I-was-Mrs.-Silk,-so-you-had-better-recognize!" was the attitude I carried. Spending and buying whatever I wanted whenever I wanted. I never took the time to stop and think about where any of the money came from and Mike was determined to keep my party going, never denying me anything. You name it, we did it. There was never a dull moment.

I guess you feel I should have known, right? Well I admit I did have a notion, but I really felt that between selling the weed, and the large construction company in West Palm Beach, from which Mike picked up a paycheck monthly things balanced themselves out. He told me that that was where he worked. I knew I had never heard him mention this job before, and with it being in Palm Beach, it was obvious he never went. Yes, I say, again, it did strike me as odd, but I thought this was just another phase of my new life. Mike's arrangement was simple, he reported in periodically to pick up whatever check they had at the plant for him, and then he would give them whatever package he had for them. Afterwards, Mike and I would go to visit his parole officer, who was pleased to see Mike was doing so well, and he allowed him to remain on the streets. I was finally experiencing how people with pull had it. Normally things had to make sense to me. Not this time—nope —I wasn't making any waves. If ever there was a Willie Lump-Lump, it was me.

I think I was just a little too excited about my new-found life to care.

I had become so good at not making waves; I didn't see Mike slipping his controlling grip around my throat. Slowly he choked every ounce of the old me out, breath by breath. I had become a new person; I was covered in gold from head to toe. I had rings on every finger, and gold chains with medallions hung around my neck. I draped my body in nothing but Louis Vuitton and Gucci, which I complemented with the three-hundred-dollar hairdos from Coconut Grove that I had become accustomed to getting. I was in the big time and never questioned how. I was in love, willing to do anything for the man who was willing to do anything for me. I was loyal, always there when he needed me and not worried about anything. I knew Silk would never let anything happen to his 'Pretty Good'.

It had been about a month since I had last heard from Kent. But I was glad; I didn't want to have another scene like the last one. Plus I was still very angry at him for cashing the checks that the insurance company mailed to our address in Syracuse, checks that were intended for me to use to pay for my service at the clinic. When he finally did call, it was because he had received the papers that stated our divorce was final. He tried to convince me otherwise. I ended our conversation that night with me asking him to please forget the past and just give the future a chance, a future that, for me, didn't include him. At that, Kent's receiver went dead without another word.

I had forgotten the Number One rule of friendship: Never forget those who have truly been there for you in your past, because you will surely see them on your way back down in the future. And Kent was truly my friend.

Kent didn't call back right away, but he did eventually call, after he heard how I had managed to ruin my relationship with the friends he and I had had for years. I knew they were concerned about me, but they were constantly saying negative things about my man— things I did not want to hear and wasn't going to stand for. So I told them all, including Fred, who had taken me to the airport that day, not to call my house ever again if they could not accept Silk.

When Kent's call came, it was late in the evening. I was glad to hear from him. For some odd reason, he was on my mind just before the phone rang. This conversation was a lot different from our last. This time, I wasn't so sure about my divorce or not seeing Kent again. After all, I really did love Kent; I just couldn't feel it anymore.

Back then, I thought you had to feel love for it to be real. I identified with the many happy families I grew up with on television. They never fell out of love, and they never argued. They were always laughing as they baked cakes and cookies to share during the holidays with family and friends. Where was that life? What was wrong with us?

Kent told me why he called, he spoke of how much he loved me and how we could work through it all. I wanted so much to agree with Kent, but my mind was swirled with thoughts of all that we had said, and all that had been done. How could we ever bounce back from the hurt? How did he think we could ever possibly make it? I just lay there in the dark; my eyes filled with tears, not saying a word, afraid I may give in. Silk, who was in the living room watching TV, came in to see who I was talking to. As the light from the hallway shone into the room, I quickly wiped my face.

"Who you talking to?"

Oh, Kent, I said, thinking nothing of it. "He just called to see how I was doing."

"Yeah, well, hang up the phone."

"Huh?"

"You heard me. Hang up the phone!" He yelled as

he threw his can of drink across the room in my direction.

Startled at what had just happened, I told Kent I had to go and hung up. Mike walked back into the living room.

A few days later, my divorce became final, granting me a wish that I had made hastily in my decree, requesting to return to my maiden name. It was a mistake, and I now refused to change. I decided I would keep the name McFadden for life, which is what I had sworn just a few years before the day Kent and I got married. To me, although all else was gone, I would still have Kent's name.

For the most part, I was still pretty happy-go-lucky when it came to a lot of things. I was just a little more careful now not to anger Mike, becoming a little less aggressive and bossy, not wanting him to blow up again. It seemed the more I relinquished, the more Mike took. He began staying out later than usual and now, instead of letting me ride with him, he would leave me home alone.

One night, while I sat at home watching TV, my favorite cousin on my dad's side called. He wanted to see if I was up to a party on the beach like we did in the old days when I was new to being an island girl. I said yes, explaining that I would have to make a stop along the way and let Silk know where I was headed.

We rode the town for twenty minutes before finally seeing Silk's car, but he was nowhere to be found. I waited fifteen minutes or so to see if he would return, then left. The party was just about over when we arrived but I wasn't ready to go home. I wanted to give Silk some of his own medicine and let him be the one at the house wondering where I was. Arrie and I hung out that night until about four a.m., just laughing and talking about the old days.

When Arrie dropped me off, Mike's car was there. Even though I really hadn't had too much to drink, I wanted to exaggerate my good time. I slurred my voice a little and sang an up beat song I couldn't get out of my head from earlier that evening.

"Hey," I said, still humming my fake tune and making sure

not to plop down on the floor next to Silk as I had done for so long in the beginning. But not this time! I sat on the sofa across the room, pretending to be half-involved in what was on television, I could tell Mike was bothered right away that I hadn't sat in my usual submissive spot at his feet.

"Who'd you go out with?"

"My cousin, Arrie."

"My cousin, right, so I look stupid to you? That nigga wants to screw you and I know it."

"No, he doesn't; Arrie is my cousin!" I said with a disgusted tone in response to his suggestion. "Nigga, I'm ya cousin," Mike responded.

"That hurt! It's not the same, things are different between us. How could you say such a cruel thing like that? I would never have done anything like this if it wasn't you. Never!"

I wanted Mike to know he had hurt me, but I didn't want a confrontation, so I got up off the sofa, pretending to be just a little woozy, and in the driest tone possible said, "Goodnight."

"Goodnight? He yelled, Brang yo' ass back here! You weren't sleepy when you were out with ya fuckin' Nigga!" Mike said as he snatched me down to the floor by my arm slamming my head against his knee. He forced me to sit there as he smoked his joint and laughed at the television.

The next morning, it was I who felt guilty. I should have never tried to make him feel unloved or that I may have possibly been with someone else. Mike had already been through a lot and it was very hard for him to trust anyone. But he had trusted me right from the start and everyone knew it.

I decided never to do that again. I wanted Mike to know that he was right in trusting me and if anyone would ever hurt him, it wouldn't be his 'Pretty Good'.

Janice E. Sullivan

Chapter Eighteen
No Turning Back

———•••◆•••———

From that day on I rode with him everywhere he went, most times sitting in the car, which was parked several blocks around the corner. Mike said he didn't want me around certain friends of his because they didn't know how to respect women. So, I waited, and trusted everything he told me.

We would make several stops during the day. Mike would run in, stay about ten or fifteen minutes, then we would be off again. Our routes never seemed to change much from day to day but it was okay with me as long as we were hanging out together and everyone knew I was "Mrs. Silk."

No matter where we went, people seemed to know Mike. If we pulled up to a store, the guys outside would run over to the car and open both doors, seeking to do any favor they could.

"Good morning, Mrs. Silk. Want me to carry that for you?"

"Mrs. Silk would you like me to wash the car?" said another one.

"Mrs. Silk-this, Mrs. Silk-that." I felt like a celebrity and didn't know why.

Mike had gotten accustomed to having me with him, he became more and more lax in where he took me. Silk decided I was finally ready to ride through an area, at that time called Dixville, which was previously off-limits for me. It wasn't a very clean area and people were everywhere, hanging out chilling, with their music blasting.

As we rode through, Silk drove slow, leaning to one side trying to be extra cool. I, too, relaxed and enjoyed cruising through the small area that was like its own little town, looking around at everyone just doing their own thing. Mike had pulled off the road and parked the car in the shade just down the street. I was leaning against the door with my back towards my window, not wanting to miss any of what was going on. When all of a sudden, out of nowhere, this thing, I mean, woman—or whatever it was—appeared at the window on my side of the car. I was so frightened by her, I immediately grabbed for the knob and rolled up the window, locking the door and yelling for Silk's help.

"What is wrong with you?" Silk asked.

"Look at this person at my window!" I yelled, still holding the door.

He smiled and greeted her, "What's up?"

"You know her I questioned?"

"Yeah, that's Gina. She's good folk; roll down ya window."

"Hey, Silk," the woman said as I rolled down the window.

"Hey, my ass, Nigga. You know not to be rolling up on my car like that, and especially with my woman in the car."

"Mrs. Silk, I'm sorry. I'm sorry, Mrs. Silk. Silk, I'm sorry."

"It's okay," I said, still leaning as far away from the window as I could get.

"Get yo' ass away from the car and let 'em know I'm around the corner!" Silk yelled after her as she scurried away. "And I ain't gonna be all day!"

Mike then took me several blocks down. He got out and told me once again he would be back. I sat there for what seemed like an hour before I decided to walk back to the store I had seen on the corner to get a drink. As I got out of the car and began walking towards the store, a black car with two white men in it pulled up alongside me, riding very slowly, the one on the driver's side rolled down his window and said, "Go home. You don't know this guy and you don't belong here." Then he rolled up the window and sped off.

I didn't finish my walk nor did I say anything to Mike when he returned, because he had told me not to get out of the car. As time went by, Silk would allow me to park closer and closer to his destinations, sometimes being right there with him while he did whatever he did, always huddled over in a corner and talking with different people.

Mike had taught me to never look into the crowd, nor ever look in anyone's face, so I'd turn my back, or pretend as though there was something in my purse that I just couldn't find. I did anything to look as though I wasn't interested in what was going on. It was about this time that I figured out he was selling something other than weed, but I still had no real idea of just how dangerous a drug it was.

One night during our ride out, while Mike was gone, I heard gunshots coming from his direction. I jumped out of the car and ran towards the sound. When I arrived, I saw Silk with a gun in his hand, beating a guy across the back and head with his pistol as he knelt on his knees. The guy was bawled in a ball trying to protect himself. He kept yelling that he didn't know who she was. I walked up closer, now trying to find out myself just who the "she" Mike was all upset over was. As I got closer to the man, he started yelling, "Mrs. Silk, help me! Tell him I didn't know, Mrs. Silk! Tell 'im, Mrs. Silk, all I said to you was 'You look pretty' that day. Tell 'im, Mrs. Silk!" the guy said muffled as Silk struck him again with his gun.

As the man fell over, I realized who he was. It was Stephen—Stephen, who I had known and hung out with from the very first time I set foot back on the Island. Stephen had been one of the few that was on the bus that day my mother took us from my dad. His father and mine had been like brothers. My mind immediately flashed back to the many nights Stephen had escorted Alicia and me to our table, using his best waiter voice, letting us eat for free—knowing it would probably cost him all the tips he would earn that evening.

"Oh, my God, Mike! what have you done?" I said reaching down for Stephen.

Mike grabbed me by the back of my shirt before I could help Stephen up and shoved me away. Yelling first at Stephen, "Nigga you gone respect mine! Don't you ever approach my woman again!" Then pushing me towards the other direction. He yelled at me.

"Didn't I tell you not to get out of the car?"

I looked back briefly, catching the eye of Stephen lying on the ground, helpless; he looked up at me through blood-filled eyes. I am not sure how Mike knew I had seen Stephen that day, but somehow he knew. I went to the store alone, intending to do a little shopping, but was interrupted when I ran into Stephen. He stopped me briefly to say hi and ask how long I was in town for. Although it had been a few years since we had last seen each other, we were still very good friends. It felt good to talk to someone who wasn't a part of the life I now had.

The conversation flowed like old times, as if not a day had gone by. When we finished, Stephen gave me a hug and was on his way. Now, somehow, that brief innocent moment had turned into this. I explained to Mike frantically, hopping to calm him down.

Then, suddenly, *Whump!* a loud sound echoed as I felt the back of Mike's hand come across my face.

"You shouldn't have been in that nigga's face anyway," he said as he placed both hands back on the wheel. I grabbed my face in disbelief, crying as the blood from my nose trickled down my face. Reaching in my purse, daring not to say a word, I grabbed a few pieces of old tissue and folded it in a ball. I placed it on my nose in an attempt to catch the warm fluid running down my face. I turned over, slumping towards my window in a muffled cry, with Mike continuing on his route as though nothing had happened.

I had pretty much signed my fate regarding where things would go from that night on. Mike had lost respect for me. He wanted and expected a fight. He started making remarks about that situation. He would say things like,

"I thought you were so tough. Now what?"

I in turn ignored him, determined not to give him the fight he wanted.

He became more possessive, treating me like property. He kept me out all times of night, hanging out on street corners or sitting in some dark hole on a side street. He would make me watch as he walked up and down the block, talking to the people that stopped him. He convinced me that he needed someone he trusted to watch his back. He gave me a 9mm glock, fully equipped with bullets that were known as cop killers. As he passed it over to me he said, "There are seventeen hollow-points in this clip. You need to know that this is for your protection as well as mine." I took the gun, feeling its massiveness in my hand, hoping the day I would have to use it would never come.

I was afraid of Mike's temper. He would go off without warning at the slightest word or stare from an onlooker. I was constantly on guard for him, being careful not to speak to anyone in a certain manner. Mike would make a spectacle of any man who remotely smiled at me in an alluring way. Sometimes making them kneel in the middle of the street and apologize for looking me in my eyes. He would make them apologize over and over again as they too were struck repeatedly with his gun, I stood watching with my gun in hand, in case any one tried to challenge his decision. Sometimes, I cried myself, wishing someone would come to our rescue.

Mike appointed me my own personal driver to take me wherever I had to go. I was constantly being watched, I was afraid to talk to anyone, not knowing what would happen. I refused to go anywhere. I demanded that I be allowed to stay home where my presence couldn't bother anyone. My family saw what was happening but no one dared to say anything. I had made my bed, causing shame to everyone. Now I would have to lie in it.

I remember the many days I spent trying to explain to my girlfriend, Alicia, who still lived on the island, why I put up with Mike.

"No one understands him!" I would say. "I know Mike has a rough exterior; but he can also be the most kind and loving person you'd ever met." She just looked at me not saying a word,

231

but her expression said loud and clear that she hoped I didn't believe my own lies. I felt in my heart that Mike knew I was miserable, and he hurt because of it. He just had no idea what to do. His mood would swing back and forth, one day consoling me, the next beating me for just about anything. I knew that that one childish night when I wanted to test his love had violated his trust. Now I would have to keep paying for it.

Mike would do everything he could to cheer me up after one of his episodes that would go too far. He would host little gatherings at the house to get people to come over. I would go along with it, not wanting to incite another outburst of rage. I knew, like me, most of the invitees were there for only one of two reasons. Either they were afraid of him and wouldn't dare not show up, or he had paid them to do a service.

I had become very sad and lonely in a town that once made me happier than I'd ever been. I had to keep my worries and fears to myself—one slip of information to the wrong person could be deadly. Everyone was always looking for a point of weakness, something that would let him or her get the jump on the other man. Anyone could be bought as far as Silk was concerned, including me. Not knowing who to trust was hard for a person such as myself. I had always had a carefree spirit and although I had always been considered smart, I was actually very naive to this new world. A world where a friend could very well be the same person holding the knife in your back.

I began calling Syracuse a lot, asking Colette, who was about the only one still speaking to me, how everyone was doing. (Funny how the place you once ran from, can suddenly seem like home again.) I was glad to talk with my old girlfriend again. I knew no matter what happened or how far I went we would still be friends in some form or another. It didn't take long for my friend Marsha to take me back into her good graces either, even after I was such a jerk.

My conversations with them would always be about the joyful moments Mike and I would share, I would leave out the part of how most of them would end in abuse. Leaving both Marsha and Colette filled with envy over my new life.

Mike, in his attempt to make things right after another of his rages, suggested I have a few of my girlfriends from Syracuse come visit. He knew I was hurting, all he could say was "Pretty Good, I'm so sorry. I don't know why I get so angry. Let me make it up to you." And I did. I called Collette and Marsha and invited them down. Mike paid for everything; he took them to all the places he had taken me upon my first visit, showing them some of most expensive hotels and beaches, making their visit the time of their life. By the end of their stay Mike had convinced them that I was happier than I ever been. They envied me, and secretly I envied them, for getting the side of him that I had fallen in love with.

It was on rare occasions like this that we would have a good time, laughing and joking all night. We would hang out on the corner, in the yard of an abandoned house in Dixville, dancing and singing. Mike was very fun-loving during these times. And if you ever caught him in the right mood, he would give you the world. I would look at him during this child-like moment and realize just how misunderstood he really was. He had only known one way of life and one set of rules: Kill or be killed—which he stuck to.

If he ever was caught "slipping," as he put it, that would be the end of him.

He would sit there with his pistol in hand, leaning back quietly, watching as Gina and "Sweet" (to Dixville locals) prepared the crab boil, so everyone else could enjoy himself or herself at Mike's expense. The parties could never make up for all the hurt he put me through, but I was just glad for the brief moments when things felt like they once were.

By now, I had become accustomed to Gina and all the others who had once frightened me so much that first day that I rolled up the car window. It seemed natural now to have several people running up to the car or flagging us down. Pregnant women, kids, you name it. They were all there walking around, late night and early morning, it didn't seem to matter. All were in search of a high that I had not yet become familiar with, nor had any clue of the danger that came along with it.

I was playing a part as I had done so many times in my life before. The Lord had sent a warning to me that day in Dixville when the mysterious car pulled along side of me, and the white man, who I found out later was part of the G.B.I. unit said I shouldn't be here, warning me about Silk. I was unable to recognize it then. I didn't know the Lord's voice, but He—God, again—was looking out. I, again, had become a victim of my surroundings. I was known on the streets and playing a role with which I wasn't familiar; but, on the other hand, I had never played a role that I couldn't win an Emmy for, and this was no different.

I would ride through town, music blasting and letting the fresh air blow on my face, draped in a picture of what everyone considered happiness. My position changed, I was responsible for some of Silk's old duties, it was me now who could be seen sitting out on the hood for everyone to see, as I watched the runners do their job, making sure they reported back to me with the money and to Silk to re-up (get more drugs).

I'd watch as that black car with the deep tinted windows would ride through slowly, causing everyone to scatter. I would sit patiently on the hood of my car and look closely at the window, waiting for it to crack just slightly enough for me to see the eyes. Then it would close again as they passed me.

The car didn't make me nervous, I hadn't been in any real trouble before, and as long as I, wasn't selling drugs, I didn't believe I was doing anything wrong—correction—anything I could go to jail for.

One day, in the wee hours of the morning, a morning when no one should have been out, Mike insisted that we go. He said this was the best time for us to be out, because no one else would be. So Mike, along with two lookouts, a runner, and me, went to work.

The fog coming in off the dock was low, and you could hardly see a block away.

I was scared, sitting in that thick fog with different cars passing by. Some stopping, others slowing as if to stop, and then speeding up. There had been several jackings (slang for robberies) lately. Some guys out of Florida had gotten word of a little town off the coast of Georgia, where there was money to be made and everyone wanted some. The jackers would pull up as if to purchase, then pull out a gun and take what little a runner would have on him. In some cases, they would take the runner hostage, making him take them to his supplier where they would then rob and kill them all.

This night, I just had a bad feeling. I kept asking Mike to let's just go home.

"Please," I said, pretending to have cramps and a headache.

"In a minute," he said.

Suddenly, a whistle came that sounded like a bird. This meant there was a car approaching. The car pulled up, slowing in the middle of the street by the first runner. The window began coming down slowly, and then there was a loud yell as all four doors on the car swung open.

"Five-O! Run!" the voice yelled from the middle of the street.

"Run? Run where?" I thought, not knowing what to do.

Everyone around me took off in different directions. I took about five steps before I heard the cries for help, as some of the guys were caught. I immediately dropped flat on my stomach, lying in a field of tall grass next to a house. I tried hard not to breathe, afraid I would be found as I heard the voices of officers all around me. I continued to lie still as a ray of light circled overhead, then landed on my face. I refused to take a breath, hoping it would glide past me if I lay still enough, but it didn't. I looked up now face-to-face with the light, which was directly on me.

I couldn't see the face of the officer because of the glare from the bright light he carried. He rustled past me, shining his light in a different area and yelling to approaching officers.

"There's nothing here; the rest got away."

I could not believe it! Why? Why had the officer not turned me in? He didn't know me, nor did I know him.

I had heard some talk of an officer helping a few of the pregnant mothers, giving them a chance to get themselves cleaned up or locked up, but, he didn't owe me anything! Was the officer setting me up? I wasn't sure; I was puzzled and worried, but not enough to tell Silk. I could only imagine what would run through his mind. Especially if I said, I had no clue of who this guy was. Although, in my heart, I knew it had to be the eyes behind the tinted window—the eyes that led to a soul—that had to be graced with the mercy of God, which allowed him to run past me that night as I lay in the field breathing so hard that I thought my heart would come through my shirt.

Once again, I was shielded by God's mercy.

The next morning, the guys who were arrested were released from jail. Neither of them had anything on them, so the most they could be charged with was loitering.

Later that afternoon I found the owner of the abandoned house, and rented it. That night, it was back to business as usual.

Brunswick had become very popular amongst the drug circuit. It was new-found territory and everyone wanted a piece. More and more traffic was coming through and Mike was the man who met the demand. We made more and more trips, taking more and more risks along the dangerous 95 South highway, determined to meet the needs of the small-time dealers who purchased their weight from Mike. Weight! you ask? Well, "weight" is what I came to know as large quantities of drugs. And that drug was crack—pure cooked up cookies of cocaine, cut into small tiny pieces for distribution. This was the role of a lifetime; a role that, in most cases, only had one ending, but I was too stupid to know it.

We had been stopped several times in the last few months, sometimes losing thousands of dollars to would-be drug officers who only wanted the cash. Leaving us to have to scrabble from every end to make up the cash that didn't belong to us in the first place. Mike would always have the dealers pay him up front, then tell them where they could pick up their drugs in a day or so. They never questioned him; I assume it was because they must have felt that his being so cautious was what had kept him in the game so long. But that wasn't it. We had been stopped so many times we had lost almost all of our money and some of theirs. The only thing left to do now was flip it, and flip it fast. So we'd take all the money he could gather, head south to Daytona turn the money into drugs, cook it up, sell it at a profit, then return with what we needed for the others.

Mike was a known felon and he drew immediate attention. Officers seemed to know him by name from town to town. It became so dangerous on the highways, we began riding separately. Me, in my brand new car, which was bought with cash right off the showroom floor, and Mike in the vehicle that had become known by the DEA. I would ride casually by, looking on as the police held Mike on the side of the road waiting for the dogs and reinforcement.

I know most of you won't believe me, but I still had no clue of how serious or how dangerous this game I was playing really was. I hadn't seen crack before; therefore, I had no idea of how it could destroy a person with just one hit. I certainly couldn't have been thinking about the jail time that comes along with this type of crime or I would have never done the things that I would later do.

I was far in the mix now. Cars and guns were registered in my name. I took shooting lessons at the range in Miami. Mike wanted me to be prepared. He said I was the only one he could trust to watch his back and I did. We'd go down to Miami, where I would sit in a hotel room for most of the day. Mike would return late afternoon in time to take me to the flea market to do some shopping till about 8:30 p.m. or so. Then he'd get a call, make a brief stop, and be back on the road.

It was tiring, constant work, and I could tell it was getting to Mike. I could see through his tough guy act. I knew he prayed for that one big score that would allow him to get out. It had become too much for him and me to handle. I think that it would have been during this time that Mike met the guy who would later become his right-hand man. Mike, for whatever reason, extended his trust to this person, taking him under his wing. Doug, was also from Miami, by way of Brunswick, and had the heart of a lion. Mike took to him immediately. I had never seen him trust anyone but me so fast.

Mike would take Doug shopping, getting him the best clothes money could buy. All the time saying nothing was too good for his "Nigga." At first, I wasn't sure what to make of Doug. But after awhile I must admit, I liked him too. I thought he was cute in a rugged sort a way. This led me to making Mistake Number Two: I introduced him to my baby sister, Dedra.

It wasn't long before he had swept her off her feet, and now, my sister, who had always wanted to be like her big sister, was in the middle of a game that neither of us knew was for keeps. She too began running cash while Mike and Doug stayed out on the corner all day keeping a watch on their investment. First she, and then I: we would take turns picking up thousands of dollars, hand-counting it and putting it in stacks on the bed. I never thought I'd ever see the day when I would get tired of counting money, but I did.

Mike was doing well. He had someone working with him, with the spirit of the game, as he called it. And he was happy. He would reward his accomplice's work on a regular basis, buying fancy new cars as gifts, or giving him a few grand to do something nice for Dedra. I, too, had fallen into my role. I had a reputation of my own, having pulled a gun on several people myself. I covered Mike's back as he chastised runners, he and Doug beating them until they were barely able to walk for smoking up the merchandise.

I would sit back in a corner, watching, as Mike, who loved to drink and party, would relax. He knew that not only I, but several others, sat watching closely with guns on their sides, waiting for any sign of trouble, which, like clockwork, was sure to happen. Mike could never go anywhere or do anything without something breaking out. Because of this, I learned to watch—and watch closely. I learned to sense when it was time to go, monitoring, Mike's behavior carefully, like I had learned to do years ago with Richard.

Some nights we would make it out without a scene and other nights we'd shoot our way out. Both of our arms drawn straight, pointing at the predator, with Mike giving the command to his guys to 'kick that nigga to sleep', as he called it, rendering whomever unconscious, while daring them to fight back. Times were wild and everything seemed to be going Mike's way. He had become reckless, starting to believe in the bigger-than-life stories everyone told about him. Each trip south was like a brand new victory. Mike began to look at each day as a game. It was him against the cops.

Mike's job was to get past the roadblocks and dog searches. Doug's job was to protect him while he did so. They were terrors, modern day wise guys, to all who got in their way. No one was expendable; we each had our own part. I remember several trips where I acted as a human moneybag, covering myself in a full body stocking then stuffing it with money until every area was filled. I would make the drop at a prearranged location then head back home. This left Dedra and Doug to complete the task of seeing the drugs safely back to Brunswick.

Every time Mike was within reach of his goal, something would go wrong. Once he was forced to leave several keys of cocaine sitting in a chair at a bus terminal. The cocaine had been stashed in a huge Shamu the Whale doll. It was obvious that the officers had received a tip about possible drugs being brought back on the bus. They showed up with the drug dogs. Mike was scheduled to be on that bus. He said something, a second sense

239

maybe, had told him to wait until everyone was on before he boarded. He was like that, when he was focused. Always being extra careful about his surroundings.

Mike taking another big hit off his joint, continued to tell his story. He said just as the last person boarded, the officers walked in with the dogs, two of the officers stood at the entrance of the depot and the other two boarded the bus with the dog. Mike said he watched as the officers asked each person to identify their luggage. Mike got up that day, walking out of the bus station, leaving well over a hundred thousand dollars in street value, sitting in the chair as he walked past the officers, not looking back. He knew someone had passed the word on his trip, but he wasn't sure who.

After one or two other small incidents, he didn't trust anyone, including me. He would accuse me of plotting with some other dealers that he felt had their eye on me. Rumors were spreading about Doug wanting to run things for himself. We found out that Doug had been taking the money from Mike's scores and purchasing drugs of his own. He would put it on the streets in direct competition with Mike. They both had become too big in their own minds, each of them feeling it was himself, not his partner, who was the reason we even had an organization to run.

Their adversaries took advantage of this now-apparent riff between the two. I tried to talk to both of them, explaining that without each other, they were nothing, but together they had a chance. I begged them not to let anything come between them; they no longer trusted each other and there wasn't anything I could do. Mike insisted that Dedra ride with us on each trip. He felt that since she was now pregnant with Doug's twins, Doug wouldn't dare try anything that might land her in jail.

So now, here I am, big sister, supposed role model for a girl who believed in everything I told her, now strapping keys of cocaine around her and my unborn nephews. I never once thought of the danger. (I must take time now to thank the Lord for not letting anything happen to her during those times. For I know I could never live with myself today if she had gone to prison.)

The Lord watches over fools and children.

We made several trips that year with my putting anyone I could talk into it, in danger.

By the time I had finished, I had risked the lives of both my brothers and my sister, and had talked Marsha into moving herself and her four little kids from Syracuse to be with me, so I could have someone that I trusted around me. I felt I couldn't trust my sister anymore; she had become just as loyal to Doug as I was to Silk. I truly believed that she and he were both up to no good. I begin hearing rumors of Mike meeting other women at Dedras' house. Looking back, I imagine it must have been an odd situation to be in; I mean, he was her cousin, and they had always been cool. But I still felt betrayed.

Silk asked me to talk to Marsha about keeping his stash at her house; He promised me that nothing would ever be sold out of her home. It wasn't very hard to convince Marsha to go along with it. She liked Mike and wanted my lifestyle from her first visit. Mike made it worth her while; he paid all her bills and put $1500 in her pocket every week. Plus, he kept her fridge supplied with all the beer she could drink. Marsha and I learned how to convert keys of powder into the deadly substance called crack. Beacons of uncut crack, shaped like cookies, filled her back room, waiting to be cut into twenty-cent size pieces to be sold on the streets.

One day, at Marsha's, I, doing what I thought was calming down what looked to be a heated discussion between Doug and Silk, jumped in the middle of the conversation as both of them sat there going back and forth over whatever had taken place. Doug became frustrated with me. He told me I needed to learn my place. "You need to learn how to sit down and shut up while men are talking," referring to him and Silk. He looked at Silk and finished with, "You let her call the damn shots while I'm the fool taking all the risks!" His chest rose up and down in anger as he breathed heavily.

You see, Doug felt I had too much control and would often make little remarks to me when Silk wasn't around, knowing to never do it in his presence. He hated making drops and having to answer to me if something came up short, but he had no choice, I handled the money. That's how it was, and that's how it was going to stay. Doug felt I had made Mike soft, telling him when to pull off or cut business for the night. I had a sixth sense that Mike trusted, which, obviously, Doug didn't.

Mike leaped out of his chair with his gun pointed at Doug's head.

"Nigga, don't you ever make the mistake of talking to her that way again."

"Silk, man, come on, man. Put the gun away, we brothers man, what you doing?" Doug said realizing he'd gone too far. Silk smiling, while slowly un-cocking the trigger, said, "Man, you know I ain't wit that! Don't ever talk to her like that again!" Doug leaned over and slowly picked up his hat.

"Yeah, man, you right, my fault. Let's go, Dedra."

"Unh-uh, Dedra, you need to stay here," I said, taking the big sister role again. Dedra, who was now in her fifth month of pregnancy waddled towards the door.

"Nah, I'm gone Jan," she said as the door closed behind her.

What I had feared most had happened; there was now a rift between Doug and Silk that was irreparable.

Marsha was constantly warning me about several girls Silk was sleeping with right under my nose. She said these same people would sit in my home, pretending to visit, while they got a free high. Marsha told me that everyone was laughing at me as I made a fool of myself, thinking it was all about me. And I did—I did think that it was all about me. No way could you have made me believe that Mike would betray my love. I wouldn't listen to Marsha and even cut her off. I cut off her money and her work. She was going against Silk again and I wasn't having it.

I knew Marsha would do exactly what her whole family had

always done. She applied for welfare, then took a job that paid her in cash. She worked as a bartender in one of the clubs where she, too, would meet the man that would destroy her life. I had no idea what was going on around me. All I knew was Mike was hurting; we needed to get back on top so we could finally get out of the game for good.

I could see fear in Mike's eyes now. He had grown tired and weary. The zeal and reckless behavior he once operated in had been replaced with extreme caution. He was fearful of some of the things he had done; he believed that one of the crack-heads he had beaten in the past would come back for revenge. But there had been so many. Which one? Which one should he be watching? It troubled him day and night; he couldn't sleep and had become jumpy. And in the game, jumpy is dangerous.

I knew it was time to get out, but I didn't know how. Mike began talking of the other trades he had, but none of them would provide any type of life style. Mike refused to be one of the legends that never made it. He had pointed at the old men (affectionately called "old G's") on the corner many times himself, telling me how important they once were. Nope, that wasn't for him—he had to go on.

Doug did eventually come back to talk with Silk. He tried to explain how he was under a lot of pressure, he said he felt as if someone was trying to set him up, and if they didn't pull together, both of them would fall. Mike wasn't sure what to think but he knew the best place to have his enemy was with him. Mike and Doug began to plan things as usual, putting Marsha back in play now. Mike wanting to eliminate as much risk as possible, decided to set Marsha up with enough crack to re-up the runners; that way he nor Doug would have to be present when the runner needed more dope. Marsha and her new man were now in charge of holding the product for that day, and, if they ran out, I would drop off more as I collected the cash from the main runner. On two occasions, Marsha came up short. She said she wasn't sure who had picked her purse. But with all the traffic in and out of her house, it was bound to happen, she added, looking at Silk.

But Silk didn't want to hear it. He said I was stupid if I could believe a crack-head would only take three or four pieces of crack if a whole bag was available. I thought I must be stupid then, because I had known Marsha all my life, I had even slept in her closet when I didn't have anywhere to go as a child, so I believed her. Silk on the other hand moved his product to the house we had rented on the corner. He decided to make it livable so the guys could have a place to crash until it was time for their shift. So that meant I had work to do.

No one knew of the move but Silk, Dedra, Doug, Marsha, her new man, and me.

Mike set up shop that night for the next day's business, putting the crack in a dark green plastic bag, and then tucking it neatly in a tree trunk across the street from the house. At the time, I didn't understand why, but I also knew not to question. That morning, when we arrived at the house the guys were out back, standing over a huge barrel with tall flames coming from it, laughing and joking, ready to go to work.

"Hey, Silk, where ma stuff at, man?" said one of the guys. "These nigga's ready to do some work."

"Hold, on Nigga you gone get ya work in, but first my baby wanted to stop off and get you niggas some breakfast."

I leaned over reaching in the back seat of the car, bringing out bags of McDonald's for everyone. Silk told the guys to eat and relax for a moment while he made a run. When he got back into the car, he told me to tell them where the stash was after he was gone, not before, he said reminding me like some child.

Mike left that day as he did so often now for hours, not saying where he had been or where he was going, but I continued to do what I was told. After the guys finished eating, I told them where the stash was and went about my work, looking around the house to see what I could do to spruce the place up.

Tim was the main runner. He controlled the guys. His job was to pick who would work on any given day, making sure that each of them was clean (not high) on their shift. He was friendly and I liked him a lot. He knocked on the door not long after I had gone in.

"Mrs. Silk," he said. "I set it out but this ain't nothing. We'll be done with this in about an hour. What's up! We dry?"

"No, I don't think so, but don't worry. You just work what you got."

"Yes, Ma'am!" he said with a loud, playful voice and a huge grin, as he practically jumped off the steps running out the door.

No sooner than his feet hit the pavement, as he was crossing the street, the cars swung around the corners from every direction. The G. B. I. agents got out. They were all dressed in black. They demanded that everyone get on the ground with our hands behind our heads.

They searched through our pockets for drugs, then handcuffed us. Several other men rushed into the house.

I could tell by their faces that they were disappointed that Silk wasn't amongst their catch. There wasn't anyone left in the house and the runner who normally carried was fresh out, except for the few pieces he kept for his own habit. I was calm, acting almost cavalier, having no clue of how serious what was about to happen really was.

They lined us up against the car, directing their aggressive form of interrogation on each of us one at a time, asking questions trying to intimidate one of us into talking.

A crowd had formed and everyone one was pointing and talking. I wasn't afraid; I felt that they had nothing on me. I'd be arrested and let go. I'd seen G. B. I. swarm a crowd before and basically they were always just looking to get lucky. Hoping to catch someone small who could lead them to someone big. And that person wasn't me; I would never tell on Mike.

While the commotion was still going on and the crowds were yelling obscenities from across the street, the car with the tinted windows pulled up and parked on the side of the road. The detective that was in charge walked over to the car. He poked his head in only for a moment, and then came back to the yard.

"Pack 'em up, they're going downtown," he said.

As the officer turned us toward the wagon. The detective that had walked over to the vehicle grabbed me by the arm and pulled me back. He walked off and whispered something to the other officer, who, in turn, came back and told the other cop that the detective had said not to take me in.

"You can let her go," he said again as the officer stood beside me with puzzled look on his face. The officer, without questioning his superior shoved me around to remove my cuffs. He told me this was my lucky day.

"I'd go home if I were you" he touted, as if upset to see me leave.

I walked off just as lost about the whole thing as he was. I couldn't explain why the man in the car let me go again. I was just as thrown off as everyone else. I knew exactly how this would look, but I wasn't going to insist he take me. Would you?

I gathered up my purse and walked down the street, not knowing where I would go because Mike had my car. He also had both sets of keys. I couldn't go to Marsha's because that would be too much like jumping out of the frying pan into the fire. I took a cab to Cynt's house and sat there with her all evening, wondering where the hell Mike was while I was about to go to jail.

When Mike came, he had already heard the news. He said, two of the runners were arrested, but the others, along with Tim, were let go or given bail. Although Mike was glad to see that I hadn't gone to jail, he wanted to know why. I couldn't explain it. All I knew was the officer in charge said not me, and I was released.

Mike was mad. He said there was talk being spread about how the police could have known of his switch so soon, and my name was at the top. I looked at him as if he was crazy. Here I am doing all sorts of stupid sh@%* for his a** and he wants to accuse me. I knew how it looked, and I understood how he felt, but I couldn't explain it then and I can't explain it now.

The only thing I knew was I had had a long day and wanted to go home. Not Mike—he wanted to put his hand on what he considered a puzzle. He would not let go. He just kept going on and on about how unusual things had been lately. He insisted we stop off and have a drink to help me calm down. Hell, I wasn't upset; I knew with all my heart I hadn't done anything wrong. It was he who wanted to keep pressing a dead issue. Reluctantly, I agreed, knowing that I should go straight home.

Mike was already high off marijuana, and he had been drinking. This, for Mike, always spelled trouble. And after the day I had had the last thing I wanted was trouble. I suggested not going to the club to which we would normally go. I wanted to go to a little spot on the corner that was known for a mature crowd and never had any real trouble. Mike was reluctant but soon agreed, just wanting to get more alcohol in his system.

When we entered the club, there was a desk blocking the entrance, which meant they were charging. Whoever was working the door had stepped away, leaving the door unattended. Mike, having to use the restroom, walked off saying he would be right back while I waited on the door attendant to return. When the man working the door returned, he began hassling me about my sneakers. He made a fuss about there being a dress code on Friday nights, adding if I gave him my number, of course, he would forget that I had on sneakers.

I was tired and didn't want any confusion.

"Sir please, we just want to have a drink and then go home. Is Mr. Demp around?" (Old man Demp was the owner.) "He knows me very well and he will tell you its okay."

"Nah, Demp can't tell me nothing, little lady," he said, walking around the desk to get closer to me.

"Look, I don't think you know who I am. I'm Silk's old lady and he's in the restroom, so just stop the bullshit before he comes out, okay! I don't want to see anyone get hurt."

"Who? never heard of um, but I'm TB!" he yelled, moving back towards the desk just the same.

As he was heading back around the desk Mike came out of the restroom. The look on his face said he thought something was happening, but he wasn't sure what. I walked over to him, meeting him halfway across the floor and putting my hand on his chest. "It's Friday, and I can't get in with sneakers." I said.

"What? You dressed better than half the mother fuckers in this club," Mike said while moving my hand from his chest and walking past me to the desk.

"My Nigga, you can't let me and my girl in for a drink?"

"Nah, My Nigga, I can't," the guy at the door said, mockingly.

"Fuck this club!" Mike said grabbing my hand to leave.

"That nigga don't know, I'll buy this club and his ass will be working for me" he said speaking loudly enough for the man at the door to hear.

"Just buy ya woman some damn shoes," the man yelled, responding to Silk's comment.

Mike let go of my hand and went back towards the desk. "What'd you say?"

"Just go on, man. Come back when you properly dressed," the guy said, sensing he had gone too far.

But it was too late. Mike reached in his side and pulled out a .357 Magnum. He struck the guy right in the mouth, saying, "Nigga, that's for being in my woman's face, and this is for fucking up my night," he said, hitting him again, this time in the head.

Blood ran from his head and mouth, but the guy kept coming. He and Mike wrestled from one corner to the next. At some point the guy struck Mike with a pistol he had pulled out from behind his back, although Mike was able to slap the gun from the guy's hand. Mike also fell, dropping his gun in plain view as well. As Mike scrabbled for the gun, I ran to the corner, putting my foot on Mike's hand so I could pick it up.

With the 357 now in my hand, I pointed down at the person. I begged him, "Look, mister, we just want to leave, okay! No more trouble."

I reached down to help Mike to his feet, backing him out of the door with my gun pointed at the same time. When we got outside, there were a few people coming in. I asked them to just stand back and let us get to the car. I got in on the driver's side, still facing the crowd waiting until Mike was in.

As we pulled out, Mike punched me in the face. He claimed I must be fucking the nigga or he wouldn't have been so comfortable getting up in my face like that. I didn't try to plea with him or explain what had really happened. Mike, upset and angry, flagged down a car riding past; he jumped out, and told me to go home. I was more than glad too. I was fed up with his tough-guy act. I went home, called my brother and cousin Arrie to help me get packed, so I could get the heck away from this damn place.

By the time they reached the house my lips had swollen up so big I could barely talk. The only thing I could do was cry as they walked through the door. They knew what I wanted. We all went upstairs, grabbing handfuls of clothes off the rack, throwing them on the bed. We gathered up all my belongings and carried them downstairs. As we all stood there, with our arms full of clothes, we heard a car coming down the drive. Everyone looked at each other and ran for the stairs, trying to hang everything back up before he could park and come in.

When Silk entered the door, we were all sitting in the living room, watching TV as I held an ice pack over my face, as if everything was okay. He had Marsha and Irene a girl Marsha had befriended who was from Dixville, with him. They both just stared at me not saying a word.

Mike tossed a bag filled with money and a few pieces of crack in my lap.

"Put this up," he said, turning his attention to the men. "What you niggas doing, man? Sitting here watching TV like a ho'."

"We just stopped by man, we about to get up." They left, declining Mike's offer to ride out with him. Mike left out after they did without saying a word, leaving Marsha and Irene with me.

After Mike left, Marsha told me that he had gathered up a group of guys and went back to the club. They shot it up, she said, only to find the man who was at the door, gone.

Too much had happened that day and I had had enough. I just wanted to be gone. I lay my head back on the couch, giving Marsha the crack.

"Keep this in a safe place, Marsha. I think your friend is a smoker," I said in a low tone after Irene was out of ear shot.

Marsha took the sack, folding it up tight and put it in her bra. She had held plenty of dope before, so I knew if anything went down, she would know what to do with it. I then rolled over, balled up on the couch, and went to sleep.

I must have been asleep for about an hour before I awoke, coughing and gagging. I wasn't sure what I was choking on, but it had the whole house smelling. I tiptoed upstairs, expecting to find Marsha's crack-head friend beaming up in my house. And if so, I was going to kick her ass. Instead, I opened the bathroom door and found my best friend on her knees with the pipe stuck in her mouth. I couldn't believe it. I didn't understand how this could happen. When did this happen? Marsha on drugs? No way, I couldn't believe it!

Marsha was high, she said all sorts of ugly things about how she was sick of kissing my behind for everything. "Mrs. Silk-this, and Mrs. Silk-that. Ho, I knew you when yo' butt was homeless!" she screamed.

I closed the door and walked away. I laid back on the couch in disbelief. Mike had been right about Marsha stealing the whole time. She was hooked on the drug everyone said had no return right under my nose, and I couldn't see it.

The next morning Marsha apologized, explaining how Curt, the guy she was dating, had got her to try it one night, claiming he was too high to tell if the product was any good. You see, Curt was what the industry called a tester. Dealers would let certain junkies try the product for free to find out how good it was. If the high was good, the word could spread like wildfire in a matter of seconds.

Well, this particular night, Marsha said Curt was all burned out. He'd tried several loads, so he'd asked her to see what it was like. Although Marsha had smoked some of the best weed and snorted some traitorous white girl (cocaine), she said this was unlike any of that, and the next thing she knew she found herself hooked. Marsha's eyes filled with water, as she begin telling me how I had turned my back on her, leaving her to fend for herself after she came down here to be with me.

Her lights and water were both off, while I, the mighty "Mrs. Silk," rode by her house each day, refusing to stop because of what she said about some nigga who was using me anyway.

"Yeah, he's using you. Ask Dedra, her and the girl hang out."

"You're lying. My sister would never do that to me."

"Yeah, right," Marsha retorted. "You're so messed up, you wouldn't have believed her even if she told you."

Marsha was right—I was messed up, but now my head was on straight and I wanted out. Mike hadn't come home that night so I called him on his cell, which during those days was the size of a shoebox, so there was no saying you left it in the car.

"I want yo' sorry @#% to come and get your clothes out of my house," I screamed through the receiver.

Mike was shocked! "Oh, no this trick didn't, he exclaimed! You better not be at the house when I get there!"

I yelled, "You the trick nigga!" and hung up.

Marsha and Irene both stared at me like I had just signed my death warrant. I grabbed the money I had lying on the table and headed out the door. Marsha and Irene tried to convince me to take along some clothes but my spirit told me to move and move fast. I jumped in my car, pulled out of the driveway, being urged once again by my sixth sense to take the back way out. I drove over the curb, heading out the other side of the complex. I was nervous as heck as I drove down the highway, afraid I would run into Silk.

Once I had made it to the hotel on the outskirts of town, I called the house. Marsha was frantic. She said she didn't understand how Mike missed me. He came up the stairs two seconds after I went down. I knew it was my God in heaven who had steered me clear that day. Had I not driven behind the house over the road, I would have bumped right into Mike. He was at the light on the corner when I called him, one minute from home. Marsha said he had torn up the house looking for me, he knew there was no way I could have gotten out without coming past him. She said he took his clothes and left, but he had put five thousand dollars on the couch for me, to make sure I could take care of myself.

I told Marsha to give it back to him and I would see her in a few. I hid out for two days, waiting on things to clear. I called Cynt's to see if everything was cool. Cynt gave me Mike's message that I could come back now, he wasn't going to bother me. I still chose to wait another day or two.

When I finally decided to come out of hiding, I went to Cynt's. We sat out on her porch, talking until Silk pulled up. My heart dropped because I knew his volatile nature.

He got out with his hands up in a sign of surrender, saying he was sorry.

"You got me, okay? What kind a cool nigga rides around with his clothes in the trunk? You got all the fellows laughing at me," he said smiling happily.

And just like that, the feud was over. We went back to the house, put his clothes away, and laughed about how I dodged him.

Silk said I had had enough vacation time, now I needed to get back to work on the house in Dixville.

I hadn't forgotten all the trouble from the other night; I

begged Mike to please leave his gun home. "If all we were going to do is work on the house then why do you need a gun?" I said, pleading my case.

Mike wouldn't agree to leave his gun, but he did agree to put it under the car seat, out of the way. That was good enough for me. At least he wouldn't get drunk and shoot anyone before they could run. Once we got over to the house, it was like old times. Mike had his trunk up with the music blasting and the guys were happy to see I was back. Somehow, they knew I kept them safe from Mike's wrath.

I went to the liquor store and bought a few cases of beer and a bottle of Remy so everyone could relax as we worked on getting the house in order. I looked around figuring out what I would need to buy to bring life to the place. I asked Silk for some money and took off with Marsha, heading for Wal-Mart.

We had gotten maybe halfway across town before I realized I wasn't going to have enough money, so I turned around and headed back to the house. As I approached the Dixville area, an ambulance flew past me, headed towards the hospital with sirens blazing. The closer I got to Dixville I began to see crowds of people running through the streets, many of them trying to flag me down.

I finally stopped at Alvin who I had done business with in the past. I could barely hear what he was saying as I rolled my window down. Then it came loud and clear.

"Silk's dead," I heard him say. I tried to understand if that was what I heard.

"Silk's dead," he said again. "T. B. shot him dead, Mrs. Silk."

"Who?" I asked, now shaking like a leaf.

"T. B. That nigga out of Miami that Silk had some beef with at the club the other night. Silk didn't have a chance Mrs. Silk. He—didn't—have—his—gun—on—him— and that nigga unloaded on him. Silk tried to run but he shot him in the leg."

Everything was coming out in a blur. I couldn't hear him any longer, but his lips kept moving. The only thing I heard was he didn't have his gun on him.

"Oh, God it's my fault," I yelled as I wheeled the car around and headed for the hospital. Knowing Silk and I both had forgotten his gun was under my car seat.

When I got to the hospital, the emergency room was filled with everyone and their momma. Silk had made a lot of enemies but he had made a lot of friends too, and they were all there. They were running around screaming and yelling as if they themselves had lost someone. There was one girl in particular who was so upset she couldn't stop throwing up. I tried to console her, getting wet paper towels to help cool her down. I thought that would make her feel better as I, too, stood in the restroom sobbing and hiding from everyone; while I waited anxiously on the doctors to come out. The young woman finally pulled herself together and left the bathroom.

Marsha smiled one of her what-a-joke smiles and said how touching it was to see both Mrs. Silks getting along so well.

I spun around as if to go after the girl who had just left, but Marsha grabbed my arm, pushing me back against the wall and pinning me down.

"Now isn't the time," she said. "You just lost your man and every drug dealer out there is waiting for you to fall weak."

She was right. I gathered myself and went back to the waiting area. I sat calmly, watching for the door to the back room to come open.

An hour or two later the doctor came out asking for Silk's wife. I stood up, walking slowly towards the doctor. "Is he—?" I stammered, trying to remain calm.

"No," said the doctor, "but he's not going to make it. If you'd like to come in you may do so now."

As I walked towards the bed, I was so startled by what I saw, I fell to the floor. The doctors and nurses rushed over to me. I came through only to collapse again, this time letting out a yell as I headed back towards the floor.

The two male nurses were bracing me on my feet when Mike, without warning, sat straight up in the bed.

"Get her out of here, she can't stand blood," he said, before collapsing himself.

Apparently the nurses were just as startled as I because they let me drop to the floor and rushed over to Mike's side, whisking him away for surgery. Mike made it through that night. It was unbelievable because he had been shot twice in the leg, twice in the back, once in the chest and head as he tried to hide under a truck. He was crawling away from the gunfire and pleading for his life while T. B., in plain view, kneeled down and aimed under the truck. He fired shot after shot until his gun, the same gun I had left on the floor that night in the club, was empty.

Witnesses said he then walked calmly back to his car and drove himself to the police station and turned himself in. The police officers that came to the hospital the next day advised me not to let anyone know that Mike had made it. They thought it would be in his best interest if I didn't announce his miraculous recovery. They feared that other drug dealers, who may want him out of the way, would suddenly flood the city causing more havoc than they were prepared for at this stage.

The last thing they said was for me not to go home for a few days, just to make sure no one was staking my house out. I was a nervous wreck and afraid for my life. After all, it was I who had held T. B. at gunpoint that night, and now, after all this, the police let him go. They claimed since no one had pressed any charges and they didn't have a weapon, nor witnesses willing to come forward, they had no case. The man went in to turn himself in and they refused to arrest him.

I was jumpy, scared even of my own footsteps. People were saying all sorts of things. Some claimed I was having an affair with T. B. and had set Mike up. I tried to make sense of him being shot down on the very same day I convinced him not to carry his gun. I, in turn, would ask: Where were all the henchmen we paid good money to watch his back? Everyone had an excuse.

Doug claimed he ran across the field to get his gun while others claimed to have been pulling up as T. B. drove off.

All I knew was Mike was lying in intensive care, almost dead. And had I not left when I did, or come back just a few seconds earlier, I, too, would have been lying on the streets that day. I am sure of it, because I was committed to my role, even if it meant playing it to the death. I shuddered every time I thought about what happened that day, replaying it over and over in my mind, never thinking to thank God that I had left.

Word doesn't take long to get around in a small town. Before morning, the news was out that Silk wasn't dead. The hospital switchboard was overwhelmed with people calling in and asking for information on where Silk was being kept. The one good thing about Silk being in intensive care was it gave me say over who would could visit and who could not.

It took three days before he could open his eyes. During that time, so many questions raced through my mind, I wasn't sure what I should do. Did I owe it to him to be faithful or would I be justified in leaving him right there in the hospital? Who could blame me? Especially after the way he cheated and made an obvious fool of me for everyone to see. I wasn't sure what to do but when he finally awoke, I was right there, standing in his face and waiting for him to answer my questions.

"Mike!" I yelled, "Who was that girl in the emergency room? I know your not cheating on me. Tell me the truth. You can blink your eye or something, but I need to know the truth."

Mike's eyes widened as I pressed on, demanding answers. His alarm went off but I was still looking at him, determined to know, as the doctors rushed in and pushed me out.

"Ma'am," the doctor said when it was over.

"He is still very much in danger. He needs his rest and for God's sake, don't upset him."

"I won't, I'm sorry. I just wanted to talk to him."

"Why don't you go downstairs and get something to eat while

we get him settled down?"

"Okay," I said looking back at Mike angry that he hadn't given me what I wanted.

When I reached the cafeteria whom should I run into but the same chick that couldn't stop throwing up the night Mike was shot. I sat down, not even in the mood to confront her.

Instead, she had the nerve to walk over to me all humble.

"Excuse me."

"Yeah," I answered.

"You're Silk's wife, right?"

"Yes."

"Thanks for the other night—"

"Yeah," I said curtly, cutting her off.

"Well I just wanted to know if he was alright."

"He's fine."

"Look," she said, "I know people are talking and you probably don't know what to believe. I understand, okay, but I knew Silk before you came to town. I'm the one who introduced him around town and we became good friends, sort of in the same business, if you know what I mean. But unfortunately, people just have to have something to talk about. My old man is 'Dollar Bill' and he's not trying to hear it, so I suggest you don't either. I'd like to see Silk if that's okay with you," she said without batting an eye.

I looked at her, wishing she had said one thing to push me over the edge but she hadn't. In fact, I knew 'Dollar Bill'. He was a small-time, wannabe dealer, who didn't have the guts to take it to the next level when things got sticky. She was so convincing, I took her number and told her if Silk was feeling better I'd let her come up for a few minutes.

Later that night, I told Silk of my meeting with Terry. This time he didn't get upset. Instead, he indulged my prying questions as he lay there with tubes in almost every part of his body, blinking his eyes once for yes, twice for no, declaring he had nothing to do with that girl.

The next day, I gave Terry a call, inviting her to the hospital to spend a short visit with Mike. When she arrived, I left the room, confident that Mike would never betray my trust. Certainly not on his deathbed, I thought as I brushed by Terry, giving Mike's hand a squeeze, no longer feeling insecure.

It took three weeks before Mike was out of intensive care. He was concerned for his life and knew there would be all kinds of would be dealers or hit men wanting to take him out while he was down. He was able to talk now that the tubes were out of his throat and he quickly began giving orders. The first thing he wanted was all of his money brought to the hospital where he was. He knew it wouldn't be long before someone would try and jack me, if they thought I may have money on me since I, of course, continued to run the business just as he had.

I prepared, cut, and weighed it, just as he had taught me. I kept track of every dime while Doug, who now felt guilty for running, made all the pickups. I did what Silk asked me and brought everything he needed to the hospital, including his arsenal. T. B. was still walking around and Silk knew in the game, if a nigga missed either, he would definitely be back, or he would never have a moment's rest worrying about his own life, constantly watching his back, afraid the man he missed, wouldn't.

More rumors surfaced as the news of Silk's recovery continued to spread. The new word was I had set Silk up after I found out about him and Terry. I kept getting the same question over and over again:

"Why had I told Silk not to carry his gun?"

"I don't know," I said. "I guess I was just sick of all the violence."

"He would have never left his weapon! He would have never done it." My aunt screamed, now so upset, she looked as if she was getting ill.

"For one, I already done told you I don't even know a T. B., so you can stop telling people you got word from the bottom [Miami] that he was my man," I said yelling back at her, not believing she could even say such a thing. "And two, did you ever think that I may have saved Mike's life? If he had had his gun, his foolish pride would have had him standing in the middle of the street like some cowboy, shooting at a man who wanted nothing more than to see him dead. My foul-up probably saved your son's life." I listened to myself speak, not knowing whether I was trying to convince me or her, as I slammed the door on my way out. I knew my aunt was upset; Mike was her only child, but that didn't give her the right to blame me.

I headed back to the hospital.

I walked in Mike's room, not sure what to say or how to act. I looked at him lying there flat on his back in pain, unable to move. I gazed at him through tear-filled eyes, remembering that night at the hospital as I walked back to pay my last respects. There had been so much blood in the room that night. Mike's body had swollen up at least ten times its normal size. I had never seen the effects of a gunshot wound before, so I wasn't prepared for what I saw. I smiled to myself as I remembered how protective he was that night. Mike was amazing. After all he had been through, he still jumped up from his deathbed to my rescue, as he had all my life. How could he think, I, who had loved him from a small child, would ever wish him harm? I stood there silently crying, knowing that there were no words that could remotely take away the pain he must be going through, both mentally and physically, as he tried to figure out fact from fiction. That night I decided to stay with him at the hospital. I didn't want to go back to the house alone. I needed to be near him.

I had the nurse bring in a few blankets, letting her know of my plans to stay. After she left the room and completed her last visit, I climbed into bed with Mike, lying on my side, just needing to be near him. As we slept, a bright light which shone through the curtain that had been pulled around the bed, awakened me. The light was coming from the hallway. Through the silhouette, I could see a male, about 5'9", and in his hand appeared to be a small object.

I yelled, "Who you looking for?"

The man took off. I jumped to my feet, grabbing my gun and running down the hall, looking for the hit man who seemed to have just disappeared into thin air. When I got back to the room, Mike was awake. He knew what had happened. He claimed he was lying there quietly, being squashed by me but not complaining.

I looked at him.

"Mike, I had nothing to do with T. B. I don't know why I had a feeling about the gun that day, but I did." I was rattling on, trying to get everything out in one breath.

"I know. I know," Mike said. "They want to make you out of the snake that they would be. They have no other way to bring you down. In many ways, you are naive and I can't afford for you to be naive." He paused for a moment, and then changed the subject.

"This is what I need you to do. I need two bodyguards I can trust, someone who can't be bought. Offer them $10,000 each and I want one with you and one to be here at the hospital with me."

I had just the right person in mind. My cousin, who had not too long ago gotten out of prison himself for killing one of our friends—I knew he couldn't be bought. I ran around that day, completing several errands for Mike, some that even took me back to that horrible spot where this nightmare had all begun.

Driving through Dixville reminded me that I had not heard from Marsha, my dear friend who had moved south looking for a way out, but instead had become trapped. As I pulled up, Marsha was sitting on the porch, rocking back and forth with a 40-oz. in her hand. I could tell she was high. I couldn't believe I hadn't seen it before. Marsha started crying the minute I stepped out of the car. I thought, "Aw, hell, I don't need this right now." I wished I could get back in the car and pull off without the drama.

"They got my kids, they got my kids!"

"Who has your kids? Marsha, what are you talking about?"

I said dryly.

"DFACS! DFACS took my babies!"

"Oh my God Marsha, what have you done?"

"Me? What do you mean, "What have I done"? You the one left us out to dry. We don't have any money, my lights and gas are out, and one of these stinking 'hoes turned me in, talking about an unfit environment." Marsha was yelling at the top of her lungs and people congregated on the corner.

"When did this happen? When do you go to court? Can you get them back?" I bombarded her with questions, never listening for an answer.

This was all too much for me. I wasn't sure how much more I could take. I had destroyed the lives of the people I loved, was in love with the man who raped me as a child, abandoned my husband, sold drugs to a mother-to-be, got myself in the middle of a death sentence, and had finally cost my friend her kids. I just wanted this whole thing to stop. I got in my car and drove off, leaving Marsha standing there yelling obscenities at me, her closest friend.

Next, I needed to find a place to hide out until Silk could get back on his feet. I rented a hotel room for us and the bodyguards, getting them rooms on either side of ours, ensuring our security.

I nursed Silk back to health, putting bandages on his wounds three times daily. I fed him, bathed him, and wiped him up after he defecated. I did anything I could to reestablish the obvious gap that had drifted between us.

Within a few weeks Silk was up and around on his crutches. Resuming his habit of taking long undercover drives through town, always with dummy cars leading the way. I, of course, was confined to the hotel with my cousin's girlfriend, who was the same girl I caught smoking crack in my home that night with Marsha. She had been brought in to keep me company.

Irene was plenty company for me, as far as I was concerned. She suffered from all sorts of emotional issues but she was nice to talk to. We sort of became confidantes and, of course, I tried to convince her that she didn't have to live like she did, constantly being beaten and always having swollen eyes and huge bruises all over her body. I guess she thought, who was I to talk? I could fool myself all I wanted in my own mind, but everyone knew, except for drugs, I was no different from her.

Irene confided in me one day about the long trips Silk would take while I sat in that small, dingy room with only her to entertain me. She told me Silk had been spending his days with Terry. Irene had gone on many trips to drop him off, taking food and alcohol to make sure they would have no need to leave once dropped off. I couldn't believe my ears. After everything I had done! I'd wipe this nigga's butt and no sooner than he could get up on his feet, he hobbled over to this ho's house.

I was furious. I couldn't wait for him to hop his butt back through the door. I was mad as hell, and intended to make everything I knew known, even though Irene had begged me not to tell. I couldn't help it, I was in a rage, I never took a moment to stop and think about what may happen to Irene.

When Silk entered, I immediately started yelling and swinging on him, thinking his ability to retaliate would be a mere drop in the bucket compared to what I would do to him. I underestimated Silk's ability to defend himself. And when it was all over, it was me who fell to the bed with my arms drawn up towards my face, attempting to ward off the blows that were still coming. I tried desperately to protect myself from Silk as he swung, viciously beating me with his crutches and bruising my legs and arms.

I lay across the bed, sobbing like a child. Not sure if I was hurting from the abuse, or the act of betrayal that I had found out about. Silk apologized, but that wasn't good enough; I needed to know why. Why would he do me like this? How could he lie on his deathbed, knowing what I felt and how much he meant to me.

His defense was sex and blow jobs. "All men want a freak," he said. He claimed he would never ask me to do anything I wasn't comfortable with. I wanted to yell, "You're the reason I'm screwed up and can't sexually relate to anyone!" but I didn't.

Instead, I admitted I wasn't the most open person when it came to sex, but I was willing to try. In addition, try I did. I spent the rest of the night proving I was just as much of a freak as she was, thinking it would keep him home.

The next morning when Silk got up, he wasn't any more in love with me than he had been before my little one-night freak show. In fact the only thing that really had happened was, I had succeeded again in giving up a part of me that was never intended to be given away in that manner. I watched Silk and his bodyguard drive off, making sure they were out of eyesight, and then, I went next door to talk with Irene. She refused to open the door.

"Go away" she said in a muffled voice. "I have to stay in my room and can't talk to anyone."

I could tell she had been crying, so I pleaded with her to open the door.

After about twenty minutes of begging, she finally opened the door. My mouth fell to the floor. Irene was hideous. Her eyes had closed so tight, she could barely see. At least four of her front teeth were missing from between her deformed, blood-bruised lips. She was covered in black and blue marks. She could barely talk, only motioning helplessly with tears rolling down her face. I couldn't bear to stay in the room with her, knowing this was my fault. I apologized and went back to my room to figure out where my life was heading and why I was allowing it.

* * *

Letting someone strike you once means you've just given them the okay to do it again.

Janice E. Sullivan

Chapter Nineteen
Which Way is Out?

From that day on I knew it would only be a matter of time before I'd have to make some serious decisions myself. Was Mike worth fighting for? Was I willing to continue being abused? These were hard questions, but they were questions I would need to answer if I didn't want to end up like Irene.

I tried to give him credit for at least having taken care of Marsha by making sure she had whatever she needed, and pulling some strings to get her a hearing for her kids.

But just the same, he was back up to his old tricks. Mike had been gone for the better part of the day. He wasn't returning any of my pages, nor had he sent anyone by with food for Irene and me. Mike had already said no deliveries and no walking around outside, so what did he expect us to do? I called Marsha:

"Hey girl, what you doing?" I said trying to act casual, knowing she was still mad at me.

"I'm watching television, why?" she said, knowing I obviously needed a favor.

"I've been paging Silk and Doug, but neither seems to answer, can you walk to the corner to see if they're out there for me?"

"Hell no, I can't walk to the corner and see if their out there for you!" Marsha was a lot more upset than I thought she would be. Considering all we had been through, I felt she, if anyone, would give me a break. Instead Marsha dug in deeper.

"Oh, so you can't at least look out your door? I said, upset at her attitude.

"No!," Marsha said, "I'm not going to look for Silk, I'm not going to call Silk, and, if he was standing at my door, I wouldn't let the nigga use my phone."

Marsha was high—I could tell by the way that she was talking, as she began talking to someone in the background.

"Can you believe this ho'? Look Mrs. Silk," Marsha said mockingly, "Because you my girl, and we go back, I guess it would be better if I told yo' dumb ass, and not someone else. Yeah, Silk was out here! Him and Terry just left, as they have every other day, with her riding around in your car like it ain't nothing."

"Oh, hell nah!" I yelled. He has me sitting in this dingy hotel, talking about for my safety, while he is gallivanting around town with some trick!

"Yep!" Marsha said, before slamming the receiver down.

I was furious, I got up got dressed and took a cab to our other car. I put my 9mm in my purse. I wasn't thinking clearly; I had had enough. I rode around town for a couple of hours hoping to run into Silk and Terry, checking any place I thought they would go. I got tired of driving so I decided to buy myself some food and liquor and just wait. I parked in an area near Terry's house, so I could see them when and if they came in. It made me so angry to think about how she played me in the hospital cafeteria that day. And me, how stupid am I for believing her? It made me sick to think of Silk and his lover. I spent the night outside her home waiting and holding my gun in my hand vowing to shoot the first one that appeared. Neither of them showed that night, and in hindsight, I am glad. It was just after daybreak when I left that morning. I had been up all night. Fatigued and distorted I drove slowly, trying to comprehend once again, why me?

When I got back to the hotel, I could see Silk hadn't been there either. He had stayed out all night. I was in a rage, my heart was filled with the pain of his betrayal. I gathered up Silk's clothes, driving back to Terry's house, I threw them all over her lawn. Although they never came to the door, I knew they were there.

I drove off that day determined once again to get away from everything that remotely had anything to do with drugs or Silk. I went back to my family, who were still sitting around drinking and talking all day as if nothing else existed in the world. We did get Marsha's kids back and the first thing I did was to put her back on a bus to New York. I couldn't sit by and watch Marsha self-destruct. Now filled with shame, I eased my way back into a comfortable environment at my brother's house. No one said a word to me about anything. And I thank them for being so kind.

Silk didn't come after me, and I didn't go anywhere I might see him. It was going on three weeks and still not a word, then one day out of the blue, Mike pulled up, saying he took off so he could clear his head. He said we needed to talk. He opened the car door for me to get in.

It would be on this very same day that T. B. would be gunned down while sitting under a tree at the corner store. He was shot with the same type of gun that was used to shoot Silk just a short time ago. No one was ever charged with the killing. Some say it was a hit man. According to an eyewitness, a masked man walked up and put the gun to his head, shooting twice before he ran off, jumping into a parked car around the corner.

It was odd to me that the very same day Silk would insist I accompany him on a shopping trip to Jacksonville, Florida, where, by co-incidence, I had been casually coaxed into tipping the cashier a crisp new one hundred dollar bill. After a few more stops to nowhere we returned home, never having the conversation Silk had implied we needed to have.

To my surprise there was a card from a detective tucked neatly in the door with a note on the back, the note requested that I come down to the station. Silk encouraged—no, he insisted— that I go immediately. He wanted the detectives to know I had nothing to hide.

When I got to the station, the detectives took turns tossing questions out at me about my supposed affiliation with T. B. and the beef that they knew existed between Silk and he. I answered their questions, acknowledging nothing of an affiliation or beef, stating I was sorry to hear about what had happened to T. B., and that we, meaning Silk and myself, had been out of town and could prove it. I was sure the cashier would remember us and my receipts showed the time and date of purchase.

Just as I finished my sentence the thought came to me just how convenient an alibi I had. I left that day, keeping my assumptions to myself, feeling more afraid for my life now than I had ever felt.

I knew that T. B. was just as connected as Silk and the game had just been taken up a notch. I became paranoid, afraid of everyone, not sure when someone could walk up from the crowd and blow my head off out of revenge for the man they hated. I started having panic attacks. I thought for sure someone was out to kill me but I didn't know who. I was afraid to eat anything I hadn't prepared for myself, fearing I could be poisoned. I couldn't even bring myself to accept food or drink from anyone, including family, afraid that they, too, may have been bought.

We were mid-way through the summer of 1992., and my panic attacks had become so real and so severe, that I thought I was losing my mind. I had seen so much, I wasn't sure what was real and what was not.

Some days I would find myself sitting at a traffic light, too scared to move, wondering if the light was green or if I just thought it was. I'd look around again, and be struck with another thought: "What if I'm really outside of the car, wandering around, crazy and out of my mind but I don't know it."

I'd turn the radio up, blasting the music trying to focus on the song, following each word, knowing that if I could recall each chorus, then I must not be crazy. It helped for a short time, but my condition got worse. This fear, this horrific fear that struck me every time I would step foot out of my house, had won. It took away my ability to drive altogether because I was afraid I would one day hurt someone. I only felt safe when I was tucked away inside my home. There was a constant battle going on inside of me. Mealtime was the worst: I had become reluctant to even eat the foods I got from the store. I would suffer attacks right after consumption. I was afraid it might have been poisoned by some other person just out for laughs. For the first time I saw the world and the people in it as the real monsters they were. And it scared me.

Losing my mind had been my worst fear ever since I wandered the streets as a teenager.

One year, when I was maybe thirteen or so, I saw a young man, who had worked for years as the neighborhood barber, lose his mind after his mother was killed in a tragic accident. It took a horrible toll on him, slowly fading him from society. He had always been well-groomed and very handsome. When he resurfaced years later he was wandering around helpless, reborn to the streets as a homeless bum. His clothes were all ragged and torn, his hair had grown out and was matted with who-knows-what. He grunted and mumbled as the kids teased him, following him as far as they were allowed to go. Maybe they didn't remember him, but I did. He had always been nice to everyone, and here he was with no one. This was an image that stayed tucked away in my mind for many years. I always wondered what could happen that was so severe it would cause you to lose your mind. With all that I had been through, I wondered if my mind had had enough. That image of the young man was resurfacing now, and it created a fear that I wasn't sure I could beat.

I kept my challenges to myself, trying to endure the best I could. I kept telling myself: "You have to function. Ignore it, ignore it," I'd repeat in my head, trying to overcome the feeling that I was losing control.

One evening, Silk called, asking if we could take a ride so we could talk. I told him no, realizing he was a big part of what I was going through. I told him I would be glad to sit and talk, but I wasn't interested in going anywhere with him. He showed up at my door angry, defiant and making his usual threats. But what he didn't know was that my panic attacks had become so big and so real, that the fear it imposed on me was far greater than anything he could ever bring.

Silk sat anxiously, telling me how he was giving serious thought to leaving and taking me with him. He had grown tired of the game, believing he had lost his edge. This was hard to say for a man who at one time in his life didn't know what fear was; he had always been ready to pay the consequences, even if one of those consequences was his life. Not anymore! He was afraid, not knowing who, if anyone, he could trust. I didn't tell Silk, but I knew in my heart, I was not interested. I was through, done, out of there as soon as I could pull it together.

Silk's phone went off as he sat, talking about all his new plans. It was his mother and she wanted him to bring some food by her house. She claimed she hadn't eaten all day and was feeling weak. This, of course, concerned Silk. He asked that I ride with him. Although I didn't want to, I reluctantly got in the car.

It was already well after dusk and would have been close to 10:00 p.m. by the time we picked up the food to head her way. I was already starting to feel a little jumpy, and I just wanted to be in my home, tucked safely away. The streets were crowded. People were hanging out, getting geared up for the night, which usually meant trouble of which I wanted no part. As we passed a well-known housing area which Mike frequented on his late night drives as part of his route, I felt the urge to duck. I knew a stray bullet, meant for him, could just as easily hit me.

Once we were past the crowd, I felt a little better. Then came the whistle: a familiar sound that I had heard oh, too often. We looked back to see one of the guys Silk had considered a brother standing in the middle of the street trying to flag him down.

"Keep going," I said. "Let's just keep going."

But Mike ignored me. "It will only take a minute."

He parked his car along the curb and walked into the shadowy center of the field, where his so-called brother had disappeared. Within seconds, sirens were ringing from everywhere. GBI agents pulled up, coming to a screeching halt, causing dust to fly as they parked. They blocked both entrances to the area, driving right through the rows of the buildings.

Detectives rushed out into the crowd, emerging with Silk. They had handcuffed his hands behind his back. He was being pushed and spun around like a trophy. The charge was possession with intent to distribute. An officer held a small plastic bag, which contained two or three pieces of crack cocaine, high over his head. He waved it, as if to signify that this time, they had him. The officer claimed to have seen Silk toss it while being more than twenty-five feet away from him in the dark.

Silk tried desperately to explain that he had just stopped off for a moment and was on his way to his mother's with dinner. He pointed at the back seat window of his car, the seats were filled with bags of restaurant food, still hot with the receipts displaying the time of purchase, but the officers had no interest in his story. To them, they had caught the big one, and their pleasure showed on their faces.

Silk had made his decision to leave this town too little, too late. He had always told me that he could never get caught slipping, as he called it, in Brunswick because he knew once they got him, they would never let him out.

Once they had Silk, they started to work on the rest of us, confiscating cars and possessions alike. They threatened me with money-laundering charges, amongst other things. Everything purchased had come through me. I received phone calls from family members and then-friends who had possessions purchased in my name that were now being taken back.

My sister called, stranded alongside the road with her laundry and kids. The car was confiscated while she was at a traffic light by AFT or the GBI agents, I wasn't sure which. My little house of cards was falling down. I was now back in Silk's life because of loyalty and necessity only. Once again, he needed me, and although I wanted out, I could not let him face this newest drama by himself. My entire life had been a soapbox and this was just another role I had to play.

Silk would need someone he trusted to stay on top of his lawyers and make sure they did the job they were paid to do. He was no fool; he had seen many a lawyer make the DA's case for them. He would also need someone to run errands if he was going to be prepared for the case he felt he could win. He was more than aware of the fact that the detectives planned to put him away for good.

The other two charges, which they had not pursued up until this point, occurred the summer before, and were now on his list of alleged crimes. The first was possession of a weapon by a convicted felon. "Piece of cake," Mike said, explaining to me how, because the gun was registered to me and found in the glove compartment of a car that I owned, they couldn't possibly pin that on him. Silk knew I would gladly swear he had no knowledge of the gun when I let him drive off that afternoon, forgetting myself that the it was in the car.

The second charge was also a possessions charge. This charge would take a little work, but Silk had a plan, since the gun was found this time in a leather, purse-like bag that a lot of the guys carried back then. Silk's plan was to get the person who was with him that day in the mall, to say the bag was his, admitting he had carelessly placed the bag down next to Silk for a brief moment, while he looked at some shoes, just a few feet away. I did what Silk asked; I talked until I was blue in the face, trying to convince my uncle Dutch to take the blame for the charge. He refused, so then, left with no choice, I did the unthinkable: I blackmailed my uncle with the threat of exposing his past life as a child molester. I told him of all the horrible nights that still plagued my memories, of how he forced himself on me, his niece, helpless and too young to defend myself. He shamefully agreed to take the rap. He held his head down as he walked away, but not once did he say he was sorry or try to explain.

I felt no remorse for what I had just done, all I knew was that Mike, not Silk, was in trouble and needed my help.

Silk expressed no concern over the third charge, stating that, based on the facts, he would never be found guilty of intent to distribute cocaine. The package found that night was twenty-five feet or more away from him, he said it was virtually impossible for him to have tossed a bag that was less than a half an ounce that distance. More importantly, he continued, there weren't any prints on the bag, so they couldn't prove possession. Not only that, he offered further, the officer who claimed to have seen the toss was driving and he would have to prove that, while driving through all the dust and maneuvering through all the people out that night, he could see Silk clearly. Mike was on a natural high; he felt things were going his way again.

When we received the police report, we found that the man the officer described in his arrest notes, had on long pants with a light colored shirt. This, according to the description would have been Mike's play brother, and not Mike. He was elated. Mike was more confident about his situation. He relaxed, making a mockery of the officers who wanted to see him sweat every chance he got. He had me put money on the books for several inmates. He took care of everyone, making the jail his own. He had the phone all day long, as he needed it, forcing me to sit by my own phone in case he called.

He would question me about my whereabouts if I missed one call. He was still flamboyant and as intimidating as ever, convincing everyone that he would get out. For my birthday, he asked me to drive by the jail where, to my surprise, he had all the other inmates standing in front of the windows. Each held up huge black letter, stretched out across the building that spelled, "HAPPY BIRTHDAY!" He stood smiling and waving his hand so I could see him. It was amazing how he could be so thoughtful and loving and within seconds be so deadly.

Although I was still impressed by Mike, I was only doing what I thought I had to. I, like many others, was afraid he would soon get out.

Months began to pass, but Mike insisted that the officers

were only prolonging his case because they knew they didn't have one. They moved him to another location, raising Mike's suspicions, knowing that even the "Po-Po" (police) could play dirty. He insisted that I not visit him until he could make sure it would be safe.

After a couple of weeks, Mike called. He asked me to come up to the jail on Saturday. Playfully, he insisted I wear a dress or skirt because he needed a little affection. I knew what Mike meant. I had often heard the girlfriends of other inmates talk about how they would go to their visits without any underwear. So, while the guard was out of the room, they could sit on the inmates' lap, allowing them to slip their penis inside, pretending nothing was going on. I had even known girls who claimed that they had actually conceived their babies while the father was locked up.

I'm sure the guards knew what was going. But they would turn their heads, most of them brought their own drugs from the very men they were locking up, so it was the 'one-favor-deserves-another' kind of setup. I was nervous about Mike's request, especially since I no longer carried the feelings I once had for him. But, I did it! I went down to a jail with no underwear on, with the intention of spreading my legs in an open area of a public place, because I feared what would happen if I didn't, and Mike beat his case. He wasn't the forgiving type, and he would look at my not doing it as betrayal: turning my back on him when he needed me is what he would say. I knew Mike would rather protect me than hurt me any day, but I also knew what he could be like when he was angry.

When I got to the prison, Mike had already assumed his position as one of the more important prisoners. The guards gave him liberties that other inmates didn't seem to have. We were put in a room by ourselves; there were no other visitors as far as I could tell, which opened up even more of an opportunity for Mike's plan to happen. We talked briefly about nothing really, just going through the motions, I guess, until it was time. Mike, deciding we'd had enough small talk, reached out for me to hug him. He placed his hands around my waist, pulling me into his lap as he gave me a kiss.

Even his kiss felt empty; it held no meaning for me as I tried to remove myself from the situation, thinking of a different place and happier time. So I could fulfill what I thought was an obligation. I opened my legs wide and slid up on Mike's lap. He slid his hand under my dress, rubbing his hands against my thighs and pubic area, attempting to put me in the mood, but it didn't work. I was too wound-up and appalled at even the thought of what he had asked me to do. Mike became angry and tried to force his manhood inside me, but he was as soft as I'd ever seen him. I rocked back and forth on his deflated manhood trying my hardest to satisfy his wishes.

He pushed me up and called to the guard. He asked if we could be allowed to go to his cell, which I thought would never happen. But the guard agreed I couldn't believe it! Here we were, in a federal jail, being escorted back to a cell, for what, I'm sure, the guard knew was a conjugal visit. Mike walked back to the cell, holding his crotch in a braggadocios manner.

I continued back to the cell with everything in me saying, "No." Lucky for me, an officer from another division showed up that day and ruined our little rendezvous. I would not understand what a divine intervention his showing up was until later.

That day, after I left the jail, I knew it was over. No more visits, no more $1,500.00 phone bills to feed his insecurities. Mike must have felt the same way, because after that his calls stopped coming and so did the letters.

I went about my life, trying to salvage everything I could of who I once was, trying to pretend the past three years had never happened. I prayed that some crazed family member from Mike's previously-slain rival wouldn't come after me.

I went to work full-time at Popeye's Chicken. I'd sit in the window of the drive-through and think how it was I, not Mike, that was now living the life of the ole' G's who didn't make it. Brunswick was a small town; most people knew how I once lived compared to how I was living now. I had to sell off most of Mike's things just so I could make it. The guys who were still in the game meant well, leaving open the offer to buy back any of Mike's equipment or jewelry when I got back on my feet. I know everyone thought I should have been embarrassed but I wasn't. I was glad. I knew if I wanted to stay in the game, I could have easily made myself available, but for me, anything other than Mike would have been a step down. So instead, I fought the good fight, taking whatever job that came, doing the best I could. I don't have to tell you that Popeye's wasn't for me. I was use to given orders not taking them.

I lost the house I was renting because I couldn't pay the rent. I was so happy that day when the Sheriff showed up to throw out my belongings that Dedra and I had already moved, every stitch by ourselves, saving me my last shred of dignity. No workers, no bodyguards, just my baby sister and me. What a difference a day makes! I moved in with my sister Dedra, realizing the time had come for me to leave Brunswick; there was nothing else left for me to do but prepare for whatever was next.

Shortly after moving in with my sister I met a guy named Harold who worked on the island at one of the restaurants. He had to be at least six or seven years younger than I, but he was very charming in an innocent kind of way. He stood about 6'2", and possibly weighed one hundred forty pounds wet. His most protruding feature, outside of that long, slender body of his, was his bright, shiny gold tooth. Harold had it placed right-square in the middle of his upper jaw. He was definitely the opposite of anything my last life represented. Harold was what you might call country slick, meaning he thought he was cool, but of course, he was no match for any of the men I had known. He wasn't a part of the mix (meaning the drug scene). It was a welcomed change.

I remember the day we all went out job-hunting. I, along with Dedra and James, had gone down to a new restaurant/hotel establishment, following a lead in a newspaper ad for help. The ad stated that they were in need of managers, cooks, and waitress's. This was a trio for us. I, of course, had years of management experience. My brother, well, he could cook and manage, and my sister had found her niche as a waitress.

We went in that day, one by one. I was first.

"Sorry, we've hired all our management staff, but we do still need cooks if you know anyone," said the man, who hadn't even looked down at my resume, before telling me I was over-qualified.

"Okay, thanks," I replied and left.

My brother was next.

"Sorry, we've hired all the cooks we need at this time," said the man who had just told me they needed cooks.

"Okay, thanks, Sir," my brother replied as he left.

Finally, my baby sister went in.

"Sorry, ah—"

"I know! You don't need any waitresses," she replied, cutting him off as she turned to walk out.

It was hard not to get angry and blow up, but we didn't. And in spite of all the adversity, we were all eventually able to get jobs. Working as a waitress (not a manager, with years of experience) allowed me to save up the money for my move. There was no way I could continue to live in this town as a law-abiding citizen with any hope of getting ahead. I learned quickly that, in the south, blacks were still being exploited. We were good enough to wait tables or clean the homes of wealthy white folks, but not good enough to run their businesses.

I sat in my room that night, happy to have another chance, glad to have a job, and to have met someone as nice as Harold. My mind drifted off to Doug, who had also been arrested shortly after Mike. He had really done a job on Dedra. She hurt more than I ever imagined anyone could over a man. His last monstrous deed was to marry our cousin in Dedra's eight month. He'd been sneaking around with her, just as Mike was sneaking around with

Terry. Wow I thought, who the hell can you trust.

I wondered what Doug and Silk might be doing at this exact time. I shook my head in disbelief. How could I have been so stupid to think our relationship was more than just some dirty, child-molester's joke? I knew how. I knew that in my heart I still hoped it was what I had envisioned from the start, which was two people that by sheer fate carried a bond and love that was stronger than blood, a love that could not be denied. I assure you now I do understand, it wasn't the latter.

I will never forget the night my relative showed up at our house as Harold and I sat watching television. She had letters in her hand addressed to her sixteen-year-old daughter from none other than—yep, you guessed it—Mike!

I became nauseous as I read his sick advances and statements that could have only been in response to a letter previously received from her. I was speechless.

"He is sick," I said. "I can't believe this."

I held my head down in shame, remembering how I stood in front of this very same person and proclaimed my love for him.

I remember clearly the words I used in defense of our relationship.

"He has loved me his whole life, this isn't what you think, we don't need your approval." I yelled. But tonight there was no defense as she stood before me with the letters in her hand.

Mike had somehow managed to sleep with not just me, but two other relatives. And each felt as strongly for him as I did, in youth and adulthood.

"He is sick." My cousin said, interrupting my negative thoughts. "And what happened is not your fault, you were too young."

I knew her only reason for telling me about those letters, was so she could have her "I-Told-You-So" moment. So, here I was, face to face with the truth. One of the worse choices I had ever made in my life just got worst. I wrote a letter to Mike that night, letting him know what a mistake of God I thought he was.

He never responded. I hoped it was because he finally felt some shame.

I called Colette looking for someone I could trust to comfort me. We had been through a lot together as kids. And no matter how many people I had met, none of them were ever the kind of friend I had found amongst those whom I knew from the bricks.

I told Colette I just needed to spend a few days with her in Syracuse before I went totally crazy.

Trying to sound concerned she quickly said yes, but I had known that girl since she was twelve; I knew that although she was truly a good friend, what she really wanted was all the details of how everything in my life was now in shambles.

When Harold and I reached Syracuse we had barely thrown our bags down before Colette started in. She didn't waste any time probing me for the details. I leaned back on the sofa, with my feet tucked neatly under me. I took a moment to take in my surroundings. Colette appeared to be doing okay: she had moved into a small, ranch-style home just a year or so earlier with her boyfriend. She looked good, too. I guess the suburban, mixed neighborhood agreed with her. I smiled to myself as I noted Colette's efforts at bringing together the two homes. Some areas were still very manly and cold, while the others had a warming, womanly touch that was clearly Colette.

Looking up from over my cup, I took a long sip of the hot tea, and began telling her everything. As I listened to myself talk, I couldn't help but think how my story sounded more like a movie drama than the happily-ever-after life I had always hoped for. I was plagued by nothing but destruction. I wanted a break, but life refused to hand me one. That evening Colette and I sat up talking about old times, sharing stories that neither of us had dared to tell the other until now. It was stupid, we knew, but we always wanted to sound as if life was great, fearing the other was doing better.

Two days had passed since Harold and I had arrived in

Syracuse, and I was beginning to feel better. Being around my old friend had been just what I needed. I believed in my heart that life was about to get a whole lot better.

Just waking up in the morning looking out the window at people who were on their way somewhere or speeding by walking briskly out for their morning exercise, gave each day a whole new meaning. The grass was a bright-green and all the trees were still clothed, even though there was a slight hint in the air that it soon would be cold. I got up to brush my teeth, this time feeling better than I had felt in a while. I was planning to try and catch up with Kent that day since I was in town, just to see how he was doing. I walked down the hall almost floating as the sunlight shone clear through the windows at the other end. I wasn't close to being prepared for the phone call I would receive, as Colette called out that the other line was for me.

"Mike has died in prison," the voice said calmly.

"What happened?" I asked my aunt, who seemed a little too casual to me to be springing something like this on me.

"AIDS!" she said, the words seeping out of her mouth like death. I fell to the floor.

"What do you mean, AIDS?" I said slowly. "When? How did he get it? It must have been after he went to jail," I said, answering my own questions. "He couldn't have had it when he was out because they would have found it when he was shot," I said, trying to convince myself he couldn't have had it while we were together.

"I don't know," she said. "We just thought you should know. I gotta run, okay?"

"Okay," I said hanging up.

I can't explain nor will I try to put into words all that I felt that day. I hadn't heard from Mike since that last visit. It was now 1993. I wondered if that was why he had really stopped calling. Had he known he was infected? Had he called me to the prison that day to take out his revenge for T. B.? I searched my mind for a clue as to when he may have contracted this deadly disease, hoping all the while that I had been spared.

I was blown away, Harold was frantic. He tried not to be upset, but how could he not be? Colette tried to offer what sympathy she could but I didn't want it.

I needed to run, just get away from everything.

I went back to Brunswick, pulled together all I had, and moved to Atlanta, bringing Harold with me. He was determined to stay by my side.

"If we have AIDS, then we have AIDS," he said. "There is nothing we can do now."

He sounded crazy; who would say that? I knew it was just his trying to sound mature. But he was right, what could we do? Who do you tell? Our decision was no one!

We went on each day after that as if nothing was wrong. Convincing ourselves that we were spared from this disease, neither one of us really wanting to know the truth.

Harold and my relationship lasted for about two years after our move. I caught him, of all people, cheating on me with some woman he met through his friends. For me, there were no more second chances. I had been used and abused enough by men. I packed his bags and threw him out.

Now I was all alone, just me and the possibility of being infected with AIDS.

It was tougher than I ever expected. At least with Harold by my side I felt as if someone would be there for me. Now, with it just being me, all I did was worry. I wasn't ready to die.

The pressure of not knowing was too great. I would put myself through wild eating frenzies if I thought I had lost even a pound, fearing it was a definite sign I had the disease. I put on tons of unneeded weight thinking it would keep my illness a secret and at bay.

I was not educated about the disease.

Janice E. Sullivan

It was a tough time to be alone. I had plenty of people around me, but I was trapped in a deadly silence where the only sound that was heard was a constant echo reminding me I could have AIDS. I tried to stay as positive as I could. I eventually agreed to go out on a date with someone from work. It wasn't meant to go anywhere; it was just supposed to get me out of the house.

I couldn't believe how refreshing this guy was. He was a honor roll student and valedictorian. He had graduated from Morehouse summa cum laude, and was getting ready to start working on his second degree at FSU next season. He was part of a huge fraternity, dressed impeccably and was working part time to help put himself through school. I was head-over-heels instantly and so was he. We spent every free minute we had together. I dreamed of what it would be like to be a senator's wife, traveling all over the world.

Carl was about seven years my junior but was very mature for his age. He and I got along so well. He knew how to hold me. He knew all the right things to say to stop my hurt. I began to let the worry of the secret I held subside. Channeling it instead into hope. I was tired of only hearing the stories of how great sex could be. My whole life I had never experienced some of the feelings Colette would tell me about. I hated sex. It would start out okay in the beginning then it would turn dirty and disgusting if it seemed my partner enjoyed it too much. Their touches would make me sick to my stomach and sooner or later it would become a problem too big to work through. I didn't want it to be that way with Carl. I wanted to get rid of my hang-ups. I prayed to be what I had heard termed as "turned out." It was a term that was supposed to mean sexually "whipped," able to be open and free with someone. Finally I had found someone who actually made me want to have sex. And have sex we did! I insisted we use condoms at first, knowing that I was still untested and unsure. Carl, however, didn't really enjoy them, so we quickly did away with that idea.

Carl was absolutely incredible. He wasn't pushy or

282

threatening. He was sweet and gentle with an unbelievable libido. We would meet each other at my apartment for just the quickest moments of sex before rushing off to work. I had opened up in more ways than one, now eager to give oral sex to the person I wanted to please so much.

I had gotten everything I'd prayed for. I loved Carl and he loved me. Harold, on the other hand, had not done so well. The girl he cheated on me with was also cheating on him. On more than one occasion I spotted him sitting outside my apartment just looking up at my window. He looked awful; I felt bad for him. But it was he, not I, who made the decision to betray our trust. Carl was cool about it at first, but quickly became irritated with Harold when he began calling. That, along with his nightly parking outside my apartment, was just too much. I explained to him that I only took the calls because I felt I at least owed Harold that much. But Carl didn't care, he felt if Harold was having a tough time, he should go home. There was nothing keeping him in Atlanta.

The following week Carl had a business trip come up and he would have to leave town for the weekend. His last words to me when he left was not to let Harold in. He didn't trust him and was worried. Carl didn't know Harold, but I did. He was harmless. He and I shared something once and I still respected that. That night Harold showed up as usual. He was crying and feeling sorry for himself. I knew he had been drinking and just wanted a friend. I owed him that much; he had been there for me through some tough times. He asked me if he could come up for awhile. He claimed he would leave, but had had just a little to much to drink and wanted to lie down. I agreed, suggesting he lie on the couch. We talked for a little bit and then he fell off to sleep. I placed a small cover over Harold and went off to bed myself. I laid on top of the covers in case I needed to get up. I must have lay there until about six a.m. Rolling over for my second snooze I bumped into a naked body. "Harold!" I yelled, "What the hell are you doing? Get out! Get up and get the F' out!" I was crazed; my heart was pounding. My only thought was what if Carl showed up now. He would never believe me. I couldn't believe it myself.

Harold was talking plenty of trash now. He wasn't sad and broken from the alcohol anymore. He was refusing to leave, stating this was his apartment too. I picked up the phone and threatened to call the police. Harold, although still talking trash, put his clothes on and left. He was yelling obscenities as I threw his shoes down the stairs, he called me crazy and deranged. And I was. I was scared to death of losing Carl because of this. I knew how important trust was and I had no intention of violating it. I just always seemed to mess up. What was wrong with me? Why was I so gullible?

When Carl returned, I didn't mention my little episode because he had insisted I stay away from Harold before he left. I said yes when he asked had Harold finally stopped coming by.

Two days later, just after one of our mid-day love scenes, Carl bent down looking for his shoes. When he stood up I couldn't believe what he had in his hand.

Carl held up a pair of men's tightie-whities. There was no lying about it, Carl wore boxers. How could Harold do that to me? I hadn't done anything to hurt him. Why would he want to ruin my life? I did all I could to explain to Carl, but he did not want to hear it. He struck me several times upside the head, then began kicking me in both my sides and stomach as I lay on the floor crying. He spat on me and called me a whore. He said he wanted to believe me but he couldn't. He said he'd have to be a damn fool to fall for what I had just said.

He walked out that day a different man than I had known before. For whatever reason he still did not break it off with me, but it was clear he didn't trust me. The sweet guy I knew was gone. Carl constantly abused me. He began fighting me in public for just about anything. If a man spoke to me and I spoke back, it would start a fight. I remember one night when we were out having dinner, a gentleman from across the room commented on how good my salad looked. Teasingly, I said "It tastes good, too," laughing lightly as he passed by with his date headed for their table. Carl blew up. He picked up the salad and dumped it on top of my head. He asked me, "How does the salad taste now, bitch?" standing over me as if waiting for me to say the wrong thing. I was mortified. I just sat there and wiped off the dressing that had dripped onto my face. I wanted to leave but Carl insisted I sit there so I could see how it felt to be made an ass of.

I did sit there, but the worst part about it was everyone else sat there too. No one, not one man, or part of management, intervened.

Carl pushed me day after day with his tirades. I had no choice but to start fighting back. We'd scuffle anywhere at any moment. Our friends hated for us to be around, because they knew without a doubt before the evening was over one of us would push the other's button. It wasn't like before; I was tired of being the punching bag. If Carl threw a drink on me I'd throw one right back on him. Our love had turned into violence, but I still couldn't find a way to let him go.

I loved him with all I had and I just couldn't see losing him over a mistake I made. I wished he could look inside me and see that I wasn't the kind of person he imagined. I could have never done what he thought. But he couldn't. And neither could any of my other friends to whom I tried to explain what had happened. They felt it was just too hard to believe.

Carl's disrespect for me grew and grew. He would have women over to his apartment, advising his roommate to just let me knock if I showed up. I'd stand there listening to the television and laughter after they thought I had walked away. I was hurting.

Here I was again. I walked slowly back to my apartment, broken and filled with self-hate for being so stupid. That day when I left Brunswick I had promised myself I would never let anyone treat me like Silk had again. But what I had said was just a sentence formed from words. I hadn't fixed *me*. I hadn't dealt with the issues that lay inside of me, only covered them up. I was again allowing myself to be beat, spit on, and cursed at in public and in private because it was my fault.

I was angry, I wanted to die. I slept all the time. I was just sick over everything, I was unable to keep anything down. I had never known a love like this.

My girl friends were worried about me. At work Carl stayed away from me and I stayed away from him. However, every so often, he would start in on me if he saw me at a table filled with men too long. Causing a scene, Carl would bump me so hard from behind that all the food would fall off my waitressing tray. It's hard to admit now, but I actually took all those blow-ups as a sign he still cared. I thought eventually he would get over his anger and things would go back to the way they were.

Two months had gone by since Carl and I had our big blowup. Although officially I wasn't sure where we stood, I would still allow Carl to show up whenever he wanted and sleep with me, knowing he was probably on his way to someone else's house as soon as he left mine. A short time afterwards I would find out that it wasn't love that had me so sick after all. I was pregnant.

I didn't understand it, I had gone through thousands of dollars of fertility treatments with Silk, spent nights practicing the rhythm method with Kent, told by the doctor's that I only had one partially-working fallopian tube and most likely could not conceive. And here I was pregnant.

I was completely thrown, but I couldn't help it. The thought of a baby inside of me brought a part of me alive I didn't know existed. I can't explain the feeling I had. I was determined to do everything I could to make sure my child had everything he or she would need.

Of course Carl, on the other hand, claimed it wasn't his; he didn't want anything to do with me or my baby. His reaction surprised me—in fact, it crushed me. There was a pain that consumed my whole being. I held my stomach. I felt a huge sense of love for the person inside of me. I rocked back and forth on the bed, my face covered in tears, as I cried so hard that my nose ran. It took two days for Carl to be a man and come by. He said he was scared, and he had really made some big mistakes. The other girl he had been seeing had also informed him—just one night before I had—that she was pregnant too. He only showed up to reason with me; he said he had too much going for himself, and that a baby would only complicate things. I understood him completely. I knew how hard he worked to get where he was. He was born and raised in Liberty City, one of the tougher areas of Miami, and had beat the odds. But I felt my baby had beat the odds too. And I wanted to keep it. I told Carl he could keep his money and that I'd be alright, but, I still wanted his support. I insisted he take me to all my appointments. And he did. Most of our visits would end in a physical fight in the room while we were waiting on the doctor. I would say something about the baby, then he would say something stupid. Then the fight would be on. When the door would swing open as the nurse or doctor would rush in, we'd be sitting there, my hair all scattered, and blood running down his arm from a fresh scratch or wound. We were a mess but I wanted him there. I couldn't bear the thought of being a mother with no baby's daddy.

When the time came to give authorization to take blood for an HIV test, I froze. I wanted to take care of my baby, but I was scared. It would take a call to Colette to help me through it. Colette herself had gotten pregnant just before her sixteenth birthday. She couldn't bare the thought of having a child, but she did what she had to do for that child. And so could I, she said giving me a verbal lashing for putting it off this long.

I had the test and waited the long five days it took back then to get an answer. I was negative. Thank God. I would have never forgiven myself if I had caused harm to my child. I spent the next couple of weeks doing everything to stay healthy.

I couldn't wait for my sonogram. I walked in the doctors office beaming that day. I would finally see the life inside of me. I lay on the table breathing easy as the tech searched for the heart beat, but she couldn't find it. I looked closely at the monitor trying to make out even the slightest features, but I couldn't. I knew something was wrong. When they called me back into my doctor's office for the results, I was crushed. They said the baby was in my tube. It wouldn't live and could possibly kill me if they didn't take it out.

That was it—no baby, no Carl—just me, left to somehow pull together this mess I called a life.

I spent a lot of time sitting back, alone in my apartment, questioning a lot of things that had happened in my life. What if that last visit with Silk had gone differently.

I closed my eyes to say my prayers, making sure to thank God, for his grace and his mercy.

Chapter Twenty
Bringing It Altogether

————•◆•————

Being alone gave me more time to realize just how messed up I really was. It had been tough the last couple of years. It's hard to wakeup one morning and realize the plans you made for your life just don't exist anymore. I thought my life with Kent would last forever, and when it didn't, I thought Silk was the answer. And when neither of them panned out I turned to Carl, and all those in between. I had spent my life giving control over who I was to someone else. Now it was time to return it back to me. I hadn't a clue as to who me really was, but for the first time, I wanted to find out.

I had played a dozen roles in my lifetime and most had been that of a menace. Now there was no script, no one controlling my lines or pulling my strings. I was left to my own interpretation of what I thought life should be. I had a choice to succeed or fail. Whatever road I chose, it would be on me this time.

I wanted to know and understand what it was that was in me that sent the signal that abuse in any form was okay.

On the outside, I was this ferrous, confident, well-kept person. But on the inside, the years of abuse and abandonment had stripped me of my self-esteem and love for myself. I was like a sponge: whatever mess you sat me in, I would soak it up. I always wanted to fit in, but, at the same time, stand out.

One day I was talking to a young man who said something to me that sounded so key to my situation. He said I was afraid of my own silence. I'd do anything not to be alone.

He was right. I had gone from 165 lbs to 220 lbs. I spent most of my money on booze, and in my eyes was nothing more than a fat drunk. And not even a good one. I did everything in my power to make sure everyone thought my house was the place to be. I had become crass—entertainingly funny, putting any and everyone at the end of my jokes trying to keep the others entertained so they would stay around me, not caring who got hurt in the process.

He explained how it wasn't enough for me to always say I deserved something better. He said the real change comes, when you believe it!

I'm sure to this day he has no idea of what that few minutes of his taking the time to care, did for me.

I went in search of myself. I wanted to peel away ugly layer after ugly layer and look each smack in the face. It was like waking up from a deep sleep or coma yelling to the top of your lungs, "I want to live!"

I had forgotten God's promise to always be by my side. I had always believed in my heart that there was something more awaiting me, something so big that God would never give it to me unless I was ready.

I began working out; I lost 40 of the unwanted pounds. The long walks I would take gave me a chance to think about everything. I understood why I always had to have a crowd. It was because I didn't like me any more than I liked the people at the other end of my jokes. I didn't like the silence. I would become bored and depressed even if I was home alone for just a little while.

I pulled away from the crowds and challenged myself to spend time with me. I was unhappy inside, suffering from depression and low self-esteem. To see me, you would think I had it going on. Always smiling, well-dressed, neatly-kept apartment, and an appetite for the good life. But, when the lights went out, and the cameras were rolled away, as the director yelled, "It's a take!" I'd bow and retreat into self-pity, completing another role. I wanted to love who I was. I wanted to be a positive contribution to my society.

I prayed for God to use me as a crossroad; I wanted to do all I could to save anyone that I could from the road that I had traveled. I felt it was so important for people to know that you don't have to be what you have lived, but, what you have lived can help you become what you want to be.

It would be some time after that I would see a pastor on television who, to me, seemed to preach his every word from my soul. It was as if he had heard every prayer, every dream, and every promise ever shared between God and me. This pastor unknowingly pulled me through one of the worst times in my life. He helped me really see me.

I knew now that it wasn't just in my head, but that, through everything, God was truly leading me to this point.

Just hearing the pastor say, "Your being here today is no accident," as I watched yet another television broadcast made me feel as if I was okay—not misplaced or thrown away as all had made me feel, but safely placed right where I was at that point and time. By the end of his hour I had untangled some of the loneliness and confusion locked inside of me. I thought intently, realizing that if this is where I'm supposed to be (an active part of God's plan), then I'm taking this all wrong. I placed value on each day of my past and accepted it for just what it was: the past.

I understood that we could delay God's plan with free will and foolish mistakes, but we could not change it! I took hold of every word that came out of that pastor's mouth. I knew now, through confirmation, that what God had spoken to me as a youth, had to come to pass. I was going to be alright. I was someone with a purpose.

The difference was, in the past I was looking for my own purpose and not God's. When I say God, please understand that I am talking about the spiritual—the God of not just one but all. There is no one face or feature that He identifies with more than another, but the spiritual sense of guidance that lives in us all—not the conjured-up figment made by man. I am a firm believer that whoever and wherever you are, God is there also.

I got out and mingled; I was determined to change my environment. I went back to the long, grueling hours of managing restaurants, which afforded me the opportunity of buying my very own home. In order to meet new friends, I joined a network marketing company called Pre-Paid Legal. These people were different from anyone I had met previously. They were inspired about life. They saw possibilities and hope instead of hopelessness without possibility. I would recommend some form of networking group to everyone, if only to acquaint yourself with yourself and your true capabilities. I realized that wealth and happiness was available to anyone who went after it. I dove in head first, quitting my job the very same week I joined. I had no clue that taking my mind off my life is what it would take to start it. I no longer saw things as they were, but for there possibilities.

Slowly but surely, a new me evolved—not in a physical sense but internally. I was becoming the person God needed to fulfill his plan. I realized how blessed I was. All my life I had been walking in the wisdom of God, for it was that wisdom and second sense that had helped me through every rough time I had ever had.

Amazingly enough, the first time I would set foot in the pastor's church, whose words had helped me so much, it would be without my knowing it. I was coming full circle with all God had planned.

I was invited to church one day by a relative who attended his church and a few others periodically, but this day she just so happened to pick his church to attend. Walking up to the church I still had no clue it was him. In fact, I had begun repeating remarks, rumors even, that I had heard about the church my niece attended. This church was only one mile down the street from where I'd been working the last two years, but I had never wanted to attend the huge, one-block building based on all that I had heard.

"I'm not sure about this church," I said as we got closer to the door.

"Why?" my niece asked. "Is it because it's a big church?"

"No," I replied. "It's just that people say that the guy in this church brainwashes people and takes their money. And I'm not about to give them my W2!" I exclaimed.

"Well," she said looking at me with a sideways smile, "Aren't you the one who always says, the truth isn't what's said, but what the facts determine?"

With that, she was right. I had learned that saying a long time ago in another life after watching guilty person after guilty person be released from jail because of a well thought-out lawyer. That saying still rang true. I shut up and we went inside. The church was huge and beautiful. The choir came out and performed magnificently. Then, it was time for the preacher. When he walked on the platform, I couldn't believe it. There he was, the man whose words had pulled me through.

I smiled as he opened his mouth and said, "WELCOME! IT'S NOT A MISTAKE YOU CAME HERE TODAY!"

That sermon, and the many that followed, brought me to this point. His preaching was like a self- help course designed just for me. I joined the church a few months later. And I must say the rumors were all wrong—especially the one about the W2.

Sermon after sermon, day after day, I was brought face-to-face with some ugly truths. Feelings I didn't know existed or thought I had gotten over, resurfaced. I realized I still hated my grandfather and grandmother, and I hadn't even begun to forgive my mother.

I may have said I forgave them, in the midst of false humility, but I never really had. I still cried uncontrollably at night. I still spent days asking the question, "Why?"

I was no more healed from the pain than they were forgiven. I had learned enough to know that just saying it brings about nothing. There has to be a new revelation of thought, which allows the mind, and then the heart, to reason, and then accept. So, I did something I'd never done before, I searched for the truth, but not my truth. I searched for the truth that is determined by the facts.

I wrestled with myself internally, trying to be sure that I wasn't looking for an excuse for my family—an easy way out of all the neglect, hurt, rape and humiliation with which I had lived. But there is no way to ever know for sure what was intent and what was not intended. The one thing I did know I summed up from all of my own failures, and that was, you don't know what you don't know. This was true for them as well. I began to understand that my grandmother had done the best she could. I could either spend my life trying to figure out what went wrong with them, or get on with making things right for me. Please know that I'm in no way excusing anyone—from any gender or age group—that practices this kind of behavior. Understand me for sure when I say: ***YOU NEED HELP!*** And if you don't get it for yourself, then I hope with everything in me some person who reads this book has the guts to get it for you. I'm just saying that I can't continue to dwell in it. It's like a cancer that must be cut out at the very root or it will continue to kill me. I accepted my past and all that came with it. I made plans for a special trip back to Brunswick to see my grandmother who had now found Jesus and was fighting her own battle with her own guilt. We cried together, as I turned over the years of hate I had held for her to the Lord. My grandmother told me that even in her worst times, she prayed for me. She said she had secretly hoped that I would have had the courage to kill my grandfather, so she herself could be free. Since that day we have remained close. It is I she now calls in her old age whenever things go wrong. And I, keeping a open heart, listen.

As for everyone else that had contributed to the pain in my life, well, all but my uncle have passed away. I didn't go to him with some speech on forgiveness, because he didn't ask for any that day when he had the chance. He will have to bear his own cross, as I have had to bear mine.

Chapter Twenty One
The Journey

In my heart I knew that God's plan could be delayed, but not denied. And that's what I hung on to.

I worked hard at getting away from my past, but it never seemed to be more than a few steps behind me. I tried to push everything other than the life I craved far away. I removed myself from the gook to which others seemed to want to hang on to. I was clueless as to how true the old adage, "You may run, but you cannot hide," really was. No matter how far or how long you run, eventually, you will reap what you have sown.

It was the fall of 1998 when I would find out just how true that was.

Late one evening I received a call from a family friend. She said that Dedra, my baby sister had been arrested for possession with intent to distribute. My heart sank. Why would she even be involved in such a thing? Hadn't she learned enough from Silk and Doug? She knew the time possessing crack carried. I was angry at her and myself. I had let her down as a sister and I knew it. I thought by making sure she had a job and a secure place to live before I left Brunswick she would be okay. I sent money back to her whenever I could, but I guess that wasn't enough. The story has it that the police raided the house as part of a sting operation. The police had a known crack-head go into the house and purchase the drug with marked money. Dedra was familiar with this crack-head and had done business with her before, so she thought nothing of it.

After the crack-head had scored she walked outside and signaled to the police that she had completed the transaction. The police then rushed in and made the bust.

Being a snitch was a small price to pay for a crack-head. It allowed them to keep their own freedom. Their loyalty was to the drug, not the police, or to the people the police were after. It was all about the next hit, and being free to get it.

I was the only one to call. My older brother would never get tied up in this foolishness. He wasn't the type to extend himself. I think it had something to do with our childhood. Something had driven a wedge between all of us. For a long time I tried to fix it, but nothing I did worked. The damage was far too deep and emotional for any of us to begin to know how to reach out.

I, as always, was expected to run to the rescue. So I did. When I got to Brunswick there was nothing I could do for my sister; she would have to face the punishment for her crime. Her twins and my niece, however, were a different story. They would come home with me.

Putting them in the car I promised myself I wouldn't make the same mistake with them I had made with my sister. I wanted their lives to be so much better than what we had known.

I enrolled them in school and spent at least two days a month having lunch with them. I joined the PTA, and committed to library duty so I could get what was termed, school bucks for the kids. I had a picture of a perfect family running around in my head, but their vision differed greatly from mine. They, on the other hand, didn't respect or appreciate anything I was trying to do.

No matter what I did it was never enough. They complained about the clothes I bought. They complained about the food I cooked. You name it, from bed-time to homework, it was always one big chore. In just a few months they had broken out my windows, kicked in the door, and stolen my jewelry and money. I didn't understand these kids anymore. I had kept them many times throughout the years and never experienced anything like this. The twins were eleven now, and their sister was turning seven. The promise of a trip to McDonald's or threat that Santa wouldn't come, were no longer useful tools. The game had changed and I was overwhelmed.

I wrote to their mother, my sister, and apologized for never truly understanding how tough being a parent was. On many nights, when I was on my way to the house, I would pull over to the side of the road just crying, filled with a feeling of dread, knowing I would have to eventually go home. How could I make it through eighteen more months of this?

I couldn't understand why they weren't grateful—kissing the ground I walked on for taking them away from that hell they were in. But they weren't, they wanted to go home. They wanted their mother. After all the neglect, they wanted their mother.

Between the kids and networking, I was exhausted. I couldn't keep up. There was no way I could get out and market my business as much, and as often, as I would need to in order to earn enough commission to keep things going. I tried to stay positive, focusing on the inspirational tapes and magazines I would get from Pre-Paid Legal. They were filled with all of these little quotes to get you back on track. Like the story about the man who mined his land for years looking for diamonds, shoveling pile after pile of coal out of his way. Exasperated, finally, he sold it to someone passing by. This person walked on the property and in two hours had found millions of dollars in diamonds just pushed in piles outside of the tunnel the man had dug for years. He, like so many, didn't realize that all diamonds start as a lump of coal. That story, would really get me back on my feet. And for another day I'd be content with trying to make it.

I spent hours glancing at the many faces in the magazines from Pre-Paid Legal. I admired those of them that had become successful doing the very same thing I was contemplating giving up.

There was this one issue in particular that always brought me back to it. It had a picture of Leroy Decosta, and somehow for whatever reason I would always end up staring at his picture. Not because I had a crush on him or anything, it was just that his picture—no, his eyes—always seemed to call out to me. I wasn't sure what our connection would be, but I felt somehow, someday, our paths would cross, for whatever reason.

That picture of him bothered me so much, I couldn't help mentioning it to my then business partner and one or two other friends, who all laughed. Everyone thought the same thing, teasing me about having a crush on Decosta, but I knew different; it wasn't a crush. I wasn't sure what it was. However I knew it wasn't a crush; Decosta was hardly my type. I had a thing for the "GQ" kind of guy—smooth-talking, yet funny, with just a slight hint of rough-neck. The type of man that could make a pair of jeans and a jacket look edible. Decosta on the other hand, looked to be slightly shy. He was always standing somewhere quietly, alone, watching whatever was going. He didn't appear to be smooth or offer any airs about himself.

Yet somehow, someway I knew Decosta and I would be involved in something together.

Around March of 1999, I would face the fact that I couldn't feed my family and pay my bills just doing what I was doing. I also knew that management was not my answer; it was just 'way too much walking, and too many hours for anyone who had a family.

In the last few months I had begun having a problem with my leg. It would just give out. I would drag it for a few minutes, then I would have to sit down. The pain was horrible. I couldn't go more than one block on some days without squatting or resting before continuing. I didn't have medical insurance so getting the problem checked was out of the question. I knew I would have to find a sit down job if I was going to make it financially and physically.

The person who recruited me hated the thought of my leaving Pre-Paid; they believed I would do well if I could just hang in there. But I was so tired of hanging.

In late March of 2000, as a last ditch effort, they convinced me to go to another convention—being held in Ada, Oklahoma. Little did I know that weekend would change my life forever.

I arranged for a babysitter and went off to that convention with only one thing in mind: I wanted to be sure I wasn't giving away my coal.

I had been to many conventions and each of them in the past had always revived me.

But not this time. I was just too tired and in too much pain. I knew in my heart this would be the last convention for me. I went through all the motions. I enjoyed seeing the people I had read about in the profiles of success. I watched as each of them walked across the stage getting award after award, wondering, "Why not me? What did they have that I didn't?"

Don't get me wrong, I was genuinely happy for each of them. I, myself, had reached the executive level in the company as well, but that didn't take away what I was feeling. I reached that level off of my own sweat and tears; I wasn't fortunate enough to have some large organization under me. That took a talent I didn't have. You had to be one of those people who could get someone to dream the dream. I was new to this; it was hard to sell someone a dream I had just begun to dream myself.

Everyone was cheering and clapping happily, but my mind was filled with thoughts of getting out of there. I was tired. I just wanted to enjoy the comforts of the suite my up-line graciously allowed me to share with them. One of the girls who had flown in with us decided to leave too. We were walking down the long corridor of the hotel just outside of the ballroom, when she teasingly gave me a nudge.

"There's Mr. Decosta," she said in a long, drawn-out voice, trying to be funny.

I just looked at her. I wished I had never told her about him.

The instant her eyes lit up I knew she was about to do something silly.

"Don't even try it," I said, half smiling but very serious.

Before I could finish my sentence she had called out to him.

"Hey, Decosta!, What's up?" she said cheerfully, as we both neared each other, coming from different directions.

"Hello ladies," he said in his Caribbean accent.

"Hi," I said dryly, not wanting my friend to make more of this than it really was.

"You ladies enjoying the convention?" he asked.

"Yes," we said harmoniously, sounding just a little too school-girlish for me.

"Dam," I thought to myself, "Isn't this great. He probably thinks we're fans of his." I began to excuse myself. My girlfriend interrupted my farewell speech.

"Decosta!" she said grabbing my arm to keep me from walking away. "Have you ever met my friend, Janice?"

"No, I can't say that I have; however, I've seen her around. It would be very hard to miss such a lovely lady." He said, stretching his hand out as if looking for a hand shake.

I wasn't feeling this scene at all; I slowly extended my hand out to reach his, expecting him to rush through the whole handshake formality. He didn't. When his hand touched mine, it was as if the room went blank and there wasn't anyone in that moment or space but us. He, still holding my hand, pulled me close to him and began asking me questions that were just a little unusual during a hand shake for me. Right there, in front of everyone, without blinking an eye. He asked if I was married. I said no. Then he asked if I drank. I said no. He continued by asking me if I smoked or had kids. And again I said no. His next response sent chills through my body.

He said that he and I had no time to waste, there were things we needed to do.

I am of a brown-skinned complexion, but I know, if I could have went pale, I would have.

He asked if we could talk for awhile. I said yes, although I was still just a little bewildered by the whole event. Excusing ourselves we walked around to a side of the hotel where there was a little less noise, but we could still hear the music playing ever so lightly. The music made the lights and shimmer coming from the pool seem almost magical.

As we walked off, I looked back at my friend, amusing myself with the thought of having an arm long enough to reach back and pick her jaw up off the floor, as she stood speechless watching us walk away.

A slight smile came across my face as I watched Decosta pull back the chair for me to sit, because in my heart I had always known this moment would come.

Incredible, right? I know. However, it actually happened just like that. I remember sitting there with him for hours feeling blown away from the events that had just taken place.

He was laid-back, and talked very confidently about who he was and what he wanted. I looked at him closely, waiting for him to do or say something that would allow me to walk off.

However, he never did. I sat there lost in his words, watching his lips move but somehow missing what he was saying. I figured I must be saying something that sounded really good myself, because he asked if I would mind if we talked awhile longer. He promised to escort me back to my group of friends, who were now enjoying the party that had moved to the corridors. I agreed, but advised him that I needed to be up early in the morning. He was a gentleman, and understood. He suggested that we walk and talk slowly, as we headed for the van that would take me back to my hotel.

Everyone had questions about what happened when I got back to the room. We all sat rolling our hair up for our early morning briefing. I tried to downplay how excited I really was, as I, too, wiped off my makeup and rolled my hair. I lay in my bed that night hardly able to sleep when suddenly the phone rang. I looked around the room trying to imagine which one of my roommates would dare have a man calling at 5 o'clock in the morning.

"Okay, hoochies, who gave out the room number?" I said smiling. "Tell Big Boy the night's over," I added.

Sandra, one of the girls traveling with us, answered the phone.

"Oh, heyyy, Decosta! You want Janice? Okay, hold on, 'Big Boy'," she said laughing as she slapped me five and passed the phone.

Embarrassed, I asked Decosta what was up. "Everything okay?"

"Yes," he said. "I'm in the lobby. Will you come down?"

"You're *where*? In the *lobby*?" I exclaimed, surprised at his visit. "Well, I've already put on my pajamas and was just about to get into bed," I said looking at the phone as I spoke.

"Please," he said. "Just come down for a moment, I want to see you as you are."

I finally agreed. "Okay," I said. "I'll be right down." I jumped up, put on my slippers, and headed for the door. Everyone turned around simultaneously screaming,

"I *know*, you are not going down there like that!"

"Yes I am too, chile'. I am tired, and guaranteed to be back in five minutes once he sees me." We all laughed as I shut the door behind me.

When I reached the lobby there stood Decosta wide awake and full of energy. His smile was even bigger than before. He grabbed my hands and told me it was just as he thought.

I was more beautiful now than he could have imagined. I kind of crooked one eye looking at him now, wondering if he was okay. And he was, he was far more than okay. In my mind's eye, I knew then, he was the one.

I would have never guessed how big a part Decosta would eventually play in my life.

It was hard to not think of him as a hero but that role did not fit him. He was more of a knight.

He was noble, giving, and humble. He was truly selfless, always looking out for the other guy.

I found out that Pre-Paid Legal for him was not his biggest accomplishment, although he and his partner were one of the first black executive directors the company ever had. His life's story expanded far beyond that.

Decosta was a native of the Virgin Islands; he came to the U. S. on a full, four-year scholarship to Indiana's Purdue University. He was sponsored by one of the "mukie-muks" (wealthy people) on the island. This was a great honor, so the pressure for him to do well was always present. He finished his four-year stint reluctantly, fulfilling the dream his grandmother, who raised him from the age of six months, had always had. But he knew in his heart that the corporate world or going back to the island as all hoped a sponsored graduate would, was not in the cards for him.

He missed the freedom he had grown up with, and the music that had fueled his soul. So he sought to fulfill his life's dream of entertaining. He was the name behind the Reggae group called Quasar. He traveled all around the world singing and dancing. It would take him almost fifteen years to realize he had to give up. The years had some how gotten past him. He had given entertaining everything he had. So sadly he put away his drums and sought out a new career in network marketing. It offered both the freedom and the money he wanted. And thank God he did.

I in the meantime, had taken a job working as a collections rep in 2001.The problems I was having with my leg had gone from not being able to walk a long distance to not being able to stand for more than a few minutes at a time. The best thing about that job was that I had insurance and could go to the doctors, so I did.

The diagnosis was spondyliosis. In short, there was a small split in my spine that would require surgery. I was horrified. What if something went wrong? How would I take care of myself? I called everyone I thought may be able to help nurse me afterwards, but my scheduled date for surgery was either inconvenient or my recovery time of about six weeks was far too long for anyone to commit to. I cried as I sat in my living room feeling the loneliness and self-pity that had crept over me. I decided to call Decosta. I wanted to share with him what the doctor had found.

I had been a little reluctant at first. Because the last two years of our relationship were done via long distance. Although intriguing, after our night in Oklahoma, Decosta returned back to Indianapolis, Indiana and I returned back to Atlanta, willing to live our lives together, but apart.

We did visit each other from time to time but we promised ourselves we would take it slow. He was special to me because he was the one guy I had met who respected whatever hang-ups I may have had about sex.

Oh sure, we tried the whole sex thing, but I found out for him it wasn't about sex.

I recall the first time he and I would attempt to make love. I didn't climax that night, or the next morning. To me, I think, he should have worked harder. But to him, it had more to do with me. He told me something that I had never heard before. He told me that he was not responsible for making me sexually happy. He said it was up to me to let go and find my own mental place of sexual freedom. Doing that, he said, would allow me to enjoy the experience.

What he said, did bear merit. I knew it was me, I was just glad he understood. I had prayed for someone who wouldn't hold sex over my head as some ultimatum.

And now, here I was, calling him to burden him with my latest situation on top of everything else. Dialing his number I cried even more as the overwhelming feeling of having no one to turn to came crashing down on me. It took me over an hour to get the full story out and calm down. By the time I had finished, Decosta had already began looking up flight information so he could be by my side as long as I would need him.

That first surgery, turned into two surgeries within six months of each other, with a two-year recovery time, due to the complications I incurred.

Most of those two years I spent on my back. I was unable to do the simplest things for myself. Decosta stayed right there never leaving my side. He put aside his childhood fear of hospitals and slept on a cot next to me every night that I was there. He fed me, bathed me, helped me down and up from the toilet even during my worst times. He cooked, cleaned, washed, and drove me back and forth to the doctors without a single complaint.

He let everything he had go; he lost his car, home, and business while taking care of me. But he never once complained. When I asked him about needing to return to Indiana, he would always say that he had lost far more in the past and wasn't worried. He knew one day he would get it all back. "But, if something happened to you," he would say, "Well, I could never get you back."

Two-and-a-half years later I was on my feet again, and slightly able to manage for myself.

We drove to Indiana and picked up all of Decosta's stuff, whom I now called Leroy, which was his first name.

Without a moment's regret showing on his face, I watched him put his few remaining items in the car.

His grandmother, who he cherished passed away a few months later on my birthday. It tore him up on the inside. Although he had other siblings, she was all he knew his whole life.

I realized at that very moment how truly blessed we were to have found each other when we did.

Who would have thought that that night when we met would led to a wonderful four-and-a-half year relationship, that later turned into the marriage I now enjoy with the most supportive man I have ever known.

We wedded May 16th of 2005 at a small church in Maryland in front of his family and friends. He knows much of what I've shared with you, but he decided long ago that he wouldn't read the manuscript until it was published. He said there was no need— he married me, and that meant all of me.

He felt if he read the book ahead of time his reaction or passing comment may sway me from writing my truth. He said there wasn't anything he couldn't endure from a stranger reading my book. However he could never live with himself, if for him, I changed the book.He loves me unconditionally, past and all.

My book is about growth, I was finally free to tell my story without fear or backlash, or without someone who claimed to love me walking out.

It's been a long road, but I believe, each of us—Colette, Marsha, Kent, Dedra, and the many others—are on our way to the life we all wanted. After I started the book I went back to Florida and located Marvin. He seemed to be doing okay. He and Carol are still together. She no longer works the streets, but he is just as active as ever. Last I heard he had fathered a set of twins with a nineteen-year-old at the age of fifty. My step sister Pam is also back in Jacksonville. She has five girls of her own who have given her eight very active grand-kids. Dedra and James, unfortunately, don't reach out to Marvin; they say there is far too much hurt from their past. I try to explain that in order for them to move on they will have to let the past be just that. But that is a lesson each of us has to learn for ourselves.

Sometimes that lesson is long and hard. Dedra, unfortunately, wound up in the system for a brief while again. She is still working through her own idea of life, and I am fine with that. I don't live in guilt like before. I just live to do the best I can from where I am. I pray for her and her children every day, for Dedra is truly my mother's daughter. She, like my mother, doesn't see the beauty in her children She feels trapped. Maybe one day- well, we'll see. I've learned what's best for her is not for me to decide. I'll leave that to a higher power.

Doug, Silk's old partner, and the father of my sister's twins, got caught up in another major drug bust. He would be tried and sentenced to Fed time, not to be released until 2012, from what I heard.

Marsha? Well, we are still good friends, although we don't have very much in common anymore. We still talk from time to time. It has been tough on her. She continued to use drugs for years after her return to Syracuse. The guy she eventually married was killed by the son's of his mistress for beating their mother in front of them. Marsha's own two boys had also succumbed to violence and crime. Both were serving time, last I heard.

My girl Colette? Well, what can I say? We are true sisters at heart. She did go on to find her father as well, although it wasn't what she expected. She embraced her past so that she could appreciate her future. She is married to a good, fun-loving man and is a grandmother to be. Life Is Good.

Kent and I have managed to remain friends through it all. He is still happily remarried and has the family he always wanted.

Both my brothers have also found something that is important to them. Each has a family now. My eldest brother Junior raised his children alone, after Sharon, falling prey to the deadly substance of crack and promiscuity, left him with no choice other than to divorce her.

As for my baby brother James, well, he was just recently married on April 29, 2006, to the mother of his four children— whom he dated for fourteen years before he felt secure enough to commit.

My eldest brother and I flew to the long-awaited event, doing whatever we could to make it as special as we could for a brother who I think deserves the world.

We all struggle daily to get through and stay above all that we have gone through. I pray that whatever separated us in the past, will fade and somehow we will find the love and closeness that should be shared amongst siblings. I want the family trips and holidays we never had. And you can be sure I will continue with every breath left in me to achieve that—not just for me, but for the generation that has to come behind me. I am forty-three now and I can say I know who I am.

I am a child of God, a positive influence on my community, a crossroads for any who shall enter into my path. I am a leader and believer in what is right; I am not afraid to neither question nor think for myself. I am an ever-willing blank page, knowing that each day is the opening of a new story.

If you learn but one thing from me or this book, please learn that God answers prayers. Maybe not when you expect Him to, but He does. So until He does, embrace life. Know that each day has a reason. Let no one steal your joy, and for God's sake, don't you ever just give it away. God Bless you, and may you too, be *saved by grace*....

Cucumbers Have Thorns & Snakes Love Strawberries

www.talktoauthor@cucumbershavethorns.com

I've Been Touched Foundation
Coming in 2009, Founder Janice E. Sullivan

Janice E. Sullivan

Prevalence of abuse

Child abuse was once viewed as a minor social problem affecting only a handful of U.S. children. However, in the late 1990s and early 2000s it has received close attention from the media, law enforcement, and the helping professions, and with increased public and professional awareness has come a sharp rise in the number of reported cases.

Because abuse is often hidden from view and its victims too young or fearful to speak out, however, experts suggest that its true prevalence is possibly much greater than the official data indicate. An estimated 896,000 children across the country were victims of abuse or neglect in 2002, according to national data released by the U.S. Department of Health and Human Services (HHS) in April 2004. Parents were the abusers in 77 percent of the confirmed cases, other relatives in 11 percent.

Sexual abuse was more likely to be committed by males, whereas females were responsible for the majority of neglect cases. The data show that child protective service agencies received about 2,600,000 reports of possible maltreatment in 2002. About 1,400 children died of abuse or neglect, a rate of 1.98 children per 100,000 children in the population. In many cases children are the victims of more than one type of abuse. The abusers can be parents or other **family** members, caretakers such as teachers and **babysitters**, acquaintances (including other children), and (in rare instances) strangers.

Although experts are quick to point out that abuse occurs among all social, ethnic, and income groups, reported cases usually involve poor families with little education.

Young mothers, **single-parent families**, and parental alcohol or drug abuse are also common in reported cases. Statistics show that more than 90 percent of abusing parents have neither psychotic nor criminal personalities. Rather they tend to be lonely, unhappy, angry, young, and single parents who do not plan their pregnancies, have little or no knowledge of child development, and have unrealistic expectations for child behavior. From 10 percent to perhaps as many as 40 percent of abusive parents were themselves physically abused as children, but most abused children do not grow up to be abusive parents.

Types of abuse

PHYSICAL ABUSE Physical abuse is the non-accidental infliction of physical injury to a child. The abuser is usually a family member or other caretaker and is more likely to be male. One fourth of the confirmed cases of child abuse in the United States involve physical abuse. A rare form of physical abuse is **Munchausen syndrome** by proxy, in which a caretaker (most often the mother) seeks attention by making the child sick or appear to be sick.

EMOTIONAL ABUSE Emotional abuse is the rejecting, ignoring, criticizing, isolating, or terrorizing of children, all of which have the effect of eroding their **self-esteem**. Emotional abuse usually expresses itself in verbal attacks involving rejection, scapegoating, belittlement, and so forth. Because it often accompanies other types of abuse and is difficult to prove, it is rarely reported and accounts for only about 6 percent of the confirmed cases.

SEXUAL ABUSE Psychologists define child sexual

abuse as any activity with a child, before the age of legal consent, that is for the sexual gratification of an adult or a significantly older child. It includes, among other things, sexual touching and penetration, persuading a child to expose his or her sexual organs, and allowing a child to view pornography. In most cases the child is related to or knows the abuser, and about one in five abusers are themselves underage. Sexual abuse accounts for 12 to 15 percent of confirmed abuse cases. In multiple surveys, 20 to 25 percent of females and 10 to 15 percent of males report that they were sexually abused by age 18.

NEGLECT Neglect, the failure to satisfy a child's basic needs, can assume many forms. Physical neglect is the failure (beyond the constraints imposed by poverty) to provide adequate food, clothing, shelter, or supervision. Emotional neglect is the failure to satisfy a child's normal emotional needs, or behavior that damages a child's normal emotional and psychological development (such as permitting drug abuse in the home). Failing to see that a child receives proper schooling or medical care is also considered neglect. Slightly more than half of all reported abuse cases involve neglect.

Where does the answer lie?

If you are like me the last page covering statistics was not only alarming, but it also help you see that the work has just begun.

My intention was to make this page a powerful resource for any one in trouble, or anyone who may have belief that someone else is in trouble. However after weeks of calls and research I've found that there really isn't anyone too call. All our searches led to other searches, all of our calls led to voice mails or numbers that no longer existed. And when someone finally did answer, we were met with information on another number that directed us to yet another number. Or the refusal to allow their information to be listed as a source. Sexual abuse and derogation are running wild in our community and yet we have no one outside of 911 or Defac's too call. When in many cases molestation is a slow and mentally crippling device.

For a long time I wasn't sure why God called me to write this book. Why he wanted me to become so embarrassingly transparent that with each tear stained page I could feel what my fingers were working so hard to express. I understand now that it is to create a dialogue that will stir up enough people that policy and laws will change. So that society will take this illness on and provide avenues and remedies for those wounded by it. That the many foundation listed as resources and advocates are forced to provide a real service with real answers when we call. A good friend once told me not to make my book just another march. "You have my promise, I won't." "What's your promise?"

Janice E. Sullivan

Diary of a Crack Addict's Aunt
by Betty J. Reedy
ISBN: 0-9646519-0-4

Book Review
by Renita Q. Ward, *Rolling Out Magazine*

Diary of a Crack Addict's Aunt is a gut-wrenching tale that is bound to spur some thoughts.The book published by Rite Word Book Publishing out of Atlanta, Georgia, documents the author's experience after inviting her drug addicted nephew, Antoine, to stay with he. The temporary living arrangement is a part of a larger rehabilitation plan for the 27-year-old young man.

The conversational journal is formatted just how a real diary might look. Some days have long detailed entries, like the day Antoine, known as "Tony" on the streets, finally arrives from his native home in Illinois … The maternal aunt drops in little nostalgic details remembering Tony when he was a little boy, the innocence in his eyes, and the joy in his smile. However, as the days wear on, Reedy painfully begins to realize the devastation rock cocaine can have on a person...

The personal entries of the author are juxtaposed with comments from Tony as well. Readers get a glimpse into his feelings and get tidbits about the racy street life. Tony, who is also the father of three, at one point writes, "when the pipe called, nothin' mattered; not my mother, not my kids—nothin'."

Such statements along with those of a beloved family make the pages turn quickly and the words linger on and on and on.

I thoroughly enjoyed this book and have shared it with my family. – *Yolanda A.*

Diary of a Crack Addict's Aunt can be purchased for a *Special Price* of **$10.00,** plus S & H (**$4.25**) when you mention *Cucumbers Have Thorns and Snakes Love Strawberries.*To Order Call
Ph:(404)758-8905. You can also visit our website, make a purchase or download the order form at www.crackdiary.com, or at Amazon.com.